Managing Organizations for Sustainable Development in Emerging Countries

Managing Organizations for Sustainable Development in Emerging Countries focuses on the main challenges and opportunities of managing firms and emerging economies in the light of sustainable development. One of the key questions of sustainable development is how organizations from developing countries are achieving their economic goals while considering, simultaneously, environmental issues like conservation of natural resources, eco-efficiency, biodiversity conservation, and climate-change mitigation. These questions are relevant for government, industry, and urban sustainability. However, in the modern literature that discusses organizational management for sustainable development, few studies focus on the reality of organizations from emerging countries. Moreover, changing environmental legislation in emerging countries (such as China and Brazil) will affect organizational managers. In this context, this book may contribute to organizational management in the search for more sustainable organizations, as well as deal with the challenges of managing organizations in the context of increased social problems, degradation of natural resources, loss of biodiversity, and climate change.

This book was published as a special issue of the *International Journal of Sustainable Development & World Ecology*.

Angappa Gunasekaran is Professor and Dean at the Charlton College of Business, University of Massachusetts Dartmouth (USA). He is also Editor in Chief of several scientific journals.

Charbel José Chiappetta Jabbour is Associate Professor, UNESP-Sao Paulo State University and Editor in Chief of *Latin American Journal of Management for Sustainable Development*.

Ana Beatriz Lopes de Sousa Jabbour is Assistant Professor, UNESP-Sao Paulo State University. She is also Deputy Editor of *Latin American Journal of Management for Sustainable Development*.

Managing Organizations for Sustainable Development in Emerging Countries

Edited by
Angappa Gunasekaran, Charbel José Chiappetta Jabbour and Ana Beatriz Lopes de Sousa Jabbour

LONDON AND NEW YORK

First published 2015
by Routledge

2 Park Square, Milton Park, Abingdon, Oxon OX14 4RN

711 Third Avenue, New York, NY 10017, USA

Routledge is an imprint of the Taylor & Francis Group, an informa business

First issued in paperback 2017

British Library Cataloguing in Publication Data
A catalogue record for this book is available from the British Library

ISBN 13: 978-1-138-85144-3 (hbk)
ISBN 13: 978-1-138-05897-2 (pbk)

Typeset in Times New Roman
by RefineCatch Limited, Bungay, Suffolk

Publisher's Note
The publisher accepts responsibility for any inconsistencies that may have arisen during the conversion of this book from journal articles to book chapters, namely the possible inclusion of journal terminology.

Disclaimer
Every effort has been made to contact copyright holders for their permission to reprint material in this book. The publishers would be grateful to hear from any copyright holder who is not here acknowledged and will undertake to rectify any errors or omissions in future editions of this book.

Contents

Citation Information

The chapters in this book were originally published in the *International Journal of Sustainable Development & World Ecology*, volume 21, issue 3 (June 2014). When citing this material, please use the original page numbering for each article, as follows:

Chapter 1
Managing organizations for sustainable development in emerging countries: an introduction
Angappa Gunasekaran, Charbel José Chiappetta Jabbour and Ana Beatriz Lopes de Sousa Jabbour
International Journal of Sustainable Development & World Ecology, volume 21, issue 3 (June 2014) pp. 195–197

Chapter 2
Influence of eco-innovation on Indian manufacturing sector sustainable performance
Satish Pandian Ganapathy, Jawahar Natarajan, Angappa Gunasekaran and Nachiappan Subramanian
International Journal of Sustainable Development & World Ecology, volume 21, issue 3 (June 2014) pp. 198–209

Chapter 3
A measure of sustainability of Brazilian agribusiness using directional distance functions and data envelopment analysis
Carlos Rosano-Peña, Patricia Guarnieri, Vinicius Amorim Sobreiro, André Luiz Marques Serrano and Herbert Kimura
International Journal of Sustainable Development & World Ecology, volume 21, issue 3 (June 2014) pp. 210–222

Chapter 4
Reverse logistics in the Chinese auto-parts firms: implementation framework development through multiple case studies
Nachiappan Subramanian, Angappa Gunasekaran, Muhammad D. Abdulrahman, Chang Liu and Danwei Su
International Journal of Sustainable Development & World Ecology, volume 21, issue 3 (June 2014) pp. 223–234

Chapter 5
Factors for implementing end-of-life product reverse logistics in the Chinese manufacturing sector
Nachiappan Subramanian, Angappa Gunasekaran, Muhammad Abdulrahman and Chang Liu
International Journal of Sustainable Development & World Ecology, volume 21, issue 3 (June 2014) pp. 235–245

Chapter 6
Social development benefits of hydroelectricity CDM projects in Brazil
Luz Fernández, Candela de la Sota, José Celio Silveira Andrade, Julio Lumbreras and Javier Mazorra
International Journal of Sustainable Development & World Ecology, volume 21, issue 3 (June 2014) pp. 246–258

Chapter 7
Sustainable development in the BRICS countries: an efficiency analysis by data envelopment
Naja Brandão Santana, Daisy Aparecida do Nascimento Rebelatto, Ana Elisa Périco and Enzo Barberio Mariano
International Journal of Sustainable Development & World Ecology, volume 21, issue 3 (June 2014) pp. 259–272

Chapter 8
Social learning for sustainability: supporting sustainable business in Brazil regarding multiple social actors, relationships and interests
Marcia Juliana d'Angelo and Janette Brunstein
International Journal of Sustainable Development & World Ecology, volume 21, issue 3 (June 2014) pp. 273–289

Chapter 9

Evaluating losses in ecosystem services in nature reserves in Sichuan, China
Yan Wang, Jixi Gao, Jinsheng Wang, Yuanzhi Wu, Changxin Zou, Meirong Tian and Hao Zheng
International Journal of Sustainable Development & World Ecology, volume 21, issue 3 (June 2014) pp. 290–301

Please direct any queries you may have about the citations to clsuk.permissions@cengage.com

Notes on Contributors

Muhammad D. Abdulrahman – Nottingham University Business School China, Ningbo, China.

José Celio Silveira Andrade – Laboratory of Global Policy Analysis, Federal University of Bahia, Bahia, Brazil.

Janette Brunstein – Center for Applied Social Sciences, Universidade Presbiteriana Mackenzie, São Paulo, Brazil.

Marcia Juliana d'Angelo – Center for Applied Social Sciences, Universidade Presbiteriana Mackenzie, São Paulo, Brazil.

Candela de la Sota – Department of Industrial Chemical Engineering and Environment, Technical University of Madrid, Spain.

Luz Fernández – Department of Industrial Chemical Engineering and Environment, Technical University of Madrid, Spain.

Satish Pandian Ganapathy – Department of Mechanical Engineering, Thiagarajar College of Engineering, Madurai, India.

Jixi Gao – College of Water Science, Beijing Normal University, China.

Patricia Guarnieri – Department of Management, University of Brasília, Brazil.

Angappa Gunasekaran – University of Massachusetts Dartmouth, Dartmouth, USA.

Charbel José Chiappetta Jabbour – Sao Paulo State University, Bauru, Brazil.

Ana Beatriz Lopes de Sousa Jabbour – Sao Paulo State University, Bauru, Brazil.

Herbert Kimura – Department of Management, University of Brasília, Brazil.

Chang Liu – Division of Economics, The University of Nottingham, China, Ningbo, China.

Julio Lumbreras – Department of Industrial Chemical Engineering and Environment, Technical University of Madrid, Spain.

Enzo Barberio Mariano – Production Engineering Department, State University of São Paulo, Bauru, Brazil.

Javier Mazorra – Department of Industrial Chemical Engineering and Environment, Technical University of Madrid, Spain.

Jawahar Natarajan – Department of Mechanical Engineering, Thiagarajar College of Engineering, Madurai, India.

Ana Elisa Périco – Economics Department, State University of São Paulo, Araraquara, Brazil.

Daisy Aparecida do Nascimento Rebelatto – Production Engineering Department, University of São Paulo, São Carlos, Brazil.

Carlos Rosano-Peña – Department of Management, University of Brasília, Brazil.

Naja Brandão Santana – Production Engineering Department, University of São Paulo, São Carlos, Brazil.

André Luiz Marques Serrano – Department of Management, University of Brasília, Brazil.

Vinicius Amorim Sobreiro – Department of Management, University of Brasília, Brazil.

Danwei Su – Division of Economics, The University of Nottingham, China, Ningbo, China.

Nachiappan Subramanian – Nottingham University Business School China, Ningbo, China.

Meirong Tian – Nanjing Institute of Environmental Science, Ministry of Environmental Protection, Nanjing, China.

Jinsheng Wang – College of Water Science, Beijing Normal University, China.

NOTES ON CONTRIBUTORS

Yan Wang – College of Water Science, Beijing Normal University, China.

Yuanzhi Wu – Shandong Provincial Key Laboratory of Soil Conservation and Environmental Protection, Linyi University, China.

Hao Zheng – College of Water Science, Beijing Normal University, China.

Changxin Zou – Nanjing Institute of Environmental Science, Ministry of Environmental Protection, Nanjing, China.

Managing organizations for sustainable development in emerging countries: an introduction

Angappa Gunasekaran[a], Charbel José Chiappetta Jabbour[b] and Ana Beatriz Lopes de Sousa Jabbour[b]

[a]University of Massachusetts – Dartmouth, Dartmouth, USA; [b]UNESP – Univ Estadual Paulista (Sao Paulo State University), Bauru, Brazil

This introduction article is for the special issue 'Managing organizations for sustainable development in emerging countries: natural resources, biodiversity, and climate change' in the *International Journal of Sustainable Development & World Ecology* and presents an introduction to the topics and summarizes accepted contributions in the special issue. The accepted works may contribute with organizational management in the search for more sustainable organizations. The works focus on the challenges of managing organizations in a context of degradation of natural resources, loss of biodiversity, and climate change. Accepted papers discuss these issues, based on the reality of emerging economies (e.g. Brazil, India, and China).

1. Introduction

Sustainable development is a type of development that meets the economic, social, and environmental needs of contemporary society without sacrificing the future generations' needs and development. According to Hopwood et al. (2005), the usual model for sustainable development is grounded on three pillars, linked to the environment, society, and economy. One of the key questions of sustainable development is how organizations from developing countries are achieving their economic goals. This is a question that considers, at the same time, environmental issues like conservation of natural resources, eco-efficiency, biodiversity conservation, and climate-change mitigation. These questions are relevant for government, industry, and urban sustainability (Zhao et al. 2013).

However, in the modern literature that discusses organizational management for sustainable development, few studies focus on the reality of organizations from emerging countries. Moreover, changing environmental legislation in emerging countries (such as China and Brazil) will affect organizational managers. For example, according to Bosetti et al. (2009), China, in particular, has doubled its emissions since the signature of the Kyoto protocol in 1997, and the country is now the largest contributor of energy-related CO_2 emissions. These authors also argue that it is now clear that developing countries, especially fast-growing regions, such as those in the so-called BRIC (Brazil, Russia, India, and China), will have a major impact on future emission dynamics and will play major roles in climate negotiations. In this context, managers from emerging economies, mainly from BRIC, will play key roles in the journey for Sustainable Development.

Subjects, such as management of natural resources (ecosystems), biodiversity, and climate change will be parts of the agenda of how organizations from emerging economies will contribute to a more sustainable society and development.

These subjects are part of the most relevant challenges for humankind and related works may provide guidelines to help the pursuit of Sustainable Development (Olsson et al. 2014).

The management of natural resources is related to ecosystem management. When implemented, it is expected that ecosystem management will protect the environment, maintain healthy ecosystems, allow for sustainable development, and preserve biodiversity (Lackey 1998).

Biodiversity, according to Sala et al. (2000), corresponds to all organisms – terrestrial and freshwater. This includes plants, animals, and microbes, on scales ranging from genetic diversity within populations, species diversity, and community diversity across landscapes. Still, according to Sala et al. (2000), changes in biodiversity affect the functioning of the ecosystem, wellbeing of human beings, and emissions of greenhouse gases. Moreover, land use can have serious consequences for endangered natural resources.

Climate change is characterized by strong scientific evidence that the average temperature of the Earth's surface is rising. This is a result of increased concentration of carbon dioxide and other greenhouse gases in the atmosphere. Global warming will lead to substantial changes in world climate, which in turn, have a big impact on human life and the built environment. Therefore, efforts must be made to reduce the use of fossil energy and to promote green energy (Omer 2008).

Hopwood et al. (2005) believe that a cause of difficulty in promoting sustainable development is guided by the lack of adequate knowledge and that there is a need to integrate economic, social, and environmental mechanisms. The lack of knowledge about how to integrate these multiple objectives in everyday organizations may be negatively affecting managers. Thus, to advance knowledge about the ways that emerging organizations can contribute to sustainable development, this special issue encouraged the submission of papers, but is not restricted to, on the following subjects:

- Climate change, as a challenge and opportunity for managers.
- Natural resource conservation and eco-efficiency in organizations.
- Best practices of managing for sustainable development.
- Environmentally responsible supply-chain management.
- Organizations and millennium-development goals.
- Managing organizations and considering biodiversity and ecological constraints.
- Responsible supply chain management.
- Marketing strategies, focusing on green issues.
- Role of environmental legislation in managing for sustainable development, and
- Challenges and opportunities for emerging economies.

It is worth noting that emerging economies have great potential to introduce major changes in the debate on sustainable development, particularly in regard to the emerging countries (Papa & Gleason 2012). In this sense, the proposition of the Call for Papers 'Managing organizations for sustainable development in emerging countries: natural resources, biodiversity, and climate change' by focusing on the discussion of the role of organizational and governmental actions is justified in the current context of the search for a more sustainable global economy.

2. A brief overview on the accepted works

For this special issue, we received submissions from authors of different countries, focusing on the reality of Brazil, India, and China. These countries are part of the BRIC group. Unfortunately, we did not receive submissions from Russia and other emerging countries. We also did not receive papers that directly covered all of the suggested subjects for this special issue. These limitations will be further discussed in the conclusion of this Introduction article. After the process of selecting the best articles, articles that make up this special issue are presented below.

The article 'Influence of eco-innovation on Indian manufacturing sector sustainable performance' develops an eco-innovation conceptual model. This model relates the management and innovative practices (antecedents) and overall sustainable performance (consequences) of eco-innovation, using an institutional theory. Using an Indian-manufacturing sector empirical data and Structural Equation Modelling (SEM) approach, this paper determines the effects of eco-innovation's antecedents and consequences. In the Indian context, this study suggests that the role of management practice is more significant, regarding eco-innovation, than innovative practices. The results reflect practitioners' view on how to increase innovation rates and to focus more on social aspects. The finding suggests that training on environment-related practices could involve innovation and social aspects in the Indian-manufacturing sector context.

The aim of 'A measure of sustainability of Brazilian agribusiness using directional distance functions and data envelopment analysis' is to estimate a set of indicators of relative efficiency in the Brazilian agricultural sector. The aim is also to satisfy the concept of Pareto optimality, simultaneous economic empowerment, ecological dimensions, and social functions. In order to accomplish this goal, the methods of Directional Distance Functions and Data Envelopment Analysis (DEA) were applied. These indicators confirm, in different ways, the hypothesis that it is possible to perform consistent productive strategies with the maximization of social welfare, despite the apparent antagonism, among these three dimensions. In addition, it is shown that efficient Brazilian states tend to combine the three dimensions in different ways.

The article 'Reverse logistics in the Chinese auto-parts firms: implementation framework development through multiple case studies' focuses on Reverse Logistics (RL) implementation issues in the Chinese auto parts manufacturing sector. Based on a comprehensive literature review and multiple case studies in Chinese auto parts firms, this paper proposes a conceptual RL framework and highlights the major implementation issues. The study suggests that Chinese RL implementation requires close government-monitoring mechanisms and incentives, top management commitment within firms, technology, and human-capabilities support.

The article 'Factors for implementing end-of-life products reverse logistics in the Chinese manufacturing sector' aims to understand and prioritize various end-of-life product reverse logistical factors from a Chinese manufacturing sector perspective. Multiple case studies in five different industries within the manufacturing sector have been carried out in order to understand views with respect to reverse logistics. Analytic hierarchy process has been employed in this study to prioritize the governing factors for the successful implementation of reverse logistics operations in the Chinese manufacturing sector. Results indicate that Chinese firms are unlikely to embark on reverse logistics operations without external factors, such as strict government legislation.

'Social development benefits of hydroelectricity CDM projects in Brazil' involved an assessment of 46 registered hydro-CDM projects, under the Kyoto Protocol, in terms of their potential impacts on the envisaged social development goals. Two case studies were also examined. The results indicate that organizations managing hydroelectric initiatives in Brazil can offer a pathway towards achieving a number of important social benefits. Successful projects were found to have good community involvement and were managed by both cooperative ventures and money-making corporations. The research also identified several challenges that hinder the hydro-CDM projects in delivering more social benefits, and the research provided a number of recommendations for the organizations to face these challenges.

'Sustainable development in the BRICS countries: an efficiency analysis by data envelopment' discusses the performance of countries in the BRICS group, regarding sustainable development. The objective of this study is to evaluate the efficiency of these countries in transforming productive resources and technological innovation into sustainable development. The proposed objective was achieved by using econometric tools, as well as the DEA method, in order to create economic, environmental, and social-efficiency rankings for the BRICS countries. This enables comparative analyses of the sustainable development of the BRICS countries. The results of such assessments can be of interest for more specific scientific explorations.

'Social learning for sustainability: supporting sustainable business in Brazil regarding multiple social actors, relationships and interests' discussed how one of the largest companies in the chemical segment in Latin America formed a network with social actors; it also discussed how the company is socially learning to deal with the dialectic between return on investments for its shareholders and benefits for its stakeholders. Therefore, research was conducted based on Boje's narrative analysis. The data was built through interviews, informal conversations, textual and audiovisual documents, and nonparticipant observation. The results discuss the concepts and describe the social learning process for sustainability (in this case, for sustainable agriculture) from the viewpoint of a profit-based organization. In this sense, the study seeks to strengthen the connection between social learning and sustainability.

'Evaluating losses in ecosystem services in nature reserves in Sichuan, China' assessed land use and the variation of ecosystem services value (ESV) during 2000–2010 in national nature reserves in Sichuan. The work analyzed the comprehensive effects of natural disasters and human activities on the decline of ESVs. Total ESV in the national nature reserves in Sichuan was approximately 2741.35 million US dollars in 2000, 2616.81 million US dollars in 2005, and 2499.06 million US dollars in 2010, representing a decrease of 242.29 million US dollars, or 8.84%, in the decade. Forestland, grassland, wetland, and water bodies played vital roles in the function of ecosystem services, with an aggregated

ESV of 99% of the total. The largest proportion of the total ESV was the protection of biodiversity at 48.6%. ESV of all land use types and single ecosystem services continued to decline during 2000–2010. A mechanism of adaptable risk prevention should be established, and unreasonable human activities should be avoided to protect ecosystems and to improve the functions of ecosystem services.

3. Final remarks

The aim of this special issue was to group a set of high-quality research on managing organizations for sustainability in emerging economies. We hope that the accepted works may inform managers from developing countries on the challenges of considering natural resources, climate change, and biodiversity during the day-to-day management. Unfortunately, we did not receive submissions from other emerging countries. We also did not receive papers that cover all of the suggested topics, mentioned in the call for papers. Thus, these national contexts and subjects may be further developed in future studies and publications.

Acknowledgments

We would like to thank all the authors who have submitted papers for the special issue and the reviewers who have reviewed manuscripts in a timely manner. Special thanks to the Editor of IJSDWE, Professor Jingzhu Zhao, and to the journal managers/publishers for their constant support, right from the beginning until the editorial process was completed.

References

Bosetti V, Carraro C, Tavoni M. 2009. Climate change mitigation strategies in fast-growing countries: the benefits of early action. Energy Econ. 31:S144–S151. doi:10.1016/j.eneco.2009.06.011

Hopwood B, Mellor M, O'Brien G. 2005. Sustainable development: mapping different approaches. Sust Dev. 13:38–52. doi:10.1002/sd.244

Lackey RT. 1998. Seven pillars of ecosystem management. Landsc Urban Plan. 40:21–30. doi:10.1016/S0169-2046(97)00095-9

Olsson L, Hourcade JC, Köhler J. 2014. Sustainable development in a globalized world. J Environ Dev. 23:3–14. doi:10.1177/1070496514521418

Omer AM. 2008. Energy, environment and sustainable development. Rene Sustain Ener Rev. 12:2265–2300. doi:10.1016/j.rser.2007.05.001

Papa M, Gleason NW. 2012. Major emerging powers in sustainable development diplomacy: assessing their leadership potential. Global Environ Change. 22:915–924. doi:10.1016/j.gloenvcha.2012.06.003

Sala OE, Chapin FS, Armesto JJ, Berlow E, Bloomfield J, Dirzo R, Wall DH. 2000. Global biodiversity scenarios for the year 2100. Science. 287:1770–1774. doi:10.1126/science.287.5459.1770

Zhao J, Zheng X, Dong R, Shao G. 2013. The planning, construction, and management toward sustainable cities in china needs the environmental internet of things. Int J Sust Dev World Ecol. 20:195–198. doi:10.1080/13504509.2013.784882

Influence of eco-innovation on Indian manufacturing sector sustainable performance

Satish Pandian Ganapathy[a], Jawahar Natarajan[a], Angappa Gunasekaran[b] and Nachiappan Subramanian[c]

[a]Department of Mechanical Engineering, Thiagarajar College of Engineering, Madurai, India; [b]Charlton College of Business, University of Massachusetts Dartmouth, North Dartmouth, MA, USA; [c]Nottingham University Business School China, The University of Nottingham Ningbo China, Ningbo, China

Manufacturing firms are striving to improve their sustainable performance in order to satisfy multiple stakeholders. Eco-innovation is a promising approach that decreases environmental impact and helps firms to increase their business value. There are several antecedents which help the firms to innovate and improve their triple bottom line performance. Among the antecedents, management and innovative practices are directly related to eco-innovation. It is not well known what practices and innovations help the firms to eco-innovate as well as to improve sustainable performance. Hence, the research objective of this paper is to identify the suitable combination of management and innovative practices that help firms to eco-innovate as well as to achieve overall sustainable performance. The paper develops an eco-innovation conceptual model which relates the management and innovative practices (antecedents) and overall sustainable performance (consequences) of eco-innovation using institutional theory. Using Indian manufacturing sector's empirical data and Structural Equation Modelling (SEM) approach, this paper determines the effect of eco-innovation's antecedents and consequences. In the Indian context, this study suggests that the role of management practice is more significant towards eco-innovation than innovative practices. The results reflect practitioners' view on how to increase innovation rate and to focus more on social aspects. The finding suggests that training on environmental related practices could tackle innovation and social aspects in the Indian manufacturing sector context.

1. Introduction

Innovation can happen anywhere in a firm and it can be referred to as 'the implementation of a new or significantly improved product (good or service), or process, a new marketing method, or a new organizational method in business practices, workplace organization or external relations' (OECD 2009). Innovation has long been seen as central to economic performance and social welfare; it is increasingly recognized as a significant driver of economic growth. Specifically, an innovation that mitigates environmental impacts and makes contribution to the sustainability is defined as eco-innovation which includes eco-product, eco-process and eco-organizational innovation (Triguero et al. 2013; Wilts et al. 2013). Two major desirable characteristics of eco-innovation are (i) one among the initiatives that contribute towards sustainable development and (ii) improves firms' competitive advantage through sustainable product and process design. Sustainable product design is achieved through design for environment, design for disassembly, etc. Process design includes optimization of production processes, reduced material, energy use and waste generation, etc.

More recently, industry leaders and policy makers have viewed innovation as the key to radical improvements when corporates are concerned more about environmental practices and performances. Recent studies have deliberately expressed that the adoptions of innovative/

Sustainable management practices are the drivers for the performance of any manufacturing industry (Nidumolu et al. 2009). Leading manufacturers having operations in the developed countries such as Apple (reduction in overall carbon foot print), Toyota (recovery and reuse of end of life vehicle components) and HP (environmental protective inks) came out with excellent eco-innovation solutions to mitigate the environmental as well as social effect.

The above examples reveal that only few firms are taking voluntary initiatives whereas several other firms are subjected to various pressures to eco-innovate and it can be classified as three major pressures such as institutional pressure (Legislation through government), coercive (to satisfy requirements of various standards and customers) and mimetic (competition from peers and competitors). To satisfy the above pressures, firms follow different strategies and practices. It is evident from previous studies that firms have adapted different management and innovative practices to achieve unique position through environmental and continuous improvement quality practices (Tidd et al. 2005; Yarong & Xin 2011; Gimenez et al. 2012).

The above discussions reveal that there are few drivers as well as pressures for firms to eco-innovate. It is also not well known what practices and innovations helped firms to overcome drivers and pressures to eco-innovate as well as to improve sustainable performance. Hence, the research objective of this paper is to identify the suitable combination of environmental and innovative practices that helps firms to eco-innovate as well as to achieve overall sustainable performance. Therefore, the study develops a conceptual model to map the influence of innovative and management practices on eco-innovation and subsequently its contribution to the sustainable performance. The model is developed using the underpinnings of institutional theory.

There are few more challenges to the research objective in the developing countries as well as to the specific industry context. There is a substantial environmental sustainability challenge, including global warming, energy demand, water and food supplies, behavioural changes, lower consumption and eco-efficiency due to depleting natural resources (Diedrich et al. 2011). This mandates a deeper understanding of society's relationship with natural resources.

The major contributions of this study are twofold: (i) develop a conceptual model to relate management and innovative practices (antecedents) and sustainable performance (consequences) of eco-innovation and (ii) empirically validate the model in a specific country and industry context to identify the suitable combination of management and innovative practices to achieve sustainable performance.

Out of several sectors in India, this study specifically focuses on manufacturing sector due to the following reasons: (i) higher potential to affect environment such as air pollution, effluent run-off and improper disposal of solid wastes; (ii) new technologies to cleaner processes as well as operations that are not proceeding at a fast enough pace to address the urgent need for environmental protection; (iii) 42.67% growth in number of manufacturing firms from 1987 to 2007 (98,379–1,40,355) (India planning commission report, 2013).

The rest of the paper is organized as follows: Section 2 reviews the literature to identify the pattern of practices on eco-innovation and the effect of eco-innovation on performances. Section 3 delineates the conceptual model development. The research methodology, especially the structural equation modelling approach, is explained in Section 4. Section 5 discusses the findings of the study. The major findings, limitations and highlights of the potential future research directions are summarized in Section 6.

2. Literature review

This section reviews the studies related to anecdotal practices and its effect on eco-innovations. In addition, this section also reviews the relevant studies to capture influence of eco-innovation on sustainable performance.

2.1. Management practice, innovation and eco-innovation

As a reaction to the international institutional pressures, organizations pay more attention to adapt management practices that such as ISO 14001, Total Quality Environmental Management (TQEM), eco-auditing and other decisions like employee training, R&D investments, etc. Cozzarin and Jeffrey (2014) stated that management practices such as human resource management focusing on flexible job definitions, cross-training and work teams, along with extensive reliance on incentive pay, result in substantially higher levels of productivity. Studies have found that there is a correlation between such management systems and labour productivity. Proper training for employee by itself increases productivity and training with management practices also increases productivity.

Since the greenhouse effect is worsening and the resource is scarce, sustainable development becomes a considerable concern in business practice (Despeisse et al. 2012). There are several drivers for enterprises to meet the need of sustainable development. The first and foremost reason for organizations is in respect to external regulatory and policy pressures which limit environment index such as carbon and toxic emission and water or air pollution level (Beske 2012; Hitchcock 2012). For example, some of the earlier initiatives are the European Union (EU) Emission Trading Scheme (Hitchcock 2012). Moreover, except the official policies and regulations, the pressure from some communities and non-governmental organizations also serves as an important force in sustainable development (Beske 2012). According to Porter (1996), in order to employ the differentiation strategy to gain competitiveness over its competitors, an enterprise has to focus on the Research and Development (R&D) with innovations to win the market share. The most important reason for such high attention on environmental factors is that they are regarded by an increasing number of companies as great opportunities to drive business efficiencies, stimulate innovation, reduce costs, improve brand positioning and enhance business communications. Also, companies may further strengthen their competency and add value to their business with those environmental benefits (O'Rafferty 2008). The use of processes like Design-for-Environment (DfE) helps to reduce the environmental impact of products from the initial stage of conceptual design (Kurk & Eagan 2008). The ideal situation being that products will be made, distributed and used without harming the environment as well as being recyclable and reusable. In terms of this eco-product innovation, designers will integrate environmental considerations at the very first step of product development which can contribute to the ideal goals of environmental friendly product (Kurk & Eagan 2008; González-García et al. 2012).

Technological development plays an important role in eco-innovation (Horbach et al. 2012), and helping companies benefit more from eco-innovation in various areas. According to Cook et al. (2012), the technological development provides new ways for sustainable development, and it has also shown that the improvement of technology can stimulate eco-innovation (Horbach et al.

2012). In addition, along with the globalization over time, sustainability has drawn attention from technical to political area, which has further developed into a mainstream in business area (Liu et al. 2012). Therefore, it is reasonable for people today to pay more attention on eco-innovation. Several attempts have been made in defining the concept of eco-innovation and generally, it illustrates that eco-innovation can result in positive environmental impacts, whether the purpose of the implementation of eco-innovation is related to the environment or not (Carrillo-Hermosilla et al. 2010). Moreover, Esty and Winston (2006) have pointed out that with environmental factors, the companies tend to be more innovative and entrepreneurial. In addition to the environmental benefits, many economic advantages should not be neglected in eco-innovation. Particularly, Boons et al. (2013) hold the opinion that the concept of sustainable innovation is much broader than eco-innovation. However, it is determined to define eco-innovation with the social aspects and in the model as well. It is commonly accepted that today's economic benefits should not be at the expense of the long-term benefits. Thus, eco-innovation is significant in the innovation system. Taking environmental, social and economic aspects into consideration, it may contribute to the whole innovation system to a large extent (Carrillo-Hermosilla et al. 2010).

2.2. Eco-innovation and sustainable performance

The existing research has discussed the measurement of eco-innovation and 'Tripple Bottom Line' separately, and this paper will build up a model to evaluate eco-innovation with the measurement of 'Tripple Bottom Line'. According to Cetinkaya et al. (2011), realistic funding and measurement are necessary for the sustainable development and thus, suitable performance measurement is significant for sustainability (Chaabane et al. 2012). However, the integration of tangible and intangible performance of eco-innovation adds to the complexity of the measurement selection (Giannakis 2007; Bai et al. 2012). 'Tripple Bottom Line' has been introduced by Elkington (1997). It advocates equal treatment of all three dimensions, economic, social and environmental aspects for sustainability (Beske 2012). Hence it would be appropriate to measure eco-innovation with social and economic performance dimensions in addition to environmental dimension. That is, triple bottom line measurement will be taken into account in eco-innovation, providing a more considerable evaluation. Triple bottom line includes economic, environmental and social performance. Table 1 summarizes the studies that have been carried out with respect to three performance measures. It is visible from Table 1 that non-economic performances have received lesser attention from researchers than economic performances.

It is evident from the literature review that various studies have proven that eco-innovation has the greatest potential to overcome environmental effect as well as social effect. It is obvious that eco-innovation has been achieved by firms by modifying their products, process, organizational level and marketing techniques. Interestingly, the researchers have not noticed any typical study which discusses the management and innovative practices (antecedents) of eco-innovation and its overall sustainable performance (consequences). Moreover, the objective of various studies is to mitigate environmental effect and not to, a larger extent, social aspects. It is argued that eco-innovation could contribute to triple bottom line performance. The above intriguing aspects have motivated the researchers to develop a conceptual model and relate antecedents and consequences of eco-innovation and to validate the model with empirical data in a specific country and industry context.

3. Conceptual model

Institutional theory aims to explain the extent to which 'individual firms' practices should mimic industry best practices versus reflects the participants' unique characteristics'. There are three major pressures within institution and they are coercive, mimetic and normative.

Coercive institutional pressures, which stem from political and legitimate forces, are exerted on a dependent firm by other organizations (on which the firm depends) and by cultural expectations in the society within which the dependent firm exists (Lai et al. 2006). In short, coercive pressures come from organizations in power (Sarkis et al. 2011). Examples of coercive isomorphism include governmental laws and regulations (Sarkis et al. 2011), standard operating procedures and rules (Dimaggio & Powell 1983), etc. The recent decades have been witnessing the increasing adoption of the coercive isomorphism to explain why companies engage in environmental management practices (Sarkis et al. 2011).

Mimetic institutional pressures are mainly from a firm's peer firms who are more successful. Firms tend to mimic or imitate their successful competitors to 'replicate their successful paths' (Sarkis et al. 2011). The core reason for firms' imitative behaviour is 'uncertainty' (Dimaggio & Powell 1983). According to Sarkis et al. (2011), globalization has been facilitating the imitation between firms, as it creates opportunities for firms to learn from international counterparts. But problems remain as 'To what extent companies can mimic industry best practices?' and 'How well the learned practices can work in other contexts?' (Ketchen Jr & Hult, 2007a, 2007b).

Normative pressures are believed to come from professionalization (DiMaggio & Powell 1983; Lai et al. 2006). Examples of normative pressures include the standards formed on a sector level or market level force individual companies in this particular sector or companies operating in this market to adopt a certain practice. In the

Table 1. Criteria in various area of study.

Sustainable Criteria		Source	Area of Study
Sustainable practices leading Sustainable Performance	Economy (Management)	Leitham et al. (2000), Ulusoy (2003), and Yang (2006)	Industrial performance studies
		Dangayach and Deshmukh (2000, 2003)	Per capita Gross National Product (GNP), Gross Domestic Product (GDP), Manufacturing (% of GDP), Per Capita Research and Development (GDR) Expenditure and Exports
		Rho et al. (2001), Singh et al. (2006)	Manufacturing Innovation Practices
			BPR (Business Process Reengineering), ERP (Enterprise Resource Planning), TQM (Total Quality Management), JIT (Just-In-Time), TPM (Total Productive Maintenance), CIM (Computer Integrated Manufacturing), QFD (Quality Function Deployment), DFM (Design For Manufacturer), PDM (Product Data Management), FMS (Flexible Manufacturing System), CAD (Computer-Aided Manufacturing) and CAE (Computer-Aided Engineering).
		Fang and Côté (2005)	Cleaner Production towards sustainability
		Meyer (2002)	Market valuation, financial measures, Non-financial measures and Cost measures
	Environment (Eco-innovation)	Fredericks (2012)	Environmental Performance Index (EPI), Sustainable Development Indicators (SDIs)
		Liu et al. (2002), Yang (2006), and Jayal et al. (2010)	Environmental studies
		Klassen and McLaughlin's (1996)	Environmental Collaboration
		Montabon et al. (2007)	Environment Management
	Socio-Economic (Innovation)	Curkovic (2003)	Environmental Responsible Manufacturing
		Despeisse, Mbaye, et al. (2012)	Sustainable Manufacturing practices such as lean manufacturing, Environmentally Conscious Manufacturing (ECM) and '4-Rs' (reduction, remanufacturing, recycling and reuse)
		Yarong and Xin (2011) and Gimenez et al. (2012)	Economic, ecological/environmental and social
		Foronda-Robles and Galindo-Pérez-de-Azpillaga (2012)	Socio-economic development and the strategies for protected natural areas
		Jayal et al. (2010)	Functionality, manufacturability, recyclability, re-manufacturability, resource utilization/economy and societal impact
		Orlitzky et al. (2003), Esty and Winston (2006), and Gimenez et al. (2012)	Environmental, Social and Corporate Governance
		Malarvizhi and Sangeeta (2008)	Social, Economic and Socio-economic

context of environmental and socially responsible practices, companies' adoption of such practices will be largely influenced by the market and consumer requirements (Sarkis et al. 2011).

Zhu et al. (2013) provide a holistic framework to analyse the institutional pressures that companies are facing and successfully relate the institutional theory with firms' environmental management systems. They divided the coercive, normative and mimetic pressures into international pressures and domestic pressures. Their findings suggest that international institutional pressures play more important role in adoption of green practices such as ISO 14001, Total Quality Environmental management (TQEM) and eco-auditing.

3.1. Model

The need for organizations to engage in environmentally responsible operations includes government policies and regulations, pressures from consumers and the life-threatening global ecosystem deterioration. Collectively, the level of institutional pressures perceived by firms has impacts on the adoption of organizational practices. In the current study, it is believed that institutional pressures act as main driver for companies to engage in different sustainable practices. Based on the institutional theory, it is aimed to develop a conceptual model as shown in Figure 1 to link management and innovative practices as the major drivers for eco-innovation and its effect in terms of sustainable performance.

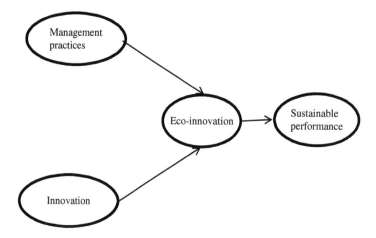

Figure 1. Atecedents and consequences of eco-innovation comceptual model.

3.2. Hypotheses development

Management and innovative practices, which are directly related to eco-innovation, are the two among several antecedents helpful for the firm to innovate and improve their triple bottom line performance. From the internal aspect within the organizations, the efforts to contribute to the environmental protection will build an image of Corporate Social Responsibilities (CSR) of organizations in customer mind (Ho & Choi 2012; Triguero et al. 2013). Data indicate that most of the surveyed organizations believe that the green efforts will have the greatest impact on 'reputation and brand' (Baskaran et al. 2011; Ho & Choi 2012). As a result of the increased brand equity and CSR reputation, organizations will be able to maintain the current customers' loyalty as well as attracting new customers. Since customer loyalty is difficult to imitate, this intangible asset will create the sustainable competitive advantages for organizations (Beske 2012; Ho & Choi 2012). Not only the efficient use of materials and energy will be considered, but also waste prevention, feasibility of recycling and expansion of product life cycle are also important elements in eco-product (González-García et al. 2012; Yang & Chen 2012). As a result, compared with the traditional product, the finished eco-product is beneficial to the sustainable development of society which in turn brings profitability for organizations. Nowadays, since some resources are non-renewable and DfE cannot solve the problem of scarce resources, organizations should come up with other strategies. Moreover, the re-manufacture of returned product can assist organizations to save material purchase costs and inventory costs and these returned products can be easily converted into saleable finished goods (Mondragon et al. 2011). Based on the above argument, the following hypothesis is postulated relating management practices and innovation.

H1: Management practices improves eco-innovation

Employing sustainable development will save costs for organizations. Although green efforts require considerable investment in R&D, the actual revenue gain will outweigh the inputs (Triguero et al. 2013). Not only does the advanced technology improves the productivity in organizations, it will also help them to avoid punishment from the tightening environmental regulation. Taking these factors of pursuing environmental friendly development into account, the word 'sustainability' addresses the efforts and concerns about relieving the impact on environment. The concept of sustainable manufacturing is that the management of materials, information and capital flows will be in line with environmental, social and economic requirements (Beske 2012; Ho & Choi 2012). For instance, Hewlett Packard innovatively removes an adhesive that makes recycling of ink cartridges challenging, which brings about 2.4 million dollars savings in two years (González-García et al. 2012). Furthermore, by simplifying the design of cartridge packaging, the materials are used more efficiently and the product cost per unit is also reduced. In order to achieve the goal, innovations serve significant function. This work addresses the significance of innovation for sustainable development. Innovative practices, especially training and investment in R&D, have significant effect on eco-innovation (Ulusoy 2003). The following hypothesis states the effect of innovative practices on eco-innovation.

H2: Innovative practices improves eco-innovation

Horbach et al. (2012) have mentioned that eco-innovation is quite successful, because research has proved that around 80.4% of eco-innovation may result in lower or constant cost, and among those eco-innovations, 32% of them even related to higher turnover. Furthermore, new business models built up related to sustainable innovations can create a win–win situation (Boons et al. 2013). For example, Liu et al. (2012) point out that compared to closed-loop supply chains that aim at improving economic benefits, sustainable supply chain management pays more attention on the coordination among social, environmental and economic dimensions. Firms' performance should be evaluated through economic, environmental and social performance (Beske 2012; Chaabane et al. 2012). A research project called 'Measuring Eco-Innovation (MEI)' taken by EU cares more about the environmental risk and pollution problems (Horbach et al. 2012). According to sustainable performance arguments, firms that eco-innovate have higher plausibility to improve on triple bottom line performance.

H3: Eco-innovation drives sustainable performance

4. Research methodology

An empirical survey is carried out to test the hypotheses. Questionnaire with standard measurement scales is used to collect the data. Given that one of the key purposes of this study is to confirm the effect of management and innovative practices that support eco-innovation and sustainable performance, a pilot test of this research is conducted with academic experts and industrial practitioners who have substantial experience in sustainability. Aiming the scope and objectives of the research, the survey instrument is developed with seven categories as follows: general respondent and company related items, environmental aspects of product and process items, items related to environmental protection practices, items corresponding to sustainable innovation practices like investments in R&D (Ulusoy 2003), measures of economic, social and socio-economic/environment performances. Initially, comments are received for the adapted questionnaire and gradually several modifications are incorporated in the questionnaire that greatly influence respondents through proper transformation of messages that conveyed in receipt of better understanding about the question, for the response scales' face and content validity. In addition, the feedback has guided in changing the order and wording of several survey items that are difficult. Further, this has insisted removal of questions of high complexity and unnecessary items. Besides the development of the questionnaire, the responses are structured with the five point Likert scale (1: strongly disagree to 5: strongly agree). The description for every scale is also elaborated and that has helped the survey's respondents to provide the most valid, consistent and reliable responses (Chachamovich et al. 2009; Patel & Jayaram 2014). The respondents of the study are executives of the manufacturing industries in the class of General manager, Works/Finance manager, Supervisor, experts from the pollution board, environmental/industrial consultants of environmental manager/auditor and environmental policy makers such as Executives from pollution board, R&D and NGOs. Respondents and organizational characteristics are given in Appendix.

4.1. Sampling and data collection

The questionnaire is distributed to the manufacturing firms (electronics, leather, textile dyeing) located in the tropical regions on the Industrial parks, special economic zones, Small Industries Promotion Corporation of Tamilnadu (SIPCOT) formed by the Government of Tamilnadu, India, with various industrial clusters in Tamilnadu, a state in southern India. The data necessary for the research are received by sending questionnaires to the contacts collected from the directory available at the Confederation of Indian Industries. The questionnaire is distributed to respondents of manufacturers through electronic mailing, hardcopies and by direct interviews. Apart from the list retrieved, contacts from several association's publications, conferences and websites are gathered. To encourage respondents' participation, as a token of gratitude, they are promised with the provision of the executive summary of the article developed through the current research. In order to increase the sample diversity, other Internet channels such as Email, online survey and MSN, etc., are also used to distribute the questionnaire.

Three remainders are sent to the respondents to complete the survey within the defined time intervals; Initial respondents (37%) are compared with the respondents whose are received next (9%) and the final respondents (54%) serve as a proxy for non-respondents. The objective values such as respondent's experience, employee size and existence of companies are taken to check for non-respondent bias and we did not notice any significant difference among early and late respondents.

4.2. Structural equation modelling approach

Fornell (1992) developed Structural Equation Modelling (SEM) approach to measure customer satisfaction in marketing studies. SEM is a method that can address several restrictions and provide a robust technique for studying interdependencies among a set of correlated variables. Malaeb et al. (2000) have identified several limitations over regression models to select SEM techniques for analysing data from experimental/observational studies and the use of the best-fit model for inference and hypothesis testing. SEM is a multivariate statistical methodology that encompasses factor and path analysis (McCune & Grace 2002; Subramanian et al. 2014). One among the multivariate statistical method is the structural equation modelling, by which the evaluation of a network of relationships between manifest and latent variables can be performed (Arhonditsis et al. 2006). Later on, use of SEM has become popular for measuring various performance measures in different domains that include examination of the relationship between factors. Numerous studies used SEM to figure out direct and indirect effects of the relationship between factors and performance (Lin 2007; Joo & Sohn 2008). There are two step approaches that are adopted in SEM for the construction of the measurement and testing the structural model (Anderson & Gerbing 1988). This study employs the SPSS 20 for confirmatory factor (Measurement) and AMOS 20 for path analysis (Testing).

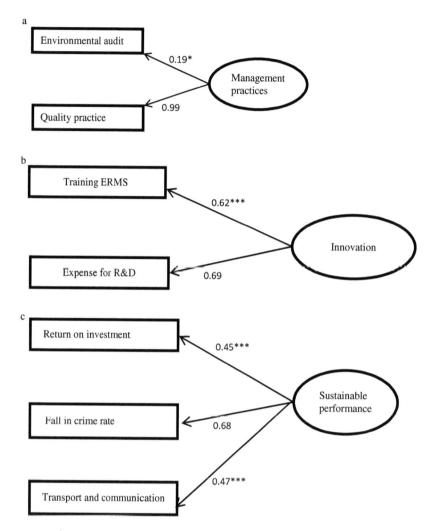

Figure 2. (a) Management practices measurement model; (b) Innovation practices measurement model; (c) Sustainable performance measurement model.
Note: $*p < 0.05$; $***p < 0.001$.

4.2.1. Measurement model – validity and reliability

Figure 2a–c shows the measurement models along with the correlation values of the constructs management practices, innovation practices and sustainable performance. Table 2 shows the constructs, composite reliability, Cronbach's Alpha and the Average Variance Extracted (AVE) of each construct. AVE is utilized to assess the discriminant validity, the square root of which should be larger than the correlations between constructs (Chin 1998).

The reliability or internal consistency is assessed through Cronbach's alpha coefficient and composite reliability. As suggested by Nunnally (1978), a value greater than 0.60 show good reliability for newly developed constructs. Measurement scales for all constructs are greater than 0.60, which means all of them have adequate

Table 2. Construct test statistics.

Constructs	Variables code	Variables	Cronbach's Alpha	Composite reliability	AVE
Innovation	C1	Training on ERMS to employees	0.625	0.5596	0.3901
	C2	Proportion of expenses from turn over for R&D activities			
Management Practices	C3	Frequency of environmental practices Audit	0.629	0.5696	0.5082
	C4	Quality/management practices			
Sustainable Performance	D2	Return on Investment	0.605	0.6618	0.3476
	E2	Fall in crime rate			
	F1	Transport and communication facilities has improved			

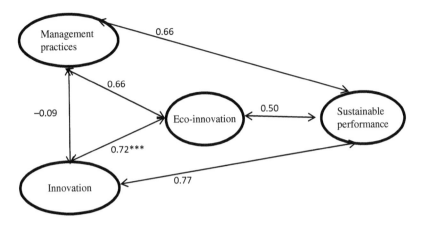

Figure 3.   Confirmatory factor analysis model.
Note: ***$p < 0.001$.

reliability. The results show that composite reliability values for all constructs are greater than 0.50, which indicate good internal consistency. The results show that all items meet the requirement.

4.2.2. Testing of structural equation models

The confirmatory factor analysis model and its fit statistics are shown in Figure 3 and Table 3, respectively. Figure 4 shows the AMOS test results of the structural equation model of antecedents of eco-innovation and its consequences. Table 4 provides the fit indices of the path model of our study given in Figure 4. The cut-offs for the fit indices recommended by Subramanian et al. (2014)

Table 3.   Fit indices of the confirmatory factor analysis model.

x^2 (df)	Normed x^2	CFI	RMSEA (% CI)	IFI
15.6 (14)	1.11	0.854	0.060	0.910

Table 4.   Fit indices of the path model.

x^2 (df)	Normed x^2	CFI	RMSEA (% CI)	IFI
21.3 (15)	1.42	0.920	0.065	0.925

given in Table 5 have been used for testing the SEM. The indices Chi-square, comparative fit index, incremental fit index and root mean square error of approximation are within the suggested cut-off.

5.   Discussions

Eco-innovation conceptual and path models that are developed in this article relate and show the influence of the two antecedents' of management and innovation on eco-innovation. The study verified path model (Figure 4) and analysed using the survey data, which is obtained through questionnaire developed to assess the sustainable performance to various practices, reveal the following:

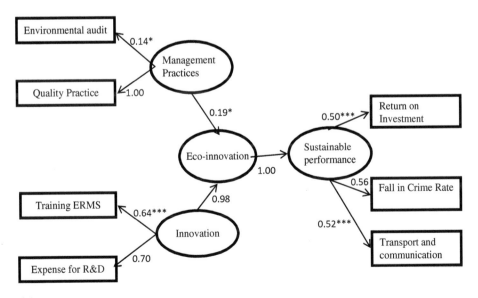

Figure 4.   Path model.
Note: *$p < 0.05$; ***$p < 0.001$.

Table 5. Description of fit indices.

Fit index	Description	Suggested cut-off
x^2	Normed chi-square: chi-square divided by degree of freedom	(0.002, 4.80)
CFI	Comparative fix index: compares the model fit with a baseline model	(0.88, 1.00)
IFI	Incremental fit index: group of goodness of fit indices that assesses how well a specified model fits relative to some alternative baseline model	(0.88, 0.98)
RMSEA	Root mean square error of approximation	(0.00, 0.13)

- The path coefficient '0.19' (10% significant level) between management practice and eco-innovation reveals that management practice is significant. It means that management practice contributes and supports eco-innovation and subsequently sustainable performance. Hence the hypothesis 'H1: Management practices improve eco-innovation' is supported.
- The path coefficient '0.98' between innovation and eco-innovation reveals that innovation is not much significant. Even though the path co-efficient is very high it is not significant as management practice. It means that the data set does not support the hypothesis 'H2: Innovation improves eco-innovation'.
- The path coefficient between Eco-Innovation and Sustainable Performance is with a value of '1.00'. This points out that the data is not sufficient enough to prove the hypothesis 'H3 Eco-Innovation drives Sustainable Performance' because companies adopt variety of quality practices. Possibility of non-supportive to our hypotheses H3 (Eco-innovation and performance) are due to the non-availability of appropriate sustainable performance measurement. Even more understanding is essential in the Indian manufacturing sector.
- Though the contribution of management practices towards improving eco-innovation is significant, it has been achieved mainly through environmental audit '0.14' rather than the quality practices '1.0' as shown in Figure 4.
- The loading of training on environmental regulation management system (ERMS) '0. 64' and expenses on R&D '0.70' on innovation indicate that the practice of them differs in large extent by the various companies.
- It is also to be noted from Figure 3 that the path coefficient between constructs between management practice and innovation is negative (–0.09) in the co-variance model, which confirms non-coexistence of management practice and innovation in most of the companies considered in the sample.

- The proactive environmental management practices will positively influence the innovative solutions to environmental challenges and improves organization's sustainability operations.
- In addition to the benefit of environmental protection, training on ERMS and R&D play a major role in sustainable performance and provides competitive advantage in product innovation, process innovation and sales growth.

The findings of Wehrmeyer and Tyteca (1998) on environmental performance measurement and the study carried out by Zhao et al. (2008) on the environmental linkages concentrate on the policies and governance, and are indicated as follows: Social and environmental responsibilities can be improved through strong legal enforcement by the government; Principal policy commitments must be supported by the governments to enhance green growth concept. They stated further that the policies should not only concentrate on environment and must embrace the social aspects of economic and negative impacts. As this study explores the linkages of management practices, innovation practices, eco-innovation and their resultant sustainable performance, it demonstrates the drivers of sustainability and the action that managers need to focus to improve sustainability, and examines the impacts of social and environmental initiatives on overall corporate profitability. This can help managers to suggest the ways to improve the measurement and management of sustainability issues, and provide guidance on how managers can translate sustainability strategies into action. However, to implement strategies generally and sustainability strategies particularly, managers need to understand better both the implications of their decisions and the actions that they can take to produce improved performance. To build sustainable strategy, Wu and Hunt (2000) suggested companies to improve the quality of its dialogue between all interested parties and stakeholders when they are preparing their environmental policy besides minimizing its impacts on the environment.

There are substantial differences in management approach and goals between eco-efficiency and eco-effectiveness. Eco-efficiency practices are generally more quantifiable measurements while eco-effectiveness has been more conceptual and qualitative. Eco-efficiency assists companies more concretely in continuous improvement by minimizing their use of resources, encouraging innovation in environmental management throughout the whole life cycle and creating tangible economic benefits. Eco-effectiveness is oriented to the redesign of the whole production and consumption system, by encouraging ecologically appropriate design of products, by closing material flows, recovering resources and using materials that result in minimal environmental impact. Eco-innovation incorporates the essence of both technological and environmental approaches towards the design and development of every aspect of process and product development. However, the innovation practices majorly concentrate towards the economic enhancement of the industry. The system of performance fails to support both the hypothesis developed for the relationship between the innovation practice and eco-innovation and also for the hypothesis developed for the eco-innovation and performance.

Socially acceptable management and innovative practices would concurrently achieve sustainable environment through eco-innovation as the primary objectives. Eco-innovation is a part of the CSR activity to magnetize the customers to realize the positive performance. It should not surprise us to find Malaysia, India and other East Asian states among the strongest supporters of initiatives to keep environmental standards, among others, out of international trade agreements (Mol 2003). An interesting note from Ooi et al. (2012) points out about the 'Ranking of the World's Most Innovative Countries'. China ranked 54, India is positioned at 56, Thailand ranked 58 and Indonesia ranked 74. It is very clear that India has to make enormous effort to increase its innovation potential. On aggregation, India is the fourth largest consumer of resources and the largest ecological destructor among those countries surveyed (Selles 2013). Indian manufacturing sector managers have to focus more on sustainable practices in future to survive.

6. Conclusion

The article delineates the inter-relation between the innovative and management practices on eco-innovation and sustainable performance in the Indian manufacturing context. A conceptual SEM has been proposed to test three hypotheses developed in the context of the practices of Indian manufacturing sector. Empirical data along with SEM approach are employed to determine the effect of eco-innovation's antecedents and consequences. The study highlights the serious challenges faced by the Indian manufacturing sector. The study identifies that Indian manufacturing sectors are well positioned in the usage of management practices. They lack in establishing their brand equity and protecting the CSR aspects. It is also obvious from the study that in future, the manufacturing sectors have to invest more on R&D activities and training to the employees related to innovative practices in order to improve sustainable performance. Furthermore, the mindset of manufacturing sector stakeholders have to change and rethink their conventional business models from lower cost to sustainability aspects to survive in the future. Few limitations of the study are with respect to sample size and the number of industries selected within manufacturing sector. Strong voluntary participation of industry leaders in future would champion the sustainability camp. Furthermore, usage of more refined sustainable performance metrics would reflect the exact status of the manufacturing firms.

Acknowledgements

The authors are thankful to the editor-in-chief, guest editors and anonymous reviewers for their critical and very insightful comments that helped to substantially improve the quality and readability of the paper. Authors wish to thank University Grants Commission of India for funding the project entitled 'Exploration and Development of Environmental Regulation Management Systems in Indian Manufacturing Industries' F.No.38-249/2009 (SR) 24 December 2009.

References

Anderson JC, Gerbing DW. 1988. Structural equation modeling in practice: a review and recommended two-step approach. Psychol Bull. 103:411–423. doi:10.1037/0033-2909.103.3.411

Arhonditsis GB, Stowb CA, Steinberg LJ, Kenney MA, Lathrop RC, McBride SJ, Reckhowa KH. 2006. Exploring ecological patterns with structural equation modeling and Bayesian analysis. Ecol Modelling. 192:385–409. doi:10.1016/j.ecolmodel.2005.07.028

Bai C, Sarkis J, Wei X, Koh L. 2012. Evaluating ecological sustainable performance measures for supply chain management. Supply Chain Manag Int J. 17:78–92. doi:10.1108/13598541211212221

Baskaran V, Nachiappan S, Rahman S. 2011. Supplier assessment based on corporate social responsibility criteria in Indian automotive and textile industry sectors. Int J Sustainable Eng. 4:359–369. doi:10.1080/19397038.2011.579360

Beske P. 2012. Dynamic capabilities and sustainable supply chain management. Int J Phys Distribution Logistics Manag. 42:372–387. doi: 10.1108/09600031211231344

Boons F, Montalvo C, Quist J, Wagner M. 2013. Sustainable innovation, business models and economic performance: an overview. J Cleaner Production. 45:1–8. doi:10.1016/j.jclepro.2012.08.013

Carrillo-Hermosilla J, Del Río P, Könnölä T. 2010. Diversity of eco-innovations: reflections from selected case studies. J Cleaner Production. 18:1073–1083. doi:10.1016/j.jclepro.2010.02.014

Cetinkaya B, Cuthbertson R, Ewer G, Klaas-Wissing T. 2011. Sustainable supply chain management: practical ideas for moving towards best practice, Vol. XVIII. London: Springer; 283p.

Chaabane A, Ramudhin A, Paquet M. 2012. Design of sustainable supply chains under the emission trading scheme. Int J Production Econ. 135:37–49. doi:10.1016/j.ijpe.2010.10.025

Chachamovich E, Fleck MP, Power M. 2009. Literacy affected ability to adequately discriminate among categories in multipoint likert scales. J Clin Epidemiol. 62:37–46. doi:10.1016/j.jclinepi.2008.03.002

Chin WW. 1998. Issues and opinion on structural equation modeling. MIS Quarterly. 22:VII–XVI.

Cook M, Gottberg A, Angus A, Longhurst P. 2012. Receptivity to the production of product service systems in the UK construction and manufacturing sectors: a comparative analysis. J Cleaner Production. 32:61–70. doi:10.1016/j.jclepro.2012.03.018

Cozzarin BP, Jeffrey SA. 2004. Human resource management practices and longitudinal workplace performance. Appl Econ Letters. 21:344–349.

Curkovic S. 2003. Environmentally responsible manufacturing: the development and validation of a measurement model. Eur J Oper Res. 146:130–155. doi:10.1016/S0377-2217(02)00182-0

Dangayach GS, Deshmukh SG. 2000. Manufacturing strategy: experiences from select Indian organizations. J Manufacturing Syst. 19:134–148. doi:10.1016/S0278-6125(00)80006-0

Dangayach GS, Deshmukh SG. 2003. Evidence of manufacturing strategies in Indian industry: a survey. Int J Production Econ. 83:279–298. doi:10.1016/S0925-5273(02)00372-9

Despeisse M, Ball PD, Evans S, Levers A. 2012a. Industrial ecology at factory level – a conceptual model. J Cleaner Production. 31:30–39. doi:10.1016/j.jclepro.2012.02.027

Despeisse M, Mbaye F, Ball PD, Levers A. 2012b. The emergence of sustainable manufacturing practices. J Production Plann Control. 23:354–376. doi:10.1080/09537287.2011.555425

Diedrich A, Uphamb P, Levidowe L, Hove SV. 2011. Framing environmental sustainability challenges for research and innovation in European policy agendas. Environ science policy. 14:935–939. doi:10.1016/j.envsci.2011.07.012

DiMaggio PJ, Powell W. 1983. The iron cage revisited: institutional isomorphism and collective rationality in organizational fields. Am Sociological Rev. 48:147–160. doi:10.2307/2095101

Elkington J. 1997. Cannibals with forks: the triple bottom line of 21st century business. Oxford: Capstone.

Esty DC, Winston AS. 2006. Green to gold: how smart companies use environmental strategy to innovate, create value, and build competitive advantage. New Haven (CT): Yale University Press.

Fang Y, Cote RP. 2005. Towards sustainability: objectives, strategies and barriers for cleaner production in China. Int J Sustainable Dev World Ecol. 12:443–460. doi:10.1080/13504500509469653

Fornell C. 1992. A national customer satisfaction barometer: the Swedish experience. J Marketing. 56:6–21. doi:10.2307/1252129

Foronda-Robles C, Galindo-Pérez-de-Azpillaga L. 2012. Working with indicators: description of states of territorial adjustment for protected natural areas. Int J Sustainable Dev World Ecol. 19:287–296. doi:10.1080/13504509.2011.626085

Fredericks SE. 2012. Justice in sustainability indicators and indexes. Int J Sustainable Dev World Ecol. 19:490–499. doi:10.1080/13504509.2012.714807

Giannakis M. 2007. Performance measurement of supplier relationships. Supply Chain Manag Int J. 12:400–411. doi:10.1108/13598540710826335

Gimenez C, Sierra V, Rodon J. 2012. Sustainable operations: their impact on the triple bottom line. Int journal Production Econ. 140:149–159. doi:10.1016/j.ijpe.2012.01.035

González-García S, Raúl García Lozano RG, Teresa Moreira MT, Gabarrell X, Rieradevall J, Feijoo G, Murphy RJ. 2012. Eco-innovation of a wooden childhood furniture set: an example of environmental solutions in the wood sector. Sci Total Environ. 426:318–326. doi:10.1016/j.scitotenv.2012.03.077

Hitchcock T. 2012. Low carbon and green supply chains: the legal drivers and commercial pressures. Supply Chain Manag Int J. 17:98–101. doi:10.1108/13598541211212249

Ho HP, Choi TM. 2012. A Five-R analysis for sustainable fashion supply chain management in Hong Kong: a case analysis. J Fashion Marketing Manag. 16:161–175. doi:10.1108/13612021211222815

Horbach J, Rammer C, Rennings K. 2012. Determinants of eco-innovations by type of environmental impact-the role of regulatory push/pull, technology push and market pull. Ecological Econ. 78:112–122. doi:10.1016/j.ecolecon.2012.04.005

Jayal AD, Badurdeen F, Dillon OW, Jawahir IS. 2010. Sustainable manufacturing: modeling and optimization challenges at the product, process and system levels. CIRP J Manufacturing Sci Technol. 2:144–152. doi:10.1016/j.cirpj.2010.03.006

Joo YG, Sohn SY. 2008. Structural equation model for effective CRM of digital content industry. Expert Syst with Appl. 34:63–71. doi:10.1016/j.eswa.2006.08.016

Ketchen Jr DJ, Hult GTM. 2007a. Bridging organization theory and supply chain management: the case of best value supply chains. J Operations Manag. 25:573–580. doi:10.1016/j.jom.2006.05.010

Ketchen Jr DJ, Hult GTM. 2007b. Toward greater integration of insights from organization theory and supply chain management. J Operations Manag. 25:455–458. doi:10.1016/j.jom.2006.05.001

Klassen RD, McLaughlin CP. 1996. The impact of environmental management on firm performance. Informs J Inst Operations Res Manag Sci. 42:1199–1214.

Kurk F, Eagan P. 2008. The value of adding design-for-the-environment to pollution prevention assistance options. J Cleaner Production. 16:722–726. doi:10.1016/j.jclepro.2007.02.022

Lai K, Wong CWY, Cheng TCE. 2006. Institutional isomorphism and the adoption of information technology for supply chain management. J Comput Ind. 57:93–98. doi:10.1016/j.compind.2005.05.002

Leitham S, McQuaid RW, Nelson JD. 2000. The influence of transport on industrial location choice: a stated preference experiment. J Transportation Res Part A. 34:515–535.

Lin II. 2007. Effects of extrinsic and intrinsic motivation on employee knowledge sharing intentions. J Inf Sci. 33:135–149. doi:10.1177/0165551506068174

Liu F, Zhang H, Wu P, Cao HJ. 2002. A model for analyzing the consumption situation of product material resources in manufacturing systems. J Mater Process Technol. 122:201–207. doi:10.1016/S0924-0136(02)00028-6

Liu S, Kasturiratne D, Moizer J. 2012. A hub-and-spoke model for multi-dimensional integration of green marketing and sustainable supply chain management. Ind Marketing Manag. 41:581–588. doi:10.1016/j.indmarman.2012.04.005

Malaeb ZA, Summers JK, Pugesek BH. 2000. Using structural equation modelling to investigate relationships among ecological variables. Environ Ecological Stat. 7:93–111. doi:10.1023/A:1009662930292

Malarvizhi P, Sangeeta Y. 2008. Corporate environmental disclosures on the internet: an empirical analysis of Indian companies. Issues Soc Environ Account. 2:211–232.

McCune B, Grace JB. 2002. Analysis of ecological communities [Internet]. MjM Software, Gleneden Beach, OR. [cited 2014 Apr 9]. Available from: www.pcord.com

Meyer MW. 2002. Rethinking performance measurement. Cambridge (UK): Cambridge University Press.

Mol APJ. 2003. Global institutional clashes: economic versus environmental regimes. Int J Sustainable Dev World Ecol. 10:303–318. doi:10.1080/13504500309470107

Mondragon AEC, Lalwani C, Mondragon CEC. 2011. Measures for auditing performance and integration in closed-loop supply chains. Supply Chain Manag Int J. 16:43–56. doi:10.1108/13598541111103494

Montabon F, Sroufe R, Narasimhan R. 2007. An examination of corporate reporting, environmental management practices and firm performance. J Operations Manag. 25:998–1014. doi:10.1016/j.jom.2006.10.003

Nidumolu R, Prahalad CK, Rangaswami MR. 2009. Why sustainability is now the key driver of innovation. Harvard Bus Rev. 87:57–64.

Nunnally JC. 1978. Psychometric theory. 2nd ed. New York (NY): McGraw-Hill.

O'Rafferty S. 2008. Designing interventions for ecodesign? Business Strategy Environ. 17:77–78. doi:10.1002/bse.610

OECD. 2009. Sustainable manufacturing and eco-innovation. Framework, practices and measurement – synthesis report. [Internet]. [cited 2014 Apr 6]. Available from: http://www.oecd.org/science/inno/43423689.pdf

Ooi KB, Lin B, Teh PL, Chong AYL. 2012. Does TQM support innovation performance in Malaysia's manufacturing industry? J Business Econ Manag. 13:366–393. doi:10.3846/16111699.2011.620155

Orlitzky M, Schmidt FL, Rynes SL. 2003. Corporate social and financial performance: a meta-analysis. Organ Stud Sage Publications. 24:403–441. doi:10.1177/0170840603024003910

Patel PC, Jayaram J. 2014. The antecedents and consequences of product variety in new ventures: an empirical study. J Operations Manag. 32:34–50. doi:10.1016/j.jom.2013.07.002

Porter ME. 1996. What is strategy? Boston (MA): Harvard Business Publishing.

Rho BH, Park K, Yu Y. 2001. An international comparison of the effect of manufacturing strategy-implementation gap on business performance. Int J Production Econ. 70:89–97. doi:10.1016/S0925-5273(00)00049-9

Sarkis J, Ni N, Zhu Q. 2011. Winds of change: corporate social responsibility in China. Social responsibility. Ivey Business J [Internet]. [cited 2014 Apr 6]. Available from: http://www.iveybusinessjournal.com/topics/social-responsibility/winds-of-change-corporate-social-responsibility-in-china#.UNINsW997tt

Selles H. 2013. The relative impact of countries on global natural resource consumption and ecological degradation. Int J Sustainable Dev World Ecol. 20:97–108. Available from: http://dx.doi.org/10.1080/13504509.2013.780190 10.1080/13504509.2013.780190

Singh LP, Bhardwaj A, Sachdeva A. 2006. Quality management practices vs. performance of SMEs: an empirical study of Indian industries. Technol Manag Global Future. 5:2393–2399.

Subramanian N, Gunasekaran A, Yu J, Cheng J, Ning K. 2014. Customer satisfaction and competitiveness in the Chinese E-retailing: structural equation modeling (SEM) approach to identify the role of quality factors. Expert Syst with Appl. 41:69–80. doi:10.1016/j.eswa.2013.07.012

Tidd J, Bessant John PK. 2005. Managing innovation: integrating technological, market and organizational change. 3rd ed. West Sussex: Wiley.

Triguero A, Moreno-Mondéjar L, Davia MA. 2013. Drivers of different types of eco-innovation in European SMEs. Ecological Econ. 92:25–33. doi:10.1016/j.ecolecon.2013.04.009

Ulusoy G. 2003. An assessment of supply chain and innovation management practices in the manufacturing industries in Turkey. Int J Production Econ. 86:251–270. doi:10.1016/S0925-5273(03)00064-1

Wehrmeyer W, Tyteca D. 1998. Measuring environmental performance for industry: from legitimacy to sustainability and biodiversity? Int J Sustainable Dev World Ecol. 5:111–124. doi:10.1080/13504509809469975

Wilts H, Dehoust G, Jepsen D, Knappe F. 2013. Eco-innovations for waste prevention – best practices, drivers and barriers. Sci Total Environ. 461–462:823–829. doi:10.1016/j.scitotenv.2013.05.096

Wu C, Hunt N. 2000. Development of environmental policy, objectives and targets. Int J Sustainable Dev World Ecol. 7:357–361. doi:10.1080/13504500009470054

Yang CJ, Chen JL. 2012. Forecasting the design of eco-products by integrating TRIZ evolution patterns with CBR and Simple LCA methods. Expert Syst with Appl. 39:2884–2892. doi:10.1016/j.eswa.2011.08.150

Yang M. 2006. Energy efficiency policy impact in India: case study of investment in industrial energy efficiency. J Energy Policy. 34:3104–3114. doi:10.1016/j.enpol.2005.05.014

Yarong Z, Xin Y. 2011. Research on the sustainable development and the objective of Chinese government performance audit. Energy Procedia. 5:1230–1236. doi:10.1016/j.egypro.2011.03.215

Zhao J, Liu H, Dong R. 2008. Sustainable urban development: policy framework for sustainable consumption and production. Int J Sustainable Dev World Ecol. 15:318–325.doi: 10.3843/SusDev.15.4:5

Zhu Q, Cordeiro J, Sarkis J. 2013. Institutional pressures, dynamic capabilities and environmental management systems: investigating the ISO 9000 – Environmental management system implementation linkage. J Environ Manag. 114:232–242. doi:10.1016/j.jenvman.2012.10.006

Appendix. General characteristics of respondents and their organization

S. No	Characteristics	Details
	Preferred Designation	Middle level managers to General manager
	Experience	8–25 years
	Organization strength	In existence for more than 5 years
	Employees (Size of the company)	50–500
	Location of firms	Tamilnadu, a state in southern India
	Type of Sector	Manufacturing
	Practices followed	Management – ISO 9001, EMS, Environmental Audit, Quality Practices
		Environmental – ISO 14000, R&D investment, Training on ERMS CSR activities

A measure of sustainability of Brazilian agribusiness using directional distance functions and data envelopment analysis

Carlos Rosano-Peña, Patricia Guarnieri, Vinicius Amorim Sobreiro, André Luiz Marques Serrano and Herbert Kimura

Department of Management, University of Brasília – UNB, Campus Darcy Ribeiro, Federal District, Brasília, Brazil

The social and environmental impacts caused by the modernization of Brazilian agribusiness have evoked a growing interest in the search of balance between social-economics development and the adequate use of natural resources, driving the country to sustainable development. Therefore, the main aim of this article is to estimate a set of indicators of relative efficiency in the Brazilian agricultural sector, which satisfy the concept of Pareto optimality, potentiates simultaneously both economic, ecological dimensions and social functions. To reach this purpose, the method of directional distance functions and data envelopment analysis was applied. These indicators confirm, in different ways, the hypothesis that it is possible to perform consistent productive strategies with the maximization of social welfare, despite the apparent antagonism among these three dimensions. In addition, it is shown that efficient Brazilian states tend to combine the three dimensions in different ways. Hence, it can be concluded that several equilibrium taken sustainable can be achieved through different actions on poverty and environmental impact reduction without necessarily generating productive inefficiencies. This result can be considered of prominent importance for sustainable development in Brazil and can also serve as a reference in the definition of goals of the plan 'Brazil without Misery' and international commitments to reduce Greenhouse Gas – GHG – in Brazil, especially for the 17 inefficient Brazilian states.

1. Introduction

The process of modernization of the Brazilian agricultural sector started between 1950 and 1960 (IBGE 2006). This transformation was strongly induced and subsidized by the government and involved the combination of extensive and intensive methods of production, including the expansion of the agricultural frontier and the rapid spread of technological innovations (IBGE 2006). As a result, the agricultural sector in Brazil presented a qualitative leap in the following years, with direct or indirect implications to all participants of this productive chain.

Because of the worldwide growing demand for agricultural products, Brazil had to broaden the scope of its historic concept of familiar agriculture, adopting a market-driven agribusiness concept and creating the roots for the Brazilian agro-industrial complex. Therefore, the modernization process that began in the middle of the last century transformed the Brazilian agricultural sector, turning the country into one of the leading producer and exporter of food in the world. According to the Food and Agriculture Organization (FAO) of the United Nations (UN), Brazil ranks as a Top 5 producer in, for instance, cereals, coarse grains, oil crop, root and tuber, fruit, fibre crop, etc. (Food and Agriculture Organization 2013).

It is important to highlight that the modernization process of the Brazilian agriculture was exclusionary, mainly because it primarily focused on large-scale production, directing efforts to emerge the country as a commodity producer, and eventually compromising the competitiveness of family farms. Small producers were relegated from credit to rural development and from technical assistance. This fact occurred even though family farms were more numerous and produced approximately 70% of the food basket in Brazil (IBGE 2006). Some studies show the rising of the Gini index related to land concentration from 0.83 to 0.85 in the 1940–1980 period (Alcantara Filho & Fontes 2009). In 2008, the index remained at 0.85, and the proportion of the total area occupied by the 50% smaller agricultural enterprises was equal to 2.2%, while the 10%, 5% and 1% larger enterprises comprised, respectively, 79.4%, 69.1% and 41.9% of the total area (Hoffmann & Ney 2010). These numbers embody a great deprivation of basic infrastructure in the agricultural field, including education, health, water access, sanitation, roads, electricity, security, and explain the high level of rural poverty, the migration of population to urban areas and misery in the suburbs of urban centres in Brazil. In 2009, even though Brazil had made some important changes to alleviate social and economic problems, 33% of the rural population still lived in poverty and 14% in extreme poverty (Grossi 2011).

There are also concerns regarding the excessive use of fertilizers and pesticides in the Brazilian agriculture and the environmental impact of the growing number of livestock.

A study from Food and Agriculture Organization (2006) draws attention to the impact that the development of agriculture has in deforestation, loss of biodiversity, pollution, depletion of water resources, desertification and soil erosion, as well as, in emissions of Greenhouse Gases (GHG), which are blamed to cause climate change and increase vulnerability of activities in agriculture.

Between 1990 and 2005, emissions of GHG in Brazil increased by 62% (Lima, Pessoa, et al. 2010). Approximately, 58% of the 2.2 billion tons of CO_2 equivalent emitted in 2005 in Brazil corresponds to activities related to changes in the use of the area reserved to forests, mainly due to deforestation and fire, and 22% to agriculture and livestock farming, which are expected to increase to 30% by 2030 (McKinsey & Company 2009).

Since some social and environmental impacts of agribusiness modernization can be considered negative externalities, it is relevant to consider not only the inputs and outputs with observable market prices, but also the undesirable, sometimes, intangible outputs, when assessing the modernization of the Brazilian agriculture. An economic sector that fosters sustainable development must simultaneously meet the needs of all stakeholders, finding a balance and a synergy of forces to mitigate risks and to reduce negative impacts to society.

Because of the importance of the Brazilian agribusiness sector not only for the country's development, but also for the worldwide supply of food, and to the perverse externalities, there is a growing interest in the search for balance between socio-economic development and the proper use of natural resources to pursue sustainable agribusiness in Brazil. Therefore, this study aims to analyse *the Brazilian agribusiness sector considering economic, ecological and social dimensions, according to non-exclusive attributes of productivity, equality and environmental responsibility.*

The main objective of this article is to identify a set of indicators of relative efficiency in the Brazilian agricultural sector, which, by following the concept of Pareto optimality, allows the simultaneous enhancement of economic, ecological and social dimensions. The research focuses on the directional distance functions (DDF) method within a data envelopment analysis (DEA) framework, using the latest available data from the Brazilian agricultural census (IBGE 2006) at the state level. The study adds results to the scarce empirical research on socio-environmental efficiency in the Brazilian agriculture.

The research follows the theme of previous studies that evaluate eco-efficiency in Brazil including Gomes and Lins (2008) and Leal et al. (2012), but differs in one important aspect. While the previous studies analyse efficiency solely from the environmental and economic perspectives, the current research assesses efficiency including rural poverty as an inalienable pillar of sustainability in emerging markets (Fredericks 2012; Hansmann et al. 2012; Ali 2013; Cosyns et al. 2013; Lyytimäki et al. 2013). The set of workable indicators shows that the method can be an interesting alternative to operationalize

the concept of sustainability and can be used to support the formulation of policies consistent with the maximization of social welfare in developing countries. Consequently, this research also presents evidence of potential improvement of sustainability in the Brazilian agribusiness.

Besides this introduction, this article is structured as follows. In Section 2, the manuscript presents the literature review, discussing concepts of sustainability and studies that use DEA to analyse this theme. In Section 3, the theoretical framework to identify the environmental efficiency is detailed. Section 4 describes the parameters and units of analysis of the environmental efficiency of the Brazilian agriculture. In Section 5, results of the research are discussed. Finally, in Section 6, the main conclusions and limitations of the study are presented.

2. Review of literature

The theme of sustainable development comes in vogue from the report of the Club of Rome entitled 'The Limits to Growth' (Meadows et al. 1972). The report pointed out that the planet would not support socioeconomic growth even taking technological advances into account, owing to the problems related to energy generation, natural resources depletion and increasing pollution. The United Nations sponsored a series of worldwide conferences and commissions to discuss sustainability of the planet, seeking for compromises and solutions. In the Brundtland Report (WCED 1987), entitled 'Our Common Future', a formal definition for sustainable development was established.

> Sustainable development is development that meets the needs of the present without compromising the ability of future generations to meet their own needs The sustainable development seeks to meet the needs of the present generation without compromising the ability of future generations to meet their own needs, which means enabling people now and in the future, to achieve a satisfactory level of social and economics development and, human and cultural fulfilment, making at the same time, a reasonable use of land resources and preserving the species and natural habitats. (WCED 1987)

Regarding this definition, Elkington (1998) proposed the concept of the 'triple bottom line' of sustainability, which is the triangulation of People, Planet, Profit, and considers seven dimensions of transformation that must occur to achieve harmonization among economic factors, environmental quality and social justice. Environmental and social problems most severely affect the vulnerable population of developing countries; however, there is yet a scarcity of research related to these regions (Seuring & Gold 2013).

Jabbour et al. (2012) highlighted that manufacturing strategy affects a company's environmental impact, which becomes relevant to analyse the relationship between environmental and operations management issues. In addition, many companies have tried to demonstrate its proactivity by implementing sustainability practices, which aim to monitor and control the impact of its operations on the environment (González-Benito & González-Benito 2008).

In this context, Montabon et al. (2007) state that companies can control their environmental impact by implementing operational, tactical and strategic level practices. The same authors found that good environmental practices imply a positive effect on firm performance. Seuring and Gold (2013) suggest the integration between environmental and social issues into approaches such as multi-criteria decision-making or optimization models as a trend for future research.

Several other approaches appear in the literature to empirically assess the concepts proposed by Elkington (1998). For instance, the study from Heyder and Theuvsen (2012) is based on a survey that explores social and environmental dimensions of 170 agribusiness enterprises of small as well as large multinational corporations in Germany. Claver et al. (2007) studied the connection between environmental management and economic performance from a perspective that includes the relationship between environmental strategy and firm performance. Govindan et al. (2013) examined the problem of identifying an effective model based on the Triple Bottom Line (TBL) approach (economic, environmental, and social aspects) for supplier selection operations in supply chains by presenting a fuzzy multi criteria approach.

In addition, several papers propose the construction of multidimensional indicators of sustainability to evaluate the performance of the agribusiness productive system. Some of these studies can be highlighted: Bockstaller and Girardin (2003), Morse et al. (2001), Munda (2005), Calker et al. (2006), Böhringer and Jochem (2007), Qiu et al. (2007), Speelman et al. (2007), Bauler (2012) and Bojacá et al. (2012).

However, many of the indicators related to the TBL have been criticized mainly due to their subjectivity. In addition, other issues can be pointed out regarding the set of attributes of the three dimensions; the methods used to choose the shape of functional aggregation and the weighting technique to establish the relative importance of attributes. Therefore, the construction of composite indicators for assessing agribusiness sustainability is still at an early stage, and new development is indeed needed (Gómez-Limón & Riesgo 2009).

Two major methods of aggregation of products, inputs and negative externalities in order to measure the socio-environmental behaviour efficiently can be found in the literature. The first method uses market prices as weights of inputs and outputs, and forecasts of shadow prices of externalities, due to the absence of a market for some undesirable products. Pittman (1983) was one of the pioneers in this stream of research, using parametric methods. Other studies can also be highlighted: Färe et al. (1993), Coggins and Swinton (1996), Swinton (1998) and Reig-Martínez et al. (2001). The second method uses endogenous weights estimated by non-parametric techniques, mainly using the DEA method. The weighting of each dimension varies from one production unit to another

and is calculated in a more flexible way with this method. This procedure assumes that the evaluated units can combine inputs and products (desirable and undesirable) differently, finding the best adaptations taking into account their specializations, which are imperative when evaluating the environmental efficiency.

The first publication using DEA and considering desirable and undesirable outputs following asymmetric shaped can be attributed to Färe et al. (1986), which adapt hyperbolic measures of efficiency. There are also other methodological approaches to address the externalities with the DEA (Tyteca 1996). Scheel (2001) compares other forms of DEA modelling of undesirable products, as for instance considering them simply as input; multiplying undesirable outputs by -1; modelling them by a positive translation of negative values; addressing them as an inverse value to output; and using the Weakly Disposable Outputs property.

More recently, Chung et al. (1997) and Färe and Grosskopf (2000) have recommended the use of an alternative approach called Directional Distance Function (DDF) as a more flexible way to incorporate externalities in the traditional production theory and in the assessment of environmental efficiency.

Thus, the rapid evolution of DEA efficiency studies which consider externalities can be proven by the large number of published papers whose object is agribusiness. Some examples of the extensive application of DDF in agriculture are found in Färe et al. (2006), which estimated efficiency of US agriculture, shadow prices of pollutants and pollution costs associated; in Kjærsgaard et al. (2009), which assessed the Danish cod fisheries; in Azad and Ancev (2010), which analysed the economic and environmental performance of a set of irrigated farms in Australia; in Picazo-Tadeo et al. (2012), which applied the method in a sample of Spanish olive farms, among others.

Unfortunately, the use of DEA method to study the sustainability of Brazilian agribusiness is still incipient, considering the importance of this segment in the national economy (Gomes 2008).

The closest reference to the present research is the study of sustainability in Brazilian agribusiness conducted by Gomes et al. (2009), using DEA models with weight restrictions, which aimed to assess the ability of farmers in maintaining their production system over time.

The use of DEA to analyse the sustainability of other sectors of the Brazilian economy is also not extensive, but in recent years, there have been a growing number of studies, as for instance, papers from Camioto et al. (2014) and Costa et al. (2013). The first study used a DEA-SBM (slack-based model) and a window analysis to evaluate the ability of industries to reduce energy consumption and fossil-fuel CO_2 emissions, as well as to increase the gross domestic product (GDP), the number of employed persons and personnel expenses. The second study uses DEA with the restrictions on virtual weights to assess the sustainability of biodiesel production with different resources.

3. Directional distance functions and data envelopment analysis

This section presents the theoretical framework of the environmental efficiency model of the study. First, the section brings the definition of the reference technology of the segment, that is, the generic form by which an input vector (input) is combined and transformed into a vector of new goods and services (output). This process is estimated by the set of production possibilities (SPP), which incorporates all the p outputs $(y \in R_+^p)$ that can be produced with the input vector $(x \in R_+^n)$ for k observed decision-making units (DMUs). Formally, the SPP can be represented as shown in Equation (1).

$$\text{SPP} = \{(x,y) | x \text{ can produce } y; x, y \geq 0\} \quad (1)$$

In addition, the SPP shall comply with the following classical properties, as formulated in Grosskopf (1986):

- $(0,0) \in \text{SPP} \Rightarrow y(0) = 0$, which means that it is technologically possible to produce anything as well as nothing
- SPP is convex, closed and admits that only finite y can be produced by finite x
- $\forall y \in R_+^p, \forall x \in R_+^n, (x,y) \in \text{SPP}, \quad y' \leq y$ and $x' \geq x \Rightarrow (x',y)$ and $(x, y') \in \text{SPP}$. This property is called *Strong Disposability of Inputs and Outputs (SDIO)*.

The strong disposability of inputs implies that, on the one hand, it is feasible to produce the same amount of output using a larger quantity of any input x. On the other hand, strong disposability of outputs suggests that it is possible to produce a minor amount of y using the same amount of x (Grosskopf 1986).

The border of SPP is comprised by the smallest possible amount of inputs to produce a given output vector or the highest possible level of production with a particular input vector. Therefore, the efficient DMUs constitute the frontier. The inefficient DMUs stay below the frontier, and the inefficiency indexes are obtained by comparing their production units with those of the efficient DMUs. It is possible to measure the inefficiency of a DMU from the minimum distance separating that unit from the efficient frontier, which defines a measure of how the unit must change its inputs and/or outputs to become efficient (Cooper et al. 2000).

The distance function of Shephard (1954), reciprocal to Farrell's (1957) Efficiency Index $(F(x,y))$, is used to estimate efficiency. The distance function oriented to outputs can be determined as $D_o(x,y) = \text{Min}\{\theta : (x, \frac{y}{\theta}) \in P(x)\}$, where $\theta \in (0,1]$ and measures the maximum proportional expansion of all outputs y that is feasible within given inputs x, that is, $y = P(x)$. The distance function oriented to inputs is defined as $D_i(x,y) = \text{Max}\{\delta : (\frac{x}{\delta},y) \in L(y)\}$, in which $\delta \geq 1$ shows in what proportion the inputs can be reduced in the input space, $L(y) = \{x : y \in P(x)\}$. When $\theta = \delta = 1$, the evaluated DMU is efficient. When the $\theta < 1$ and $\delta > 1$, the DMU is inefficient. Thus, the relationship between the distance function and Farrell's Efficiency Index, calculated by the DEA method, is represented as $D_o(x,y) = [F_o(x,y)]^{-1}$ and $D_i(x,y) = [F_i(x,y)]^{-1}$.

Considering the social and environmental externalities, the new output vector $(u \in R_+^m)$ is divided into desirable and undesirable $u = (y,b)$ elements, where, respectively, y is the first subvector and $b \in R_+^q$ is the second. Thus, $\text{SPP} = \{(x,y,b) \in R_+^{n+p+q}\}$ and $m = p + q$, which according to Färe et al. (2006), two additional properties must be satisfied:

- $\forall y \in R_+^p, \forall b \in R_+^q, b = 0 \Rightarrow y = 0$ (null-jointness). This property indicates that production of desired outputs involves the generation of undesired outputs;
- $\forall y \in R_+^p, \forall b \in R_+^q, \quad (x,y,b) \in \text{SPP} \Rightarrow (x, \alpha y, \alpha b) \in \text{SPP}, \quad 0 \leq \alpha \leq 1$. This property, called *Weak Disposability of Outputs (WDO)*, suggests that the proportional reduction of both types of outputs is possible, but the elimination of separately undesirable outputs is impossible in the efficient frontier.

Therefore, in the weak disposability, the reduction of externalities is linked to a productive cost and, in this case, to three types of trade-offs imposed by the scarcity of resources: between production and pollution, between production and equality and, consequently, between pollution and equality.

The trade-off between production and pollution results from the lack of fully clean technologies and from the existence of environmental regulations, which implies that the elimination of pollutants involves compensation. This cost, measured in terms of opportunity, can be considered as the reduction in the value of the optimal production to comply with the regulation.

The trade-off between production and equality emerges because, in order to the society to obtain equality, a unit must sacrifice resources that could increase production. In contrast, if production is prioritized, society will have to sacrifice equality. The trade-off between equality and pollution stems from the other conflicts between.

The trade-offs of the model can be elucidated graphically. Figure 1 assumes that the evaluated DMUs $(A, B, C, D, E \text{ and } F)$, using a given amount of input (x), produce a desirable output (y) and generate an environmental or social externality (b). The area OABCDE represents the SPP^{wdo}, where efficient frontier is comprised by segments OA, AB, BC and CD. This means that the efficient frontier (OABCD) is composed of different efficient allocations on a Pareto perspective. The DMUs in the efficient frontier cannot produce one more desirable output or one less undesirable output without reducing the amount of another desirable production, given the allocation of inputs and the current technology.

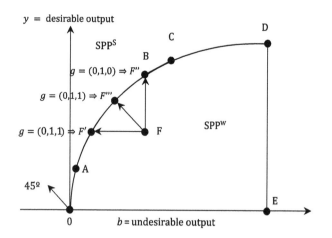

Figure 1. Trade-off between production and equality.

The most concerning issue in the analysis is the level of inefficiency of other units, particularly in a context of great need for accountability and rationality in the use of available resources and generation of undesirable sub-products. If the resources are not efficiently allocated, the DMU will be one point, as for instance F, located below the efficient frontier. Every change made to take the unit F to a point between F' and F''' will be a progress towards Pareto optimality, since it improves the behaviour in a dimension without worsening the situation in others.

Formally, assuming constant returns to scale and strong disposal of desirable outputs, the SPP that satisfies the property of weak disposal of undesirable outputs is $SPP^w = \{(x, y, z) \in R_+^{n+p+q} : Xz \leq x, Yz \geq y, Bz = b, z \in R_+^k\}$, where the intensity vector z represents the relative weights of each DMU in the definition of the reference hyperplane, $x = (x_1, x_2, \ldots, x_n)$ is the input vector used in order to produce the vector $y = (y_1, y_2, \ldots, y_p)$ and the vector $b = (b_1, b_2, \ldots, b_q)$. Consequently, $X_{(nxk)}$, $Y_{(pxk)}$, $B_{(qxk)}$, respectively, represent the matrices of inputs, of desirable outputs and of undesirable outputs from a sample of k DMUs analysed.

The levels of environmental inefficiency of a DMU can be calculated using the method proposed by Chung et al. (1997), which introduced the concept of DDF, an extension of the distance function defined by Shephard (1954):

$$\vec{D} = (x, y, z; g_x, g_y, g_b)$$
$$= \max\{\beta : (x - \beta g_x, y + \beta g_x, b - \beta g_b) \in SPP\} \quad (2)$$

The distance function estimates the optimal value of β, which must be greater than or equal to zero. This relation gives a wide range of workable indicators that represent different objectives linked to, for instance, economic, social and ecological development, according to the direction established by the vector g defined a priori by the researcher. In particular, β can indicate the percentage in which the evaluated DMU could increase all desirable products and reduce, simultaneously, the inputs and the negative externalities until the SPP frontier, when the vector g is $(g_x = 1, g_y = 1, g_b = 1)$. If $\beta = 0$, the evaluated unit is socio-environmentally efficient. For each DMU, β and z are calculated by solving the following linear programming problem (LPP).

$$\vec{D}_k^w = (x_k, y_k, b_k; -g_r, g_y, -g_b) = \text{Max } \beta \quad (3)$$

Subject to:

$$(1 + \beta g_y) \times y_k \leq Yz \quad (3.1)$$

$$(1 - \beta g_b) \times b_k \leq Bz \quad (3.2)$$

$$(1 - \beta g_x) \times x_k \geq Xz \quad (3.3)$$

$$z_k \geq 0 \quad (3.4)$$

Aspiring to know how much can be added to desired output of F with the same level of environmental impact and use of inputs, that is, determining $g = (g_x = 0, g_y = 1, g_b = 0)$, the LPP will make a projection of F at the point $F' = [b^F, Y^F \times (1 + \beta g_x)]$, according to Figure 1.

For each directional vector established a priori, depending on the goals that the decision-maker must pursue, the DDF allows the calculation of different measures of sustainability, which satisfy the Pareto optimality concept. This flexibility is particularly important to estimate the set of performance indicators that may simultaneously enhance the economic, ecological and social dimensions. Table 1 shows eight possible combinations of the directional vector with their different goals.

Table 1. Directional vectors and goals on economics and socio-environmental behaviour.

No.	Combinations		Goals
1	$\vec{D}_{io}^w$	(1, 1, 1)	Maximize y and minimize simultaneously x and b.
2	$\vec{D}_o^w$	(0, 1, 1)	Maximize y and minimize b with fixed vectors of x.
3	$\vec{D}_b^w$	(0, 0, 1)	Minimize b with fixed vectors of x and y.
4	–	(0, 0, 0)	Maintain the *Status quo*.
5	$\vec{D}_{iy}^w$	(1, 1, 0)	Maximize y minimize x with fixed vectors of b.
6	$\vec{D}_{oi}^w$	(1, 0, 0)	Minimize x with fixed vectors of y and b.
7	$\vec{D}_{ib}^w$	(1, 0, 1)	Minimize b and x with fixed vectors of y.
8	$\vec{D}_y^w$	(0, 1, 0)	Maximize y with fixed vectors of x and b.

4. Units and parameters of analysis

The study uses data from 33 DMUs, segregated by the 27 Brazilian states, 5 geographic regions and the overall country. The variables of the model comprise three inputs, one desirable output and two undesirable outputs. The choice of inputs and outputs is based on previous mentioned studies in Sections 1 and 2. The starting point is based on the following principle: agricultural activities of territorial units are seen as any other productive function, represented by the technical relationship between a set of productive factors or inputs that are combined to generate a given set of desired outputs. This process has negative environmental and social impacts measured, respectively, by a proxy associated with global warming and a variable that reflects the impossibility of access or lack of resources to meet basic human needs. In this study, positive externalities, such as the creation of employment and income, are not taken into account.

Based on Gomes (2008), the inputs of the model are:

- x_1 – employed persons divided by the total area (km^2) of enterprises;
- x_2 – agricultural inputs (fertilizers, seeds and seedlings, packaging, pesticides, medicines and animal feed, electricity, fuels, raw materials, among others). In all cases, US\$ 416 was adopted per total area of enterprises (km^2); and
- x_3 – estimated capital by depreciation of fixed capital assets (machinery, implements, buildings, facilities, among others). In all cases, US\$ 416 was adopted per total area of enterprises (km^2).

Considering the three dimensions of sustainability, the outputs selected were:

- y (desirable output) – Value of total production at US\$ 416 per total area of enterprises
- b_1 (social undesirable output) – Thousands of poor people in rural area, in 2006
- b_2 (environmental undesirable output) – Values of emissions of GHG, in 2006 in CO_2 tons-equivalent, divided by the total area of enterprises

The first four variables were obtained from the Brazilian Agricultural Census (2006), published by the Brazilian Institute of Geography and Statistics (IBGE 2006). The source of the fifth variable b_1 is the Institute for Work and Society of Brazil, which estimates the number of poor people and the poverty line based on the National Household Sample Survey of Brazil. This limit, according to the place of residence, includes the value of the food basket and the minimum amount to meet all the other basic needs: housing, clothing, hygiene, health, education, transport, leisure, among others.

The sixth variable b_2 was estimated based on four reports of GHG emissions from the agricultural segment, developed by the Brazilian Agricultural Research Corporation (Embrapa) considering the following elements:

- Methane emissions from enteric fermentation and manure of livestock management (Lima, Pessoa, et al. 2010)
- Methane emissions from rice cultivation (Lima, Ligo, Pessoa, Luiz, et al. 2010)
- GHG emissions from the burning of agricultural waste (Lima, Ligo, Pessoa, Neves, et al. 2010)
- Nitrous oxide emissions from agricultural soils and manure (Alves 2010)

It is important to emphasize that these reports calculate GHG emissions by Brazilian regions and states in 2006, except for the emission of nitrous oxide (N_2O) from agricultural soils and manure management. This latest report only gives (N_2O) emissions from 1990 to 2006 in Brazil. Therefore, considering the rate of growth of these emissions in the last 10 years in Brazil and, records by Brazilian states in 1995, values of (N_2O) for 2006 were estimated. With each GHG emissions were also calculated tons of equivalent CO_2 based on metric of Global Temperature Potential (GTP).

Table 2 shows the units (Brazilian States) contemplated, the data and the descriptive statistics of the selected variables. Note that Mato Grosso and Amapá have the lowest levels in inputs per km^2, Distrito Federal has the highest level of production, Amapá, the fewest number of poor people and Mato Grosso, the lower GHG emissions.

5. Results

Considering the parameters described in the previous section, the optimal set of indicators was estimated, representing the different goals in relation to economic, social and environmental performance, following the order of Table 1. In Table 3, the values of $\vec{D}_{io}^{w}(1,1,1,1,1,1)$ show a high level of environmental inefficiency, with an average of 0.155. In addition, these values suggest how much desirable production can increase simultaneously, reducing inputs and negative externalities. Taking into account global values of the segment, the increment of desirable production may be 5.9%, the reduction of employed persons 10.4%, the reduction of agro inputs 6.6% and the reduction in capital 7.8%. The poverty alleviation and GHG emissions can be reduced, respectively, to 15.6% and 4.1%, as shown in Table 3. These results show that, in the period under review, if inefficient Brazilian states had adopted the best practices, it would make possible to foster an agriculture that potentiates the economic, ecological, and social dimensions. Therefore, the apparent antagonism among these three attributes does not prevent the formulation of policies that could be consistent with maximization of social welfare.

In the first part of Table 4, the indicator $\vec{D}_{yb}^{w}$, defining the percentage in which the Brazilian states could increase the desirable output and, simultaneously, reduce the

Table 2.   Units, data and descriptive statistics of selected variables (2006).

No.	DMUs	x_1 - People.	x_2 - Input.	x_3 - Capital.	y - Production	b_2 - No. poor people.	b_2 - GHG
1	Rondônia	3335	7831	3864	10,214	73,964	0.071
2	Acre	2852	3121	2886	9964	61,902	0.031
3	Amazonas	7337	3973	1284	17,899	220,406	0.023
4	Roraima	1736	2.989	1187	5819	10,834	0.024
5	Pará	3526	5087	1797	14,847	313,491	0.048
6	Amapá	1499	0.385	0.549	11,470	4866	0.025
7	Tocantins	1237	7372	2271	5352	63,897	0.039
8	Maranhão	7633	7245	1526	24,027	978,882	0.037
9	Piauí	8750	6254	2010	13,968	573,779	0.035
10	Ceará	14,465	10,535	3471	48,575	807,135	0.041
11	Rio Grande do Norte	7764	6435	3795	35,164	234,974	0.033
12	Paraíba	12,961	13,699	4068	37,592	276,660	0.038
13	Pernambuco	17,389	34,700	4434	88,685	804,538	0.055
14	Alagoas	21,426	46,460	5787	155,247	492,473	0.077
15	Sergipe	18,157	58,566	4866	71,954	132,752	0.063
16	Bahia	7971	18,735	2474	28,838	1,623,194	0.042
17	Mato Grosso do Sul	0.703	12,961	3592	11,855	74,283	0.070
18	Mato Grosso	0.750	22,577	3316	20,085	150,180	0.020
19	Goiás	1628	20,363	4950	24,304	107,878	0.028
20	Distrito Federal	8883	85,391	34,947	172,222	26,448*	5.502
21	Minas Gerais	5810	35,085	6731	57,705	447,522	0.050
22	Espírito Santo	11,189	32,192	12,024	82,563	96,620	0.148
23	Rio de Janeiro	7695	22,640	10,170	60,903	529,212	0.845
24	São Paulo	5453	81,020	14,419	152,821	181,737	0.229
25	Paraná	7308	55,061	5506	103,999	180,471	0.085
26	Santa Catarina	9462	58,259	22,835	146,911	49,796	0.204
27	Rio Grande do Sul	6098	46,899	15,074	82,644	217,451	0.024
	Sum	203,016	705,838	179,834	1,495,629		7.887
	Average	7519	26,142	6661	55,394		0.292
	Maximum	21,426	85,391	34,947	172,222	1,623,194	5.502
	Minimum	0.703	0.385	0.549	5352	4866	0.020
28	North	3022	5761	2231	11,223	749,360	0.045
29	Northeast	10,184	16,262	2773	37,587	5,924,387	0.042
30	Midwest	0.973	19,397	3876	19,114	332,341	0.050
31	Southeast	6053	48,609	9505	88,417	791,744	0.080
32	South	7033	51,556	12,681	99,853	447,718	0.053
33	Brazil	5021	25,264	5384	43,590	8,245,550	0.059

Note: In the Distrito Federal, only the number of poor people is given. Its rural value was estimated considering the non-urban population percentage (3.38%).

Table 3.   Indicator of socio-environmental efficiency $\vec{D}_{io}^{w}(1,1,1,1,1,1)$ and the goals of improvement for each analysed units.

DMUs	$\vec{D}_{io}^{w}$	$(1-\beta) \times x_1$	$(1-\beta) \times x_2$	$(1-\beta) \times x_3$	$(1-\beta) \times b_1$	$(1-\beta) \times b_2$	$(1-\beta) \times y$
Rondônia	0.549	1.504085	3.531781	1.742664	33,357.764	0.032021	15.821486
Acre	0.359	1.828132	2.000561	1.849926	39,679.182	0.019871	13.541076
Amazonas	0.082	6.735366	3.647214	1.178712	202,332.71	0.021114	19.366718
Roraima	0.424	0.999936	1.721664	0.683712	6240.384	0.013824	8.286256
Pará	0.324	2.383576	3.438812	1.214772	211,919.92	0.032448	19.657428
Amapá	0.000	1.499	0.385	0.549	4866	0.025	11.47
Tocantins	0.563	0.540569	3.221564	0.992427	27,922.989	0.017043	8.365176
Maranhão	0.130	6.64071	6.30315	1.32762	851,627.34	0.03219	27.15051
Piauí	0.390	5.3375	3.81494	1.2261	350,005.19	0.02135	19.41552
Ceará	0.000	14.465	10.535	3.471	807,135	0.041	48.575
Rio Grande do Norte	0.000	7.764	6.435	3.795	234,974	0.033	35.164
Paraíba	0.189	10.511371	11.109889	3.299148	224,371.26	0.030818	44.696888
Pernambuco	0.098	15.684878	31.2994	3.999468	725,693.28	0.04961	97.37613
Alagoas	0.000	21.426	46.46	5.787	492,473	0.077	155.247
Sergipe	0.035	17.521505	56.51619	4.69569	128,105.68	0.060795	74.47239
Bahia	0.292	5.643468	13.26438	1.751592	1,149,221.4	0.029736	37.258696
Mato Grosso do Sul	0.220	0.54834	10.10958	2.80176	57,940.74	0.0546	14.4631

(*Continued*)

22

Table 3.   (Continued).

DMUs	$\vec{D}_{io}^w$	$(1-\beta)\times x_1$	$(1-\beta)\times x_2$	$(1-\beta)\times x_3$	$(1-\beta)\times b_1$	$(1-\beta)\times b_2$	$(1-\beta)\times y$
Mato Grosso	0.000	0.75	22.577	3.316	150,180	0.02	20.085
Goiás	0.124	1.426128	17.837988	4.3362	94,501.128	0.024528	27.317696
Distrito Federal	0.000	8.883	85.391	34.947	19,374.254	5.502	172.222
Minas Gerais	0.115	5.14185	31.050225	5.956935	396,056.97	0.04425	64.341075
Espírito Santo	0.129	9.745619	28.039232	10.472904	84,156.02	0.128908	93.213627
Rio de Janeiro	0.162	6.44841	18.97232	8.52246	443,479.66	0.70811	70.769286
São Paulo	0.000	5.453	81.02	14.419	181,737	0.229	152.821
Paraná	0.000	7.308	55.061	5.506	180,471	0.085	103.999
Santa Catarina	0.000	9.462	58.259	22.835	49,796	0.204	146.911
Rio Grande do Sul	0.000	6.098	46.899	15.074	217,451	0.024	82.644
Average	0.155						
Sum		181.74944	658.90089	165.75109	7,365,068.8	7.561216	1584.6511
Δ%		−10.476	−6.649	−7.831	−15.618	−4.131	5.952
North	0.403	1.804134	3.439317	1.331907	447,367.92	0.026865	15.745869
Northeast	0.000	10.184	16.262	2.773	5,924,387	0.042	37.587
Midwest	0.107	0.868889	17.321521	3.461268	296,780.51	0.04465	21.159198
Southeast	0.029	5.877463	47.199339	9.229355	768,783.42	0.07768	90.981093
South	0.000	7.033	51.556	12.681	447,718	0.053	99.853
Brazil	0.000	5.021	25.264	5.384	8,245,550	0.059	43.59

Table 4.   Indicator of socio-environmental efficiency $\vec{D}_{yb}^w(0,0,0,1,1,1)$ and $\vec{D}_b^w(0,0,0,0,1,1)$ and goals of improvement of each analysed units.

DMUs	$\vec{D}_{yb}^w$	$(1-\beta)\times b_1$	$(1-\beta)\times b_2$	$(1-\beta)\times y$	$\vec{D}_b^w$	$(1-\beta)\times b_1$	$(1-\beta)\times b_2$
Rondônia	0.74	19,378.568	0.018602	17.751932	0.85	11,020.636	0.010579
Acre	0.48	32,065.236	0.016058	14.766648	0.69	19,065.816	0.009548
Amazonas	0.12	194,398.09	0.020286	20.011082	0.35	143,263.9	0.01495
Roraima	0.50	5471.17	0.01212	8.699405	0.69	3347.706	0.007416
Pará	0.54	143,578.88	0.021984	22.894074	0.86	45,456.195	0.00696
Amapá	0.00	4866	0.025	11.47	0.00	4866	0.025
Tocantins	0.79	13,610.061	0.008307	9.564024	0.88	7603.743	0.004641
Maranhão	0.22	761,570.2	0.028786	29.360994	0.63	361,207.46	0.013653
Piauí	0.61	223,773.81	0.01365	22.48848	0.84	91,230.861	0.005565
Ceará	0.00	807,135	0.041	48.575	0.00	807,135	0.041
Rio Grande do Norte	0.00	234,974	0.033	35.164	0.00	234,974	0.033
Paraíba	0.29	196,981.92	0.027056	48.418496	0.56	122,283.72	0.016796
Pernambuco	0.10	720,866.05	0.04928	97.90824	0.20	643,630.4	0.044
Alagoas	0.00	492,473	0.077	155.247	0.00	492,473	0.077
Sergipe	0.04	127,972.93	0.060732	74.544344	0.07	123,459.36	0.05859
Bahia	0.46	881,394.34	0.022806	42.016966	0.66	555,132.35	0.014364
Mato Grosso do Sul	0.61	29,118.936	0.02744	19.06284	0.81	14,113.77	0.0133
Mato Grosso	0.00	150,180	0.02	20.085	0.00	150,180	0.02
Goiás	0.19	86,949.668	0.022568	29.018976	0.50	53,723.244	0.013944
Distrito Federal	0.00	19,374.254	5.502	172.222	0.00	19,374.254	5.502
Minas Gerais	0.20	35,8017.6	0.04	69.246	0.54	206,307.64	0.02305
Espírito Santo	0.15	81,837.14	0.125356	95.195139	0.32	66,184.7	0.10138
Rio de Janeiro	0.41	310,647.44	0.496015	86.055939	0.91	48,158.292	0.076895
São Paulo	0.00	181,737	0.229	152.821	0.00	181,737	0.229
Paraná	0.00	180,471	0.085	103.999	0.00	180,471	0.085
Santa Catarina	0.00	49,796	0.204	146.911	0.00	49,796	0.204
Rio Grande do Sul	0.00	217,451	0.024	82.644	0.00	217,451	0.024
Average	0.24				0.38		
Sum		6526,089.3	7.251046	1636.1416		4,853,647	6.675631
Δ%		−25.230	−8.063	9.395		−44.392	−15.359
North	0.75	184,342.56	0.01107	19.685142	0.91	64,444.96	0.00387
Northeast	0.00	5,924,387	0.042	37.587	0.00	5,924,387	0.042
Midwest	0.32	226,656.56	0.0341	25.192252	0.71	98,040.595	0.01475
Southeast	0.05	750,573.31	0.07584	93.014684	0.26	589,849.28	0.0596
South	0.00	447,718	0.053	99.853	0.00	447,718	0.053
Brazil	0.00	8,245,550	0.059	43.59	0.00	8,245,550	0.059

negative externalities with the same level of inputs, has an average value of 0.24. This result shows that an effective strategy with economic, social and environmental responsibility could increase production of the agribusiness sector by 9.4% and decrease the percentage of poor people and the emissions of GHG by, respectively, 25.2% and 8.1%. This potential is feasible in the 17 Brazilian states, where there is $\vec{D}_{yb}^w > 0$.

In the second part of Table 4, the indicator $\vec{D}_b^w$, related to the rate at which the Brazilian states could reduce the negative externalities with the same level of input and production, has an average value of 0.38. This result suggests an estimated reduction in poverty and emissions of GHG by, respectively, 44.4% and 15.3%. This evidence from the study, of prominent importance to sustainability, can serve as a reference in the definition of goals to the Brazilian federal governmental as well as of commitments to international standards regarding reduces in GHG emissions in the country.

Results indicate that another interesting strategy may emerge if producers direct efforts to increase productivity,

i.e., the ratio products/inputs, without changing the negative externalities. This strategy can be designed with the assistance of the indicator $\vec{D}_{iy}^w$, which has an average value of 0.17, as shown in Table 5. Thus, with the same level of environmental and social impact, the segment can increase the desired output by 6.8% and reduce, in parallel, the three inputs, employed personnel, agricultural inputs and capital, by, respectively, 12%, 7.5% and 8.6 %.

In Table 5, from the second indicator, the most interesting unit must be the largest producer. The indicator $\vec{D}_i^w$ shows the capability of reducing human resource and property costs by 0.26 on average, without affecting the level of production and the environmental impact. Whether the 17 inefficient Brazilian states adopt best practices, the reduction in human resources would be 20.2%, in input factors would be 13.3%, and in capital would be 14.1%.

The indicator $\vec{D}_{ib}^w$ can be obtained from the directional vector, which seeks to minimize externalities and agricultural inputs with a fixed vector of a desired product. The average value of this indicator is 0.23, as shown in

Table 5. Indicator of socio-environmental efficiency $\vec{D}_{iy}^w(1,1,1,1,0,0)$ and $\vec{D}_i^w(1,1,1,0,0,0)$ and goals of improvement of each analysed units.

DMUs	$\vec{D}_{iy}^w$	$(1-\beta) \times x_1$	$(1-\beta) \times x_2$	$(1-\beta) \times x_3$	$(1-\beta) \times y$	$\vec{D}_i^w$	$(1-\beta) \times x_1$	$(1-\beta) \times x_2$	$(1-\beta) \times x_3$
Rondônia	0.54	1.521	3.571	1.762	15.770	0.70	1.001	2.349	1.159
Acre	0.43	1.634	1.788	1.654	14.219	0.60	1.155	1.264	1.169
Amazonas	0.10	6.603	3.576	1.156	19.689	0.23	5.679	3.075	0.994
Roraima	0.49	0.894	1.539	0.611	8.641	0.65	0.606	1.043	0.414
Pará	0.34	2.320	3.347	1.182	19.925	0.48	1.819	2.625	0.927
Amapá	0.00	1.499	0.385	0.549	11.470	0.00	1.499	0.385	0.549
Tocantins	0.56	0.549	3.273	1.008	8.328	0.71	0.360	2.145	0.661
Maranhão	0.12	6.717	6.376	1.343	26.910	0.19	6.206	5.890	1.241
Piauí	0.48	4.533	3.240	1.041	20.701	0.60	3.491	2.495	0.802
Ceará	0.00	14.465	10.535	3.471	48.575	0.00	14.465	10.535	3.471
Rio Grande do Norte	0.00	7.764	6.435	3.795	35.164	0.00	7.764	6.435	3.795
Paraíba	0.23	9.967	10.535	3.128	46.276	0.44	7.258	7.671	2.278
Pernambuco	0.13	15.163	30.258	3.866	100.037	0.22	13.633	27.205	3.476
Alagoas	0.00	21.426	46.460	5.787	155.247	0.00	21.426	46.460	5.787
Sergipe	0.07	16.886	54.466	4.525	76.991	0.26	13.491	43.515	3.615
Bahia	0.25	5.970	14.033	1.853	36.076	0.36	5.093	11.972	1.581
Mato Grosso do Sul	0.21	0.557	10.278	2.848	14.309	0.33	0.473	8.723	2.417
Mato Grosso	0.00	0.750	22.577	3.316	20.085	0.00	0.750	22.577	3.316
Goiás	0.15	1.390	17.390	4.227	27.852	0.31	1.131	14.152	3.440
Distrito Federal	0.00	8.883	85.391	34.947	172.222	0.00	8.883	85.391	34.947
Minas Gerais	0.12	5.101	30.805	5.910	64.745	0.23	4.474	27.015	5.183
Espírito Santo	0.18	9.197	26.462	9.884	97.259	0.34	7.362	21.182	7.912
Rio de Janeiro	0.16	6.479	19.063	8.563	70.526	0.27	5.640	16.595	7.455
São Paulo	0.00	5.453	81.020	14.419	152.821	0.00	5.453	81.020	14.419
Paraná	0.00	7.308	55.061	5.506	103.999	0.00	7.308	55.061	5.506
Santa Catarina	0.00	9.462	58.259	22.835	146.911	0.00	9.462	58.259	22.835
Rio Grande do Sul	0.00	6.098	46.899	15.074	82.644	0.00	6.098	46.899	15.074
Average	0.17					0.26			
Sum		178.591	653.021	164.262	1597.391		161.981	611.940	154.423
Δ%		−12.031	−7.482	−8.659	6.804		−20.213	−13.303	−14.130
North	0.39	1.831	3.491	1.352	15.645	0.51	1.496	2.852	1.104
Northeast	0.00	10.184	16.262	2.773	37.587	0.00	10.184	16.262	2.773
Midwest	0.10	0.880	17.535	3.504	20.949	0.16	0.817	16.293	3.256
Southeast	0.03	5.865	47.102	9.210	91.158	0.06	5.666	45.498	8.897
South	0.00	7.033	51.556	12.681	99.853	0.00	7.033	51.556	12.681
Brazil	0.00	5.021	25.264	5.384	43.590	0.00	5.021	25.264	5.384

Table 6. Indicator of socio-environmental efficiency $\vec{D}_{ib}^{w}(1,1,1,0,1,0)$ and $\vec{D}_{l}^{w}(0,0,0,1,0,0)$ and goals of improvement of each analysed units.

DMUs	$\vec{D}_{ib}^{w}$	$(1-\beta) \times x_1$	$(1-\beta) \times x_2$	$(1-\beta) \times x_3$	$(1-\beta) \times b_1$	$(1-\beta) \times b_2$	$\vec{D}_{y}^{w}$	$(1-\beta) \times y$
Rondônia	0.71	0.970485	2.278821	1.124424	21,523.524	0.020661	2.43	35.074876
Acre	0.53	1.346144	1.473112	1.362192	29,217.744	0.014632	1.12	21.113716
Amazonas	0.15	6.229113	3.373077	1.090116	187,124.69	0.019527	0.18	21.085022
Roraima	0.60	0.70308	1.210545	0.480735	4387.77	0.00972	1.47	14.378749
Pará	0.49	1.79826	2.59437	0.91647	159,880.41	0.02448	0.96	29.10012
Amapá	0.00	1.499	0.385	0.549	4866	0.025	0.00	11.47
Tocantins	0.72	0.34636	2.06416	0.63588	17,891.16	0.01092	2.58	19.138752
Maranhão	0.23	5.87741	5.57865	1.17502	753,739.14	0.02849	0.30	31.211073
Piauí	0.56	3.84125	2.745506	0.88239	251,888.98	0.015365	1.28	31.833072
Ceará	0.00	14.465	10.535	3.471	807,135	0.041	0.00	48.575
Rio Grande do Norte	0.00	7.764	6.435	3.795	234,974	0.033	0.00	35.164
Paraíba	0.32	8.839402	9.342718	2.774376	188,682.12	0.025916	0.47	55.109872
Pernambuco	0.18	14.276369	28.4887	3.640314	660,525.7	0.045155	0.22	108.01833
Alagoas	0.00	21.426	46.46	5.787	492,473	0.077	0.00	155.247
Sergipe	0.07	16.922324	54.583512	4.535112	123,724.86	0.058716	0.07	77.206642
Bahia	0.45	4.368108	10.26678	1.355752	889,510.31	0.023016	0.83	52.658188
Mato Grosso do Sul	0.36	0.449217	8.282079	2.295288	47,466.837	0.04473	0.57	18.553075
Mato Grosso	0.00	0.75	22.577	3.316	150,180	0.02	0.00	20.085
Goiás	0.22	1.26984	15.88314	3.861	84,144.84	0.02184	0.28	31.157728
Distrito Federal	0.00	8.883	85.391	34.947	19,374.254	5.502	0.00	172.222
Minas Gerais	0.21	4.60733	27.822405	5.337683	354,884.95	0.03965	0.26	72.7083
Espírito Santo	0.23	8.637908	24.852224	9.282528	74,590.64	0.114256	0.30	106.91909
Rio de Janeiro	0.28	5.548095	16.32344	7.33257	381,561.85	0.609245	0.39	84.472461
São Paulo	0.00	5.453	81.02	14.419	181,737	0.229	0.00	152.821
Paraná	0.00	7.308	55.061	5.506	180,471	0.085	0.00	103.999
Santa Catarina	0.00	9.462	58.259	22.835	49,796	0.204	0.00	146.911
Rio Grande do Sul	0.00	6.098	46.899	15.074	217,451	0.024	0.00	82.644
Average	0.23						0.51	
Sum		169.1387	630.18524	157.78085	6,569,202.8	7.366319		1738.8771
Δ%		−16.687	−10.718	−12.263	−24.736	−6.602		16.264
North	0.57	1.287372	2.454186	0.950406	319,227.36	0.01917	1.35	26.351604
Northeast	0.00	10.184	16.262	2.773	5,924,387	0.042	0.00	37.587
Midwest	0.19	0.785211	15.653379	3.127932	268,199.19	0.04035	0.24	23.682246
Southeast	0.06	5.714032	45.886896	8.97272	747,406.34	0.07552	0.06	93.633603
South	0.00	7.033	51.556	12.681	447,718	0.053	0.00	99.853
Brazil	0.00	5.021	25.264	5.384	8,245,550	0.059	0.00	43.59

Table 6. The reduction in externalities and input factors also increases environmentally responsible productivity. In Table 6, indicator $\vec{D}_{ib}^{w}$ shows that poverty and GHG can be mitigated by, respectively, 24.7% and 6.6%; whereas employed staff can be reduced by 16.6%; capital resources by 12.2%, and agricultural inputs by 10.7%.

Finally, results of the study can be used to estimate to know how much production can be increased by keeping the other variables constant. The indicator $\vec{D}_{y}^{w}$ shown in Table 6 has an average value of 0.51 and suggests that an efficient management could increase production by 16.2%.

Summarizing the analysis of the results, the study shows a high level of relative inefficiency of Brazilian agribusiness. The federal states of Tocantins, Rondônia and Roraima are the worst performers. In addition, only 10 Brazilian states, highlighted in Table 6, achieved the best performance in all environmental efficiency indicators: São Paulo, Santa Catarina, Paraná, Rio Grande do Sul, Distrito Federal, Mato Grosso, Rio Grande do Norte, Alagoas, Ceará, and Amapá. It should be emphasized that many of these states stand out in at least one of the selected variables, as seen in the previous section and others are linear combinations of those notable states, establishing the efficient frontier. This result reveals that some efficient units tend to be more responsible than others in terms of social and environmental dimensions.

Additionally, some explanations for this high level of social and environmental inefficiency can be suggested: (1) High technical inefficiency, since the DEA-CCR oriented to output model, without considering the environmental and social impacts, estimated an average of 1.78. In this case, only four states (Amapá, Alagoas, São Paulo and Paraná) are efficient. This result implies that the Brazilian agricultural production could increase 78% if states adopt best practices; (2) The very poor social indicators in Brazil: high poverty, low education, high concentration of income and land; (3) The large regional inequality; (4) Little recognition, by the population, of environment as a public good; (5) Failure and ineffectiveness of state to enforce environmental standards and public policies of agricultural assistance, especially to the small producer.

Despite these potential explanations, analysis of the causes of low social and environmental inefficiency behaviour is beyond the scope of this study.

6. Concluding remarks

From a sustainable development perspective, the social and environmental impacts of the modernization of Brazilian agribusiness have generated a growing concern in the search for balance between socioeconomics development and the appropriate use of natural resources. In this context, this research contributes to the discussion of sustainable development in the agribusiness sector of one of the largest food producer in the world. Because of the important role Brazil plays as an importer and exporter of agricultural products, changes in efficiency in the country's productive process may have a significant impact on agricultural commodity prices all over the world.

By applying DDF and DEA methods, the study evaluated the environmental efficiency of different states in Brazil. It is important to highlight that one of the main motivations of this research was the lack of references in the literature using these combined methods focused on the Brazilian agribusiness. The study of Brazilian states can shed light to identify sources of inefficiencies, indicating the need for further research. Since the study showed large variability in the efficiency levels of the states, it would be interesting to confront performance with specific characteristics of the DMUs. For instance, climate, soil, instruction level of population, GDP per capita, educational constraints and human development index of the states could be used to explain agribusiness efficiency. In this context, the study presents some limitations as, for instance, the focus on DMUs of a single country and the small number of variables used in the model. Nevertheless, there are arguments that may weaken these limitations: the leading position of Brazil in the agribusiness and the limited number of available environmental and social data. It should also be emphasized that the choice of variables followed, for instance, Gomes and Lins (2008) and Gomes et al. (2009).

As for the results, the research estimated a set of environmental performance indicators, which, by satisfying the Pareto optimality concept, could simultaneously enhance economic, ecological and social dimensions. These indicators confirm, in different ways, the initial hypothesis that it is possible to establish consistent productive strategies that are compatible with the maximization of social welfare, despite the apparent antagonism among these three dimensions.

In addition, this study shows that efficient Brazilian states tend to combine the three dimensions in different ways. Hence, several optimal points can be obtained from different actions to reduce poverty and environmental impact without necessarily generating productive inefficiencies. This result can be considered of prominent importance for sustainable development in Brazil and can also serve as a reference in the definition of goals for the Brazilian government in an internal context as well as in the choice of international GHG emission standards to which the country could commit itself. Reducing inefficiencies in 17 states would probably enhance productivity of the agribusiness in Brazil and at the same time promote a sustainable social and environmental development.

Finally, it is worth noting that there is a great potential for research regarding the use of DDF in a DEA framework, mainly in the agribusiness sector, where an increase in productivity can occur at the expense of jeopardizing enhancements in other dimensions. Further studies can take advantage of this tool to estimate the shadow prices of pollution reduction and rural poverty. Also, studies that could explore the availability of time series data would allow the definition of dynamic models, which shifts the central issue of environmental efficiency to other very important problems such as the evolution of indicators through the years and the nature of their trajectories in the long term. Panel data would therefore make possible the study of state or country-level variables that, through time, could explain the impact not only in agribusiness production, but also in the environment and social welfare.

References

Alcantara Filho JL, Fontes RMO. 2009. A formação da propriedade e a concentração de terras no Brasil. R. Heera. 4:63–85.

Ali ASM. 2013. Targeting the poorest in developing countries: components of multidimensional deprivation in Luxor, Egypt. Int J Sustain Dev World Ecol. 20:504–511. doi:10.1080/13504509.2013.842946

Alves BJR. 2010. Emissões de óxido nitroso de solos agrícolas e de manejo de dejetos [Internet]. Relatório de Referência. Brasília: Empresa Brasileira de Pesquisa Agropecuária – Embrapa. [cited 2014 Mar 25]. Available from: http://www.cetesb.sp.gov.br/userfiles/file/mudancasclimaticas/geesp/file/docs/publicacao/nacional/2_comunicacao_nacional/rr/agricultura/brasil_mcti_solos_agricolas.pdf

Azad MAS, Ancev T. 2010. Using ecological indices to measure economic and environmental performance of irrigated agriculture. Ecol Econ. 69:1731–1739. doi:10.1016/j.ecolecon.2010.04.003

Bauler T. 2012. An analytical framework to discuss the usability of (environmental) indicators for policy. Ecol Indicators. 17:38–45. doi:10.1016/j.ecolind.2011.05.013

Bockstaller C, Girardin P. 2003. How to validate environmental indicators. Agri Sys. 76:639–653. doi:10.1016/S0308-521X(02)00053-7

Böhringer C, Jochem PEP. 2007. Measuring the immeasurable – a survey of sustainability indices. Ecol Econ. 63:1–8. doi:10.1016/j.ecolecon.2007.03.008

Bojacá CR, García SJ, Schrevens E. 2012. Investigating the technical sustainability of farming systems with correlational biplots. Int J Sustain Dev World Ecol. 19:361–368. doi:10.1080/13504509.2012.671194

Calker KJV, Berentsen PBM, Romero C, Giesen GWJ, Huirne RBM. 2006. Development and application of a multi-attribute sustainability function for Dutch dairy farming systems. Ecol Econ. 57:640–658. doi:10.1016/j.ecolecon.2005.05.016

Camioto FDC, Mariano EB, Rebelatto DADN. 2014. Efficiency in Brazil's industrial sectors in terms of energy and sustainable development. Env Sci Pol. 37:50–60. doi:10.1016/j.envsci.2013.08.007

Chung YH, Färe R, Grosskopf S. 1997. Productivity and undesirable outputs: a directional distance function approach. J Environ Manage. 51:229–240. doi:10.1006/jema.1997.0146

Claver E, López MD, Molina JF, Tarí JJ. 2007. Environmental management and firm performance: a case study. J Environ Manage. 84:606–619. doi:10.1016/j.jenvman.2006.09.012

Coggins JS, Swinton JR. 1996. The price of pollution: a dual approach to valuing SO2 allowances. J Environ Econ Manage. 30:58–72. doi:10.1006/jeem.1996.0005

Cooper WW, Seiford LM, Tone K. 2000. Data envelopment analysis: a comprehensive text with models, applications, references and Dea-Solver software. Boston (MA): Kluwer Academic Publisher.

Costa AO, Oliveira LB, Lins MPE, Silva ACM, Araujo MSM, Pereira Jr. AO Jr, Rosa LP. 2013. Sustainability analysis of biodiesel production: a review on different resources in Brazil. Renew Sust Energ Rev. 27:407–412. doi:10.1016/j.rser.2013.06.005

Cosyns H, Damme PV, Wulf RD. 2013. Who views what? Impact assessment through the eyes of farmers, development organization staff and researchers. Int J Sust Dev World Ecol. 20:287–301. doi:10.1080/13504509.2013.806372

Elkington J. 1998. Cannibals with forks – the triple bottom line of 21st century business. Gabriola Island: New Society Publishers.

Food and Agriculture Organization. 2006. Livestock's long shadow environmental issues and options. Rome: Food and Agriculture Organization of the United Nations. 978-92-5-105571-7.

Food and Agriculture Organization. 2013. World food and agriculture. Rome: Food and Agriculture Organization of the United Nations. 978-92-5-107396-4.

Färe R, Grosskopf S. 2000. Theory and application of directional distance functions. J. Prod Anal. 13:93–103. doi:10.1023/A:1007844628920

Fare R, Grosskopf S, Lovell CAK, Yaisawarng S. 1993. Derivation of shadow prices for undesirable outputs: a distance function approach. Rev Econ Statist. 75:374–380. doi:10.2307/2109448

Färe R, Grosskopf S, Pasurka C. 1986. Effects on relative efficiency in electric power generation due to environmental controls. Res. Energ. 8:167–184. doi:10.1016/0165-0572(86)90016-2

Färe R, Grosskopf S, Weber WL. 2006. Shadow prices and pollution costs in U.S. agriculture. Ecol Econ. 56:89–103. doi:10.1016/j.ecolecon.2004.12.022

Farrell MJ. 1957. The measurement of productive efficiency. J. R Stat Soc Ser A (General). 120:253–290. doi:10.2307/2343100

Fredericks SE. 2012. Justice in sustainability indicators and indexes. Int J Sust Dev World Ecol. 19:490–499. doi:10.1080/13504509.2012.714807

Gomes EG. 2008. Uso de modelos DEA em agricultura: revisão da literatura. Engevista. 10:27–51.

Gomes EG, Lins MPE. 2008. Modelling undesirable outputs with zero sum gains data envelopment analysis models. J Oper Res Soc. 59:616–623. doi:10.1057/palgrave.jors.2602384

Gomes EG, Mello JCCBSd, Souza GdSeS, Meza LA, Mangabeira JAdC 2009. Efficiency and sustainability assessment for a group of farmers in the Brazilian Amazon. In: Annals of Operations Research.

Gómez-Limón JA, Riesgo L. 2009. Alternative approaches to the construction of a composite indicator of agricultural sustainability: an application to irrigated agriculture in the Duero basin in Spain. J Environ Manage. 90:3345–3362. doi:10.1016/j.jenvman.2009.05.023

González-Benito J, González-Benito Ó. 2008. Operations management practices linked to the adoption of ISO 14001: an empirical analysis of Spanish manufacturers. Int J Prod Econ. 113:60–73. doi:10.1016/j.ijpe.2007.02.051

Govindan K, Khodaverdi R, Jafarian A. 2013. A fuzzy multi criteria approach for measuring sustainability performance of a supplier based on triple bottom line approach. J Clean Prod. 47:345–354. doi:10.1016/j.jclepro.2012.04.014

Grossi MD. 2011. A questão agrária, a agricultura familiar e a probleza no Brasil [Internet]. In: Miranda C, Tiburcio B, editors. Pobreza Rural: concepções, determinantes e proposições para a construção de uma agenda de políticas públicas; Brasília; p. 79–82. [cited 2013 Oct 27]. Available from: http://www.iicaforumdrs.org.br/iica2010/adm/adm/imagens/arquivos/Edicao%20Especial_Serie%20DRS_baixa%20resolucao.pdf.

Grosskopf S. 1986. The role of the reference technology in measuring productive efficiency. Econ J. 96:499–513. doi:10.2307/2233129

Hansmann R, Mieg HA, Frischknecht P. 2012. Principal sustainability components: empirical analysis of synergies between the three pillars of sustainability. Int J Sust Dev World Ecol. 19:451–459. doi:10.1080/13504509.2012.696220

Heyder M, Theuvsen L. 2012. Determinants and effects of corporate social responsibility in German agribusiness: a PLS model. Agribusiness. 28:400–420. doi:10.1002/agr.21305

Hoffmann R, Ney MG. 2010. Estrutura fundiária e propriedade agrícola no Brasil, grandes regiões e unidades da federação. Brasília: Ministério do Desenvolvimento Agrário.

IBGE. 2006. Censo Agropecuário [Internet]. Rio de Janeiro: Instituto Brasileiro de Geografia e Estatística – IBGE. [cited 2014 Mar 25]. Available from: ftp://ftp.ibge.gov.br/Censos/Censo_Agropecuario_2006/Segunda_Apuracao/censoagro2006_2aapuracao.pdf.

Jabbour CJC, Silva EMd, Paiva EL, Santos FCA. 2012. Environmental management in Brazil: is it a completely competitive priority? J Clean Prod. 21:11–22. doi:10.1016/j.jclepro.2011.09.003

Kjærsgaard J, Vestergaard N, Kerstens K. 2009. Ecological benchmarking to explore alternative fishing schemes to protect endangered species by substitution: the Danish Demersal Fishery in the North Sea. Environ Res Econ. 43:573–590. doi:10.1007/s10640-008-9251-7

Leal IC Jr, Garcia PAdA, D'Agosto MdA. 2012. A data envelopment analysis approach to choose transport modes based on eco-efficiency. Environ Dev Sust. 14:767–781. doi:10.1007/s10668-012-9352-x

Lima MAd, Ligo MAV, Pessoa MCPY, Neves MC, Carvalho ECd. 2010. Emissão de gases de efeito estufa na queima de resíduos agrícolas [Internet]. Relatórios de Referência. Brasília: Empresa Brasileira de Pesquisa Agropecuária – Embrapa. [cited 2014 Mar 25]. Available from: http://www.cetesb.sp.gov.br/userfiles/file/mudancasclimaticas/geesp/file/docs/publicacao/nacional/2_comunicacao_nacional/rr/agricultura/brasil_mcti_queima_residuos_agricolas.pdf.

Lima MAd, Ligo MAV, Pessoa MCPY, Luiz AJB, Neves MC, Maia AH. 2010. Emissão do metano do cutivo de arroz [Internet]. Relatório de Referência. Brasília: Empresa Brasileira de Pesquisa Agropecuária – Embrapa. [cited 2014 Mar 25]. Available from: http://www.cetesb.sp.gov.br/userfiles/file/mudancasclimaticas/geesp/file/docs/publicacao/nacional/2_comunicacao_nacional/rr/agricultura/brasil_mcti_arroz.pdf.

Lima MAd, Pessoa MCPY, Neves MC, Carvalho ECd. 2010. Emissões de metano por fermentação entérica e manejo de dejetos de animais [Internet]. Brasília: Empresa Brasileira de Pesquisa Agropecuária - Embrapa. [cited 2014 Mar 25]. Available from: http://www.cetesb.sp.gov.br/userfiles/file/mudancasclimaticas/geesp/file/docs/publicacao/nacional/2_comunicacao_nacional/rr/agricultura/brasil_mcti_fermentacao_enterica.pdf.

Lyytimäki J, Tapio P, Varho V, Söderman T. 2013. The use, nonuse and misuse of indicators in sustainability assessment and communication. Int J Sustain Dev World Ecol. 20:385–393. doi:10.1080/13504509.2013.834524

McKinsey & Company. 2009. Caminhos para uma economia de baixa emissão de carbono no Brasil [Internet]. São Paulo. [cited 2014 Mar 25]. Available from: http://veja.abril.com.br/40anos/ambiente/pdf/relatorio-mckinsey.pdf.

Meadows DH, Meadows DL, Randers J, Behrens IIIWW. 1972. The limits to growth. New York (NY): Universe Books.

Montabon F, Sroufe R, Narasimhan R. 2007. An examination of corporate reporting, environmental management practices and firm performance. J Oper Manage. 25:998–1014. doi:10.1016/j.jom.2006.10.003

Munda G. 2005. "Measuring sustainability": a multi-criterion framework. Environ. Dev. Sustain. 7:117–134. doi:10.1007/s10668-003-4713-0

Morse S, McNamara N, Acholo M, Okwoli B. 2001. Sustainability indicators: the problem of integration. Sust Dev. 9:1–15. doi:10.1002/sd.148

Picazo-Tadeo AJ, Beltrán-Esteve M, Gómez-Limón JA. 2012. Assessing eco-efficiency with directional distance functions. Eur J Oper Res. 220:798–809. doi:10.1016/j.ejor.2012.02.025

Pittman RW. 1983. Multilateral productivity comparisons with undesirable outputs. Econ J. 93:883–891. doi:10.2307/2232753

Qiu H, Zhu W, Wang H, Cheng X. 2007. Analysis and design of agricultural sustainability indicators system. Agri Sci China. 6:475–486. doi:10.1016/S1671-2927(07)60072-8

Reig-Martínez E, Picazo-Tadeo A, Hernández-Sancho F. 2001. The calculation of shadow prices for industrial wastes using distance functions: an analysis for Spanish ceramic pavements firms. Int J Prod Econ. 69:277–285. doi:10.1016/S0925-5273(00)00018-9

Scheel H. 2001. Undesirable outputs in efficiency valuations. Eur J Oper Res. 132:400–410. doi:10.1016/S0377-2217(00)00160-0

Seuring S, Gold S. 2013. Sustainability management beyond corporate boundaries: from stakeholders to performance. J Clean Prod. 56:1–6. doi:10.1016/j.jclepro.2012.11.033

Shephard RW. 1954. Cost and production functions. Nav Res Log Quart. 1:171.

Speelman EN, López-Ridaura S, Colomer NA, Astier M, Masera OR. 2007. Ten years of sustainability evaluation using the MESMIS framework: lessons learned from its application in 28 Latin American case studies. Int J Sustain Dev World Ecol. 14:345–361. doi:10.1080/13504500709469735

Swinton JR. 1998. At what cost do we reduce pollution? Shadow prices of SO_2 emissions. Energ J. 19:63–83. 10.5547/ISSN0195-6574-EJ-Vol19-No4-3

Tyteca D. 1996. On the measurement of the environmental performance of firms – a literature review and a productive efficiency perspective. J Environ Manage. 46:281–308. doi:10.1006/jema.1996.0022

WCED. 1987. Report of the World Commission on Environment and Development: Our Common Future. United Nations World Commission on Environment and Development – WCED.

Reverse logistics in the Chinese auto-parts firms: implementation framework development through multiple case studies

Nachiappan Subramanian[a,b], Angappa Gunasekaran[c], Muhammad D. Abdulrahman[d], Chang Liu[e] and Danwei Su[e]

[a]The University of Nottingham Ningbo China, Ningbo, China; [b]Nottingham University Business School China, Ningbo, China; [c]Charlton College of Business, University of Massachusetts Dartmouth, Dartmouth, NH, USA; [d]Nottingham University Business School China, Ningbo, China; [e]Division of Economics, The University of Nottingham Ningbo China, Ningbo, China

In recent years, the implementation of reverse logistics (RL) in automobile manufacturing has drawn extensive interest from the Chinese government that has launched relevant take-back and environmental regulations and pilot projects. This study focuses on RL implementation issues in Chinese auto-parts manufacturing sector. Based on comprehensive literature review and multiple case studies in the Chinese auto-parts firms, this paper proposes a conceptual RL framework and highlights the major implementation issues. The purpose of this paper is to draw an overall picture of RL in the Chinese context, highlighting implementation issues in the auto-parts sector. Our study suggests that Chinese RL implementation requires close government monitoring mechanism and incentives, top management commitment within firms, technology and human capabilities support.

Introduction

In today's competitive economy, firms are surrounded by a unique environment filled with challenges and opportunities. Businesses face stringent operational requirements that include Clean Development Mechanism (CDM) of the Kyoto Protocol for sustainable development and emission reduction (especially in developing nations), environmental protection legislations of Waste Electrical and Electronic Equipment (WEEE) directive in the EU, the End-of-Life Vehicles (ELVs) take-back policies of Germany, the Universal Waste Rule (1995) of North America and Japan's Extended Producer Responsibility (EPR) law, amongst other similar legislations. Basically, these regulations require businesses to contribute to the three main dimensions of sustainability called the Triple Bottom Line (3BL), namely environmental, social and economic sustainability (Sarkis et al. 2010; Ulutas et al. 2012; Karakosta et al. 2013). Only those firms that understand these unique challenges and are prepared to timely grasp the associated opportunities stand a better chance of gaining long-term strategic competitive advantages that result in subsequent enormous business success.

One of the key potential and pivotal approaches for businesses to substantially achieve the 3BL is reverse logistics (RL). In this study, RL refers to the backward flow of used products from the end users (i.e. the consumers) to the starting point of forward logistics (i.e. the original manufacturers). RL is critical for business success and business sustainability for a number of important reasons that include (1) increasing scarcity of natural resource as well as limited capacity of the earth's resource bearing and for its absorption of waste; (2) the substantial economic value that can potentially be gained from assets recaptured, reused and recycled; (3) increasing global demand for green products; (4) government regulations and associated severity of the penalty for non-compliance; and (5) the growing pressure from socially concerned NGOs demanding corporations be more socially responsible and take better care of the environment (Skouloudis & Evangelinos 2012; Valentinov 2013; Kannan et al. 2014). Firms are therefore forced, externally by consumers and social actors and internally by own desire for long-term growth, to invest in and implement RL.

RL is not entirely a new concept. Many developed nations, especially the United States, Germany and Japan, already have well-developed and sophisticated RL system in some of their industrial sectors like the automobile and electronic products manufacturing (Yan & Yan 2011; Bai & Sarkis 2013). However, RL is only recently gaining attention (starting middle of 1980s) in China (Ye et al. 2013). The late start to RL implementation in China has resulted in its poorly shaped practice in terms of physical system construction, management system formulation, regulated market development and consumer mentality cultivation (Yan & Yan 2011). This is clearly not a sustainable foundation upon which China, the world's largest automotive manufacturer and market, can compete, especially in the long-term, when compared with developed nations such as the United States, Europe and Japan. Establishing an effective long-term competitive advantage based on effective RL practices is therefore crucial for the Chinese auto-parts makers.

While most past studies on RL have focused on developed Western nations (Ravi et al. 2005; Jayaraman & Luo 2007; Sarkis et al. 2010), the few studies on China have mostly focused on electrical and electronic waste (Liu et al. 2006; Lai & Wong 2012; Wang & Chen 2013). The study by Zhao and Chen (2011) compare the Chinese and Japanese laws on ELVs and the process of handling such laws in the respective countries. The study gave an overall present situation of scrap automobiles between Japan and China, and ELV laws of the two nations. It however did not show the road map of how to deal with scrap automobile RL issues in China. Similarly, Zhang et al. (2011) examined remanufacturing issues that Chinese automotive industry face with respect to barriers such as restrictive policies and regulations, scarcity of technologies and consumer acceptance of remanufactured products. The study did not examine in-depth details of specific RL issues faced by the automobile firms. Zhao et al. (2013) investigated the financial implications of recall announcement in China without any link to RL issues. From the above discussions, it is evident that specific study is essential to identify the issues related to Chinese auto-parts firms and the intricate details about RL implementation.

This paper develops an RL implementation framework and highlights the major implementation issues in Chinese auto-parts firms. The primary objectives of this study are threefold: (1) to carry out a comprehensive literature review on automotive RL implementation issues to serve as standard benchmark in analysing RL in Chinese context; (2) to conduct case studies in two leading Chinese auto-parts firms, based on established global RL practices, to find out their RL development status, the challenges/barriers they face in their attempt at RL implementation; and (3) to offer a direction for future development with respect to RL practices specifically in the auto sector.

The rest of this paper is organized as follows: 'Literature review' section gives a comprehensive literature review of the various issues associated with implementation of RL. 'Methodology' section delineates the methodology, companies' profile and case study results. 'RL implementation framework and discussion' section presents the discussion and proposes RL reference framework that highlights the major issues across RL stages. 'Concluding remarks' section provides our concluding remarks with direction for future studies.

Literature review

The Chinese State Bureau of Quality Technical Supervision launched the Logistics National Standard of People's Republic of China (PRC) on 1 August 2001. The standard classifies RL into two separate categories: (1) returned logistics refers to the flow of physical objects from the demand side back to the supply side, including the backflow of defective products for repairs and refunds,

and the backflow of packaging materials for reuse and (2) waste material logistics refers to the flow of physical objects that have lost their original use value in the process of various economic activities from end users to specialized disposal sites after being collected, classified, processed, transported, stored and delivered (China Federation of Logistics and Purchasing 2007). In other words, RL is not only about value recapture in defective or obsolete products, but also the recycling of waste materials for the purpose of reducing resource usage and waste generation.

RL implementation issues with auto-parts manufacturers

Gonzalez-Torre et al. (2010) summarized and categorized issues within the automotive industry as industry-specific/external issues and organizational-specific/internal issues. The external issues are those related to common forces within the industries including government's reluctance to enforce relevant laws and regulations, consumer's reluctance to send back used cars to the initial collection points and other automobile manufacturers' reluctance to carry out RL activities. By contrast, internal issues exist within an organization. It mainly includes a manufacturer's lack of the following: technical and managerial know-how, commitment from top management, effective information system, adequate financial resource and enough RL professionals. In addition to the two groups of issues/barriers, the fundamental characteristics of RL – high uncertainty level in terms of volume and quantity of returned products – increases the difficulty of managing an RL system efficiently to a great extent. The uncertain flow is likely to cause huge transportation costs because of the increased delivery time and the small delivery volume associated with mileage. Furthermore, the uncertainty in the quality of returned vehicles can lead to much higher collection, sorting and handling costs compared with forward logistics as quality diagnosis and quality evaluation are required before making disposal decisions (Tibben-Lembke & Rogers 2002; Sheriff et al. 2012, 2013).

Despite the above uncertainties associated with RL, its implementation and practice has bright prospects in China, especially within the automotive industry. For example, the RL difficulties arising from low volume could be significantly minimized in China as the country is now the world's leading automotive producer and market (Zhang et al. 2011; Zhao & Chen 2011; Liao et al. 2013). According to the global credit rating agency Moody's, China's vehicle growth rate is estimated to jump by up to 10% for 2014, pulling global demand by 4.8% (France-Presse 2013). Furthermore, China is now reported to have huge and growing size of ELVs which is further projected to reach 6.4 million by 2015 (Xiang & Ming 2011; Zhao & Chen 2011). The above coupled with increasing global vehicle manufacturers setting up vehicle plants in China could lead to reasonable flow of economic recovery quantity of used and/or ELVs and further encourage car owners to return ELVs back to designated initial collection points (ICPs) in future. Likewise, the increased costs associated with non-uniform physical conditions of returned cars can be reduced by effective gate-keeping that avoids extra costs of unnecessary transportation and scrap storage (Rahman & Subramanian 2012). All these should consequently help minimize overall quality issues, all things being equal.

Comparison of auto-parts RL practice

In some developed nations including Germany, the United States and Japan, a benign circulation system has been developed which starts from product design, goes through product manufacturing and selling and ends in ELVs recycling (Yan & Yan 2011). The maturity of such systems is reflected in the number of specialized dismantling companies, the rigour of government regulations enforcement and the rate of resource recovery. First, these developed nations all have large numbers of ELVs dismantling enterprises that possess high dismantling capability. For example, there are around 12,000 such dismantling companies in the United States, more than 4000 in Germany and about 5100 in Japan (Jiang 2009). In fact, the realization of efficient vehicle RL in America was heavily due to its numerous dismantling enterprises (Jiang 2009). In Germany especially, very strict certification appraisals on dismantling enterprises in aspects of technology, environmental measures, company scale, etc., are carried out to ensure the positives of setting up such institutions.

Second, these nations all have comprehensive laws and regulations regarding waste reduction and resource recovery. Europe in particular is leading the way in its drive to reduce ELVs waste by developing regulations such as the ELVs Directive, the Restriction of Use of certain Hazardous Substances Directive, and the Waste Electrical and Electronic Equipment Directive, which requires manufacturers and distributors to take-back environmentally hazardous products and packaging materials for reuse or recycle (Jiang 2009). In fact, the European legislation on take-back and recycling of WEEE equally affects any firm anywhere in the world wanting to sell into the European markets (Haanaes et al. 2011). Similarly, the used car ordinance in Germany requires that the last owner of an automobile deliver it to a collection centre, and the Commercial and Industrial Waste Avoidance and Management Act requires that the producer is responsible for the end-of-life disposition of their products, including reuse and recovery (Gotzel et al. 1999 in Guide & Wassenhove 2001). Japan has also launched a number of regulations including the Norms of ELVs Recycle and Reuse and the Car Recycling Directive to normalize the auto recovery industry (Jiang 2009). Third, these nations have all achieved high resource recovery rate. Approximately 80%, on average, of the total weight of vehicles has been recycled for the purpose of value recovery (Jiang 2009). Specifically, for example, average

recycling rate in EU countries was 84.1% in 2000, and in the United States, 95% of ELVs and vehicle trucks go to the recycler after retiring (Auto Alliance 2013).

China, however, is known for a general lack of effective control and support for natural resources (Qian et al. 2011; Cao et al. 2014). For example, despite rapid growth in the amount of China's ELVs, estimated to be at 4.8 million in 2010, the collection rates of ELVs was very low (estimated at 40%) with 60% of the ELVs officially unaccounted for due to ineffective government regulation and control (Zhao & Chen 2011). It is therefore imperative that this situation is exhaustively examined and changed to be in line with global sustainability practices.

The ELVs recovery sector in America has a relatively different market regime from that of most EU nations or Japan. While automobile recycling is mostly mandated by law and often cut down firms' profitability in the latter two countries, it has long been a voluntary and profitable sector in the United States. This is partially due to the special legislation regime in the United States which focuses more on encouraging rather than mandating enterprises to execute recycling and reuse activities. The United States achieved this situation mainly through its municipalities offering tax credits or taking the responsibility of the collection of used vehicle products (Guide & Wassenhove 2001). It is not surprising therefore that automotive recycling was reported to be the 16th largest industry in the United States and operated profitably at an estimated $25 billion per year in 2010 (Jody et al. 2010; Auto Alliance 2013).

In contrast, the RL of ELVs in China is far less developed and confronts many problems. In 2007, the supposed number of scrapped cars was estimated to be between 3 and 6 million, but only 380 thousand units were dismantled (Yan & Yan 2011). By early 2004, only about 10% of ELVs had been dismantled in China, implying that the rest remained in use illegally (Chen 2005). All these, however, were in the face of rapid automobile sector growth, with the automobile number growing rate estimated at 10% to 15% between 2010 and 2025 (Zhang & Zhang 2010). The volume of in-use vehicles in China reached 105.78 million in 2011 (National Bureau of Statistics of China 2012). Such large number poses tremendous pressure on the development of perfect ELVs recovery sector, without which the rampant solid waste and the resultant severe environmental pollution will become disastrous and capable of reversing past economic gains.

Therefore, to attain sustainable development in the Chinese auto-parts sector, there is an urgent need for both the auto-parts companies and the Chinese government to re-evaluate and change their current development strategy. This is imperative as sustainable development requires changes in both the socio-technical systems and the wider society (Kemp et al. 2007; Baskaran et al. 2011).

Methodology

This study involves qualitative research and uses inductive multiple case studies. According to Yin (2009), case studies are particularly suited for the understanding of real-life events. Case studies feature face-to-face interactions with key company insiders, whereupon direct and in-depth knowledge can be obtained. The key insider information is crucial for understanding the current issues and, more importantly, insights on the standing issues of RL in the Chinese automobile (auto-parts) sector. Literature suggests that a qualitative multiple case study research approach is more appropriate for studying phenomena that can lead to the development of robust new theories (Elsbach & Kramer 2003; Eisenhardt & Graebner 2007). Eisenhardt's (1989) recommendation of 4–10 cases that a researcher should select has become a popular benchmark. However, other researchers have countered this suggestion, arguing that a smaller number of cases can provide greater and richer opportunities for in-depth observations (Dyer & Wilkins 1991; Narasimhan & Jayaram 1998). In fact, Dyer and Wilkins (1991) argued that single case studies enable the capturing of much greater detail of the context within which the phenomena under study can occur.

This study investigates two Chinese auto-parts companies. The choice of these two cases was deliberate and based on key criteria that (1) the two companies are key representatives of the auto-parts industry, being amongst the largest automobile parts manufacturers in China. Both companies are suppliers to a number of global auto brands and have well-established logistics and supply chain management departments (see Table 1); (2) the products of both companies belong to an established remanufacturing category, requiring RL for take-back and/or recovery (Steinhilper et al. 2011); (3) the variation in size of the two firms (facilities, global reach and annual turnover) is likely to provide rich information on the RL phenomenon being studied and to produce a really convincing account of what is being observed due to the heterogeneous representation (Miles & Huberman 1994; Curtis et al. 2000).

Six responses were obtained from the two Chinese auto-parts manufacturers, with three respondents representing each auto-part firm. The format adopted was a combination of structured questionnaire and a semi-structured interview with key informants (R&D manager, shop-floor manager, logistic manager/design engineer) in each company investigated. The questions were related to RL design, collection points, economic gains, components they remanufacture, dismantling of collected components, whether they do on their own or outsource, quality of returned products and diagnosis, drivers and barriers of implementation, importance – implementation of technical know-how, availability of financial resources, human resource, management commitment, arrival of returned products and the disposition options they have. Figure 1 presents the general framework of the methodology adopted in this study. Specifically, the framework includes the following steps:

Step 1: Literature review: Comprehensive literature review on RL, with key priorities on global trend in sustainability in automotive industry with respect to RL practices.

Step 2: Identification of major RL implementation issues and benefits: Identification, through literature review, of major RL issues – drivers and barriers in general – specifically within the global automotive industry.

Step 3: Identification of China's RL implementation issues: Identifying RL implementation issues in Chinese context by comparing and contrasting China's auto industry RL and other sustainability efforts with global RL issues.

Step 4: Data collection: Identification of representative auto-parts firms with capability, resources and international business experiences for participation in the study. A combination of structured questionnaire and a semi-structured interview with key informants (R&D manager, shop-floor manager, Logistic Manager/design engineer) in each company investigated.

Step 5: Qualitative text analysis: A qualitative analysis was adopted based on the comprehensive interviews, site visits and data collected from investigated auto firms.

Table 1. Company and respondent profile.

Profile items	Company A	Company B
Type of organization	Joint venture	Private
Annual turnover	¥3878 million (US$633 million)	¥1360 million (US$222 million)
Number of production facilities	30	17
Number of total employees	600	1642
Number of employees working in logistics and SCM	13	21
Environmental certification	ISO 9000/01/02 ISO 1400/1/2	ISO 9000/01/02 ISO 1400/1/2
Main clients	Renault Nissan Toyota, Volkswagen AG, GM, BMW	GM, Ford, Toyota, Volkswagen, Dongfeng Motor, Fuji Ya, Valeo
Respondent position	R&D department manager, shop-floor manager and logistic manager	R&D manager, shop-floor manager and design engineer
Number of years working in logistics and SCM	3.5	13

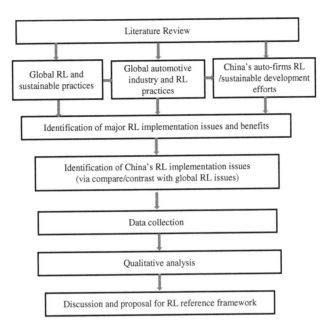

Figure 1.   General framework of study methodology.

Step 6: Discussion and proposal for RL reference frame-
work: Discussion of our findings and the development
of RL reference framework in Chinese context.

Companies' profile

Company A was established in 1992 (and restructured in
1997). The Group's core business is exterior auto-parts of
passenger vehicle in Mainland China. The company is a
supplier to many world-renowned international auto-
makers. Company A has an extensive production network
covering most of the auto markets in China; the Group has
established over 30 production facilities in the Eastern,
Southern, Northern and Central Regions of China.
Outside the domestic market, Company A has production
facilities in the United States, Thailand and Mexico,
enabling it to expand its overall overseas sales. Company
A has introduced many advanced production lines and the
processes such as extrusion, bending, injection and surface
treatment to its production facilities. Company A also has
an attractive corporate social responsibility (CSR) profile
consisting of several environmental and societal oriented
activities which show the company's commitment to good
corporate citizen.

Company B is a private-owned enterprise that specia-
lizes in both auto-parts manufacturing and mould designing, developing and manufacturing. It has a total asset of
700 million RMB and more than 1600 employees.
Company B has built long-term coordination with many
well-known automobile enterprises and final automotive
producers including General Motor, Ford, Toyota,
Volkswagen, Dongfeng Motor, Fuji Ya and Valeo. It established a national-level central lab, a high-tech R&D centre
and a postdoctoral work centre within the company. In

addition to technology, Company B possesses a number of
environmental and quality certifications, including
ISO9000, QS-9000, TS16949 and ISO14001.

Case studies results

Overall, the two management teams held nearly opposite
attitudes towards the idea of RL implementation. The
R&D manager from Company A emphasized the concept
of enterprise self-discipline to a great extent. The manager
explained his company's achievements in the field of CSR
and sustainable development with a noticeable sense of
pride and show-off to the team of investigators. On the
opposite side, Company B's managers hold a more con-
servative attitude towards RL. Their business growth philosophy is mostly focused on the development of more
comprehensive and/or more value-added assembles.
Consequently, the two manufacturers vary to some extent
in terms of their current RL implementation status.

Company A is interested in RL because of government
regulations, recaptured economic value and increasing
demand for green products. Company A views all of the
above criteria as equally important. The second key important issue for Company A is about asset (technology)
protection concern for RL products. This is closely followed by perceived uncertainty of the volume of ELVs
returned, uniformity of physical condition of returned
ELVs and the lack of technical know-how about dismantling and remanufacturing. These issues, in the order
listed, were the three biggest impediments for RL implementation in Company A. Company A additionally admits
that it also suffers from a lack of human resources and
management commitment to RL. This finding is in line
with literature which suggests that lack of internal management support is a major barrier to RL implementation

(Ravi et al. 2005; Chung & Zhang 2011; Abdulrahman, Gunasekaran, et al. 2014; Abdulrahman, Subramanian, et al. 2014).

To eliminate or at least minimize these barriers, Company A believes that all the choice options provided in our questionnaire will be very helpful mechanisms for addressing their RL issues. These mechanisms are broadly divided into three categories as follows:

Mechanism 1: Three types of economic support: (1) government financial subsidies in the form of tax deduction or funds allocation from local government, (2) capital investment sharing through corporation with business partners and (3) greater internal capital allocation.

Mechanism 2: Three types of knowledge support: (1) technical support from specialized RL enterprises, (2) professional knowledge support from RL talents and (3) integrated information system support that incorporates all relevant logistics parties.

Mechanism 3: Three types of managerial support: (1) proactive cooperation with motivated ICPs in terms of collecting ELVs, (2) top managers' strategic commitment and (3) adequate technical training for front-line workers.

The responses from Company B are similar to those of Company A, but with slight variation in the degree of importance associated with each of the different choices. Company A's manager agrees that government regulations and asset protection are the two most important RL driving forces, followed by three others that are (1) economic value, (2) customers' demand and (3) resource scarcity. In terms of barriers, Company A identified all five options on the questionnaire: (1) volume uncertainty, (2) quality uniformity, (3) lack of professional and expertise, (4) lack of enough capital input and (5) lack of management commitment to be equally highly important.

There are two important differences between the two auto-parts manufacturers investigated in terms of their motivations for RL implementation. Company B's motivation to engage in take-back and reuse of packaging materials is to reduce raw material cost. In contrast, however, Company A's motivation is a mix of internal company's consciousness and external pressures from its customers. Company A's managers appear to care much more about CSR, a mentality the company claimed has led to the creation of its in-house specialized by-products' recycling unit to conduct centralized processing of by-products. Besides its self-consciousness, Company A continues to experience significant external pressures from its environmentally conscious consumers (mainly European automobile companies) to alleviate negative environmental impacts and to reduce resource inputs for production to the lowest level. Second, Company B's logistics chain consists of several third parties. The company outsources the handling of its waste by-products to waste disposal companies, sells recyclable items to recycling companies and buys all of its needed materials from raw material

suppliers. By doing this, Company B transfers the responsibility of value recapturing in used items and appropriate disposal of hazardous wastes/scraps to third party service providers. In contrast, Company A seems to have a more integrated supply chain. For example, besides the internal by-products disposal, Company A has begun to build a self-owned packaging company as well as a transportation company. Although Company A has not started to collect used products from consumers for reuse, the set-up of internal transportation unit increases the feasibility of used products collection by the company in the future.

The two companies converged with respect to RL impediments that regards used-products take-back and associated quality limitations. Both companies feel it is extremely difficult, if not impossible, to reclaim used items from the hands of consumers. The management of both companies emphasized that given their vast and geographically dispersed market coverage, it would be almost an impossible task to recover used products from the hands of their widely dispersed customers. In addition, and given both companies' core business as auto-parts manufacturing, the added value of such parts is relatively low which creates a major disincentive for engaging in recycling and remanufacturing.

Table 2 summarizes the significant issues discovered from the present case study, regarding the development of RL at these two Chinese auto-parts firms, in comparison with the overall situation in two developed regions, namely the United States and the European Union. The table reveals various activities in RL and it is interesting to see that ELV recovery ratio and dismantling approach is almost invisible in Chinese auto sector, whereas it is very well practised in developed nations. Customer demand for green products and asset protection motivates Chinese auto sector to focus on RL compared to well-known drivers such as regulation and economic value recapture. There are numerous barriers in China about quality of RL products, technology and management commitment when compared to Western counterparts.

RL implementation framework and discussion

Given the current situation in China, an auto-parts manufacturer will have to incorporate several parties, including whole-vehicle manufacturers, automobile retailers and specialized dismantling enterprises into an integrated system so as to make the reverse flows effective (Jiang 2009). Moreover, a critical prerequisite is an advanced information system which tracks consumers' information in terms of purchased car brand and mode, purchasing time, purchasing place (the retailor), post-sale services record and contact information (Rahman & Subramanian 2012). With all these records, ELVs and defective vehicles can easily be tracked and acquired by the retailers from the car owners. After acquisition, the used cars should be sent to professional dismantling enterprises to be disassembled and sorted in line with the original parts manufacturer's policy. Finally, all the parts should be sent back to their

34

Table 2. Auto-parts RL implementation issues.

Issues	Auto-parts manufacturers		EU nations	The United States
	Company A	Company B		
Raw material recycled	Steel, aluminium, plastic and rubber	Steel, aluminium, plastic and rubber	N/A	N/A
Auto-parts recovered	Electronic equipment	Engines, chassis and electronic equipment	N/A	N/A
ELV recovery ratio	N/A	N/A	On average, about 85% of total vehicle weight has been recovered and reused in 2009 (Eurostat 2012)	About 80% of vehicle weight has been recovered and reused (Jiang 2009)
Returned product acquisition and the initial collection point	Retailer and scrap centre	N/A	Is a waste stream system where manufacturers are regulated to take back all their vehicles after use from consumers (Guide & Wassenhove 2001); car owners typically deliver ELVs to scrap vehicle centres (Jiang 2009)	Is a market-driven system where consumers are motivated by financial incentives to return ELVs (Guide & Wassenhove 2001) often to the second-hand vehicle retailers (Jiang 2009)
Dismantling approach	N/A	N/A	ELVs are usually dismantled by professional dismantling enterprises	
Disposition options that most often used	Raw material recycling and reusable parts remanufacturing	Raw material recycling	Necessary technology both mastered; all possible methods are ready to be used and the propel disposal method is decided according to the specific quality condition of returned vehicles	
Logistics parties that involved to great extent	Specialized dismantling enterprise, original auto-manufacturer and scrap centre	Raw material supplier, date centre and third party logistic enterprise	Scrap vehicle centre and dismantling enterprises	Second-hand vehicle retailers and dismantling enterprises
The primary motivations	Regulations, economic value recapture and consumer demand	Regulations, economic value and asset protection	Strict and various number of EU regulations	Manufacturers mainly driven by considerable economic value of RL activities without law
The main barriers	Uncertainty of both volume and quality returned and the lack of technique mastery of dismantling and remanufacturing	Uncertainty of both volume and quality returned, the lack of the following: technique mastery of dismantling and remanufacturing, investments and management commitment	N/A	N/A

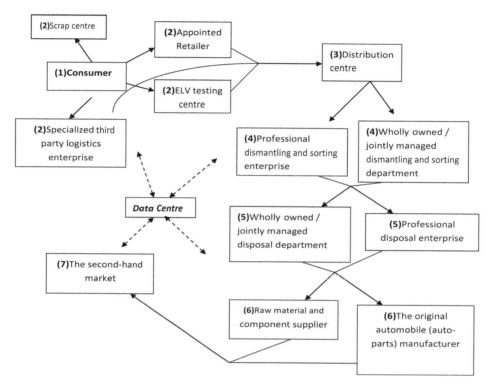

Figure 2. Chinese RL implementation framework.

manufacturers to be recovered (Rahman & Subramanian 2012). The dismantling fee is reasonable to be co-borne by the parts manufacturer and the whole-vehicle enterprise as both parties can benefit from this activity – the part manufacturer can shrink its production costs and the automobile enterprise can in turn enjoy a better price offer of car components. The various stages in RL implementation issues are depicted as an RL implementation framework as shown in Figure 2.

ELVs Reverse flow: (1) →(2) →(3) →(4) →(5) →(6) →(7).
Here,

(1) represents the consumer (starting point of reverse flow);
(2) represents the ICPs;
(3) represents distribution centre;
(4) represents ELVs dismantling and sorting points;
(5) represents ELVs disposal points;
(6) represents recovery of raw materials, reusable parts at recovery points (component supplier/original equipment manufacturer (OEM)); and
(7) represents second-hand markets
⟶ : Reverse logistics of ELVs
◄- -► : Information flow

Despite the existing issues and flaws, China's vehicle manufacturers still have very good reasons to embark on RL implementation. Amongst these reasons is the huge volume of ELVs or near-ELVs in the society that provide opportunities to leverage this new market and win a profitable business. Of course, a firm has to first equip itself with essential technology and management knowhow of RLs and remanufacturing, as well as with sufficient facilities and equipment. The important implementation issues that need to be addressed are discussed below based on Figure 1.

Consumer (as the starting point of RL flow)

Chinese consumers typically lack the level of environmental consciousness and the motivation needed to return ELVs through correct channels on one's own free will (Yan & Yan 2011). To solve this problem, universal environmental education should be enhanced and appropriate incentives should be provided to car owners to encourage returns. Second, laws and regulations on vehicle recycling are incomplete and the implementation is not that effective in China (Yan & Yan 2011). It would therefore be necessary to complete and strengthen enforcement of the relevant laws and regulations.

Retailer/testing centre (initial collection points – ICPs)

The Chinese consumers should dispose their ELVs or auto parts to an approved retailer, instead of selling it to informal recyclers. In China, it is common for consumers to sell their obsolete auto products to the informal recyclers because they gain much more value out of the sales. However, to avoid uncertainty in the product quality, it is better to ensure such products go through testing at an approved testing centre. This ensures that complications in the later stages of RL can be avoided as proper sorting is done at this stage to segregate the material into those to be recycled, remanufactured or recovered.

Distribution centre

A few Chinese firms use specialized dismantling enterprises while most firms outsource their distribution to third parties. Since RL is at nascent stage in China, extensive research is needed that specifically includes contextual factors in developing an efficient RL network with proper initial collection point, centralized return centre and processing centre, amongst others. Similarly, the routing has to be developed based on effective collection strategies. Integrated location, allocation and routing modelling would be most appropriate for manufacturers to take back their products.

Dismantling and sorting

Laggard recovery technology, limited numbers and scale of qualified dismantling firms as well as the scarcity of professional technical workers are major impediment to dismantling and sorting issues in China (Yan & Yan 2011). Currently, there are more than 1000 vehicle dismantling enterprises with more than 50,000 employees in China. Nonetheless, a great majority of those enterprises operate at an extremely small scale – no more than 100 units annually. Moreover, technical workers make up for only about 20% of total employees in this sector and only 6.7% of the technical workers possess middle- or high-level technical certificates (Yan & Yan 2011). Uncertainty of both volume and quality of returned and the lack of skilled manpower available for dismantling and remanufacturing will have to be addressed through proper integrated data management system to enhance the RL implementation in China

Disposal (ELVS disposal points)

There is limited disposal capacity for dismantling. A large proportion of ELVs are actually resold at a profit illegally to the second-hand markets or to poor regions, resulting in the unreasonably low recycling volume of ELVs (Yan & Yan 2011). In 2001, the first official government regulation, the Chinese ELV standard, was launched. The standard stipulates vehicle owners sell ELVs to certified vehicle recycling enterprises. The certified vehicle recycling enterprises dismantled ELVs into parts, and directly reuses, remanufacture or recycle them in the form of material or recovered energy, or dispose them properly in landfills, depending on the physical conditions. However, there is still no specific clause normalizing environmental requirements of vehicle recycling in terms of, for instance, environment-friendly disposal of non-degradable parts such as plastics, rubber and waste oil. Consequently, most of these harmful wastes are simply burned and dumped, and this severely aggravates soil and underwater

pollution. Burning and/or improper burying has huge negative impact on air pollution, urban ecosystems and agriculture (Bell et al. 2011). Strict enforcement of existing regulation would give more mileage to disposal of product.

Recovery (recovery of raw materials, reusable parts at components supplier/OEM)

As China is still in the initial stage of used vehicles remanufacturing (Zhang et al. 2011), the Chinese administrative rules on remanufacturing imposes some limitations on remanufacturing enterprises. For example, Chinese rule prohibits other remanufacturing enterprises, apart from the officially appointed 14 firms and the major 5 assemblies, from acquiring ELVs and dismantling business. Nonetheless, China has moved forward in the field of auto-parts remanufacturing. In 2006, for example, China's National Development and Reform Committee (NDRC), the Ministry of Science and Technology (MOST) and the Environmental and Protection Administration (EPA) jointly released a key take-back and remanufacturing policy, The Technical Policy for Automotive Production Recovery of China (Zhang et al. 2011). Similarly, in 2008, the Chinese NDRC introduced the Administrative Rules for Auto-parts Remanufacturing Pilots and selected 14 enterprises (3 automobile enterprises and 11 auto-parts enterprises) including First Auto Work (FAW), Cherry and JAC (Anhui Jianghuai Automobile Co., Ltd.) to be the first batch of remanufacturing pilots. The primary focus of these pilot programmes is the trial of remanufacturing of the five major assemblies, which were usually destroyed and melted, and the recovery of used parts to the original level of performance and quality. These initiatives will hopefully help China in future to expand it abilities to develop, test and acquire dedicated remanufacturing technologies that would make remanufacturing practice economical for auto-parts and automobile enterprises.

Market (second-hand markets)

In China, ELVs remanufactured parts should only re-enter the market through after-sales service channel instead of directly entering the retailing market. Remanufacturing enterprises are further required to obtain the trademark rights of parts/components they intend to remanufacture from the original manufacturers of such used parts before commencing work on them (NDRC 2008). Moreover, the NDRC and the Ministry of Public Security of China have jointly launched a series of notifications to regulate the ELVs recovery market and to ensure legal and proper disposals of ELVs since year 2001. The Chinese ELVs standard launched in June 2001 declared that the ELV recycling industry should be specially controlled and the ELV recycling enterprises should be administered under a qualification cognizance system. The statute requires vehicle owners to sell their ELVs to qualified recycling enterprises. These certified recycling firms are then to destroy and melt the 'five supervised assemblies of vehicles' including engine, power transmission box, steering, axle, and chassis, and then to recycle the five major assemblies as metal materials. Other parts, with the exception of the 'major five', can be sold again as secondary parts with compulsory labels illustrating 'ELV reuse parts' (NDRC 2008).

In spite of the above limitations, we fully agree with Chen (2005), who has noted that while ELVs recovery in China faces major problems, its liberalization in the long-run is inevitable. We believe that liberalizing ELVs recovery to allow all automobile enterprises that are interested in and have the capabilities to freely engage in remanufacturing business will stimulate the growth of vehicle remanufacturing in China into a profitable business. We believe that this liberalization will occur in the near future when such circumstances as technique innovation, infrastructure construction, core components, remanufacturing known-how, resources shortage and environmental crisis become well established and Chinese firms realize the considerable amount of economic value to be gained from the practice.

Concluding remarks

Although extensive literature exists on RL, extant studies are concentrated on developed countries with relatively little attention devoted to developing countries such as China – despite China being touted as the 'global factory'. Moreover, extant RL literature is dominated by studies on electrical and electronics industries. This study contributes to RL literature through the narrowing of existing gap by focusing on one of the world's largest manufacturing industries, the automotive industry. This study examines RL issues in the Chinese auto-parts sector using two case studies. Until now (and other than the government funded domestic pilot projects in China), there is no existing auto-parts RL framework that is adapted to the Chinese context. The findings of this study demonstrate that RL development in Chinese auto-parts sector is limited, evidenced by the poor RL implementations in the two relatively large Chinese auto-parts companies investigated. Our results indicate that the most practised sustainability activity in Chinese auto-parts firms centres on raw material recycling only. The study further established a number of obstacles the Chinese auto-parts firms face with respect to technology and expertise, market order discipline and regulation, amongst others.

Basically, auto-parts firms are unwilling to invest in the establishment of RL infrastructure and systems. This is mainly because of the unfavourable Chinese consumers' sentiments on remanufactured products and/or recycled items seen to be of significantly lower quality compared with new products, amongst other reasons.

The study proposes key ways by which the auto-parts firms can minimize RL issues that they face, including government economic incentives such as subsidies and tax

reduction for RL and remanufacturing related activities, and internal investment on knowledge/talent training and managerial support.

Despite the relevant and useful contributions of this study to the sustainable practices literature and RL practices in the Chinese auto-parts sector, further investigations are warranted, especially given that China is only at the starting point of RL practices. While our study is based on two relatively large firms, the nature of the case study implies that our findings must be treated with caution and further large-scale empirical studies that use robust methodologies are needed for effective generalization of RL practices in Chinese auto-parts sector.

Acknowledgements

The authors would like to thank the Ningbo Science and Technology Bureau, under the Innovation Team Project (Grant No. 2011B1006), for sponsoring this research. The authors are also grateful to the special issue editors and the anonymous reviewers for their critical and very insightful comments that have helped in improving the quality of this paper.

References

Abdulrahman MD, Gunasekaran A, Subramanian N. 2014. Critical barriers in implementing reverse logistics in the Chinese manufacturing sectors. Int J Prod Econ. 147:460–471. doi:10.1016/j.ijpe.2012.08.003

Abdulrahman MD, Subramanian N, Liu C, Chengqi S. 2014. Viability of remanufacturing practice: a strategic decision making framework for Chinese auto-parts companies. J Clean Prod. doi:10.1016/j.jclepro.2014.02.065

Auto Alliance. 2013. Automotive Recycling-Your car's afterlife: A look at the automotive Recycling Industry. [Internet]. [cited 2013 Jul 15]. Available from: http://www.imlachs.com.au/common/I/imlachscomau/images/Article%20-%20Auto%20Alliance%20Recycling.pdf

Bai C, Sarkis J. 2013. Flexibility in reverse logistics: a framework and evaluation approach. J Clean Prod. 47:306–318. doi:10.1016/j.jclepro.2013.01.005

Baskaran V, Nachiappan S, Rahman S. 2011. Supplier assessment based on corporate social responsibility criteria in Indian automotive and textile industry sectors. Int J Sust Eng. 4:359–369. doi:10.1080/19397038.2011.579360

Bell JNB, Power SA, Jarraud N, Agrawal M, Davies C. 2011. The effects of air pollution on urban ecosystems and agriculture. Int J Sust Dev World Ecol. 18:226–235. doi:10.1080/13504509.2011.570803

Cao H, Tang M, Deng H, Dong R. 2014. Analysis of management effectiveness of natural reserves in Yunnan Province, China. Int J Sust Dev World Ecol. 21:77–84. doi:10.1080/13504509.2013.786764

CFLP. 2007. Logistics terms – National Standard of PRC (author's translation). [Internet]. [cited 2013 Apr 11]. Available from: http://old.chinawuliu.com.cn/oth/content/200701/200721418.html

Chen M. 2005. End-of-life vehicle recycling in China: now and the future. JOM. 57:20–26. doi:10.1007/s11837-005-0146-6

Chung S, Zhang C. 2011. An evaluation of legislative measures on electrical and electronic waste in the People's Republic of China. Waste Manage. 31:2638–2646. doi:10.1016/j.wasman.2011.07.010

Curtis S, Gesler W, Smith G, Washburn S. 2000. Approaches to sampling and case selection in qualitative research: examples in the geography of health. Soc Sci Med. 50:1001–1014.

Dyer WG, Wilkins AL. 1991. Better stories, not better constructs, to generate better theory: a rejoinder to Eisenhardt. Acad Manage Rev. 16:613–619.

Eisenhardt KM. 1989. Building theories from case study research. Acad Manage Rev. 14:532–550.

Eisenhardt KM, Graebner ME. 2007. Theory building from cases: opportunities and challenges. Acad Manage J. 50:25–32. doi:10.5465/AMJ.2007.24160888

Elsbach KD, Kramer RM. 2003. Assessing creativity in Hollywood pitch meetings: evidence for a dual-process model of creativity judgments. Acad Manage J. 46:283–301. doi:10.2307/30040623

Eurostat. 2012. End-of-life vehicles: reuse, recycling and recovery, Totals. [Internet]. [cited 2012 Apr 14]. Available from: http://appsso.eurostat.ec.europa.eu/nui/submitViewTable Action.do

France-Presse A. 2013. Strong China demand to boost global car sales by 4.8%, Moody's says. [Internet]. [cited 2014 Feb 15]. Available from: http://www.industryweek.com/demographics/strong-china-demand-boost-global-car-sales-48-moodys-say

González-Torre P, Álvarez M, Sarkis J, Adenso-Díaz B. 2010. Barriers to the implementation of environmentally oriented reverse logistics: evidence from the automotive industry sector. Br J Manage. 21:889–904. doi:10.1111/j.1467-8551.2009.00655.x

Guide RD, Wassenhove VL. 2001. Managing product returns for remanufacturing. Prod Oper Manage. 10: 142–155.

Haanaes K, Ming TK, Hopkins MS, Arthur D, Reeves M, Kruschwitz N, Balagopal B, Velken I. 2011. Sustainability: the 'embracers' seize advantage. MIT Sloan Manage Rev. Winter:7–27.

Jayaraman V, Luo Y. 2007. Creating competitive advantages through new value creation: a reverse logistics perspective. Acad Manage Persp. 21:56–73. doi:10.5465/AMP.2007.25356512

Jiang M. 2009. Construction of integrated network for both forward logistics and reverse logistics. Shaanxi: Chang'an University.

Jody BJ, Daniels EJ, Duranceau CM, Pomykala JA, Spangenberger JS. 2010. End-of-life vehicle recycling: state of the art of resource recovery from shredder residue. [Internet]. [cited 2013 Jul 22]. Available from: http://www.es.anl.gov/Energy_systems/CRADA_Team/publications/End%20of%20life%20vehicle%20recycling%20Technology%20review.pdf

Kannan D, Jabbour ABLS, Jabbour CJC. 2014. Selecting green suppliers based on GSCM practices: using fuzzy TOPSIS applied to a Brazilian electronics company. Euro J Oper Res. 233:432–447. doi:10.1016/j.ejor.2013.07.023

Karakosta C, Marinakis V, Letsou P, Psarras J. 2013. Does the CDM offer sustainable development benefits or not? Int J Sust Dev World Ecol. 20:1–8. doi:10.1080/13504509.2012.752768

Kemp R, Loorbach D, Rotmans J. 2007. Transition management as a model for managing processes of co-evolution towards sustainable development. Int J Sust Dev World Ecol. 14:78–91. doi:10.1080/13504500709469709

Lai K-H, Wong CWY. 2012. Green logistics management and performance: some empirical evidence from Chinese manufacturing exporters. Omega. 40:267–282. doi:10.1016/j.omega.2011.07.002

Liao K, Deng X, Marsillac E. 2013. Factors that influence Chinese automotive suppliers' mass customization capabilities. Int J Prod Econ. 146:25–36. doi:10.1016/j.ijpe.2013.01.014

Liu X, Tanaka M, Matsui Y. 2006. Electrical and electronic waste management in China: progress and the barriers to overcome. Waste Manag Res. 24:92–101. doi:10.1177/0734242X06062499

Miles M, Huberman A. 1994. Qualitative data analysis. London: Sage; p. 34.

Narasimhan R, Jayaram J. 1998. Reengineering service operations: a longitudinal case study. J Oper Manage. 17:7–22. doi:10.1016/S0272-6963(98)00029-1

National Bureau of Statistics of China. 2012. Statistical Communiqué of the People's Republic of China on the 2011 National Economic and Social Development. [Internet]. [cited 2013 Apr 11]. Available from: http://www.stats.gov.cn/english/newsandcomingevents/t20120222_40278 6587.htm

[NDRC] National Development and Reform Committee. 2008. Auto-parts remanufacturing pilot officially launched [Internet]. [cited 2014 Apr 08]. Available from: http://www.eobus.com/news/1589.htm

Qian G, Guo X, Guo J, Wu J. 2011. China's dairy crisis: impacts, causes and policy implications for a sustainable dairy industry. Int J Sust Dev World Ecol. 18:434–441. doi:10.1080/13504509.2011.581710

Rahman S, Subramanian N. 2012. Factors for implementing end-of-life computer recycling operations in reverse supply chains. Int J Prod Econ. 140:239–248. doi:10.1016/j.ijpe.2011.07.019

Ravi V, Shankar R, Tiwari M. 2005. Analyzing alternatives in reverse logistics for end-of-life computers: ANP and balanced scorecard approach. Comput Ind Eng. 48:327–356. doi:10.1016/j.cie.2005.01.017

Sarkis J, Helms M, Hervani A. 2010. Reverse logistics and social sustainability. Corp Soc Resp Environ Manage. 17:337–354. doi:10.1002/csr.220

Sheriff KMM, Gunasekaran A, Nachiappan S. 2012. Reverse logistics network design: a review on strategic perspective. Int J Logist Syst Manage. 12:171–194. doi:10.1504/IJLSM.2012.047220

Sheriff KMM, Nachiappan S, Min H. 2013. Combined location and routing problems for designing the quality-dependent and multi-product reverse logistics network. J Oper Res Soc. doi: 10.1057/jors.2013.22

Skouloudis A, Evangelinos K. 2012. A research design for mapping national CSR terrains. Int J Sust Dev World Ecol. 19:130–143. doi:10.1080/13504509.2011.606338

Steinhilper R, Freiberger S, Albrecht M, Käufl J, Binder E, Brückner C. 2011. New technologies for remanufacturing of automotive systems communicating via CAN bus. In: Hesselbach J, Herrmann C, editors. Glocalized solutions for sustainability in manufacturing. Berlin: Springer.

Tibben-Lembke RS, Rogers DS. 2002. Differences between forward and reverse logistics in a retail environment. Supply Chain Manage Int J. 7:271–282. doi:10.1108/13598540210447719

Ulutas F, Alkaya E, Bogurcu M, Demirer GN. 2012. Determination of the framework conditions and research – development needs for the dissemination of cleaner (sustainable) production applications in Turkey. Int J Sust Dev World Ecol. 19:203–209. doi:10.1080/13504509.2011.606550

Valentinov V. 2013. Corporate social responsibility and sustainability: insights from Boulding and Luhmann. Int J Sust Dev World Ecol. 20:317–324. doi:10.1080/13504509.2013.808282

Wang L, Chen M. 2013. Policies and perspective on end-of-life vehicles in China. J Clean Prod. 44:168–176. doi:10.1016/j.jclepro.2012.11.036

Xiang W, Ming C. 2011. Implementing extended producer responsibility: vehicle remanufacturing in China. J Clean Prod. 19:680–686. doi:10.1016/j.jclepro.2010.11.016

Yan X, Yan L. 2011. The present development situation and counter measures of waste automobile reverse logistics in

China. Log Sci-Tech No.1 [Internet]. [cited 2013 Apr 12]. Available from: http://en.cnki.com.cn/Article_en/CJFDTOTAL-LTKJ201101036.htm

Ye F, Zhao X, Prahinski C, Li Y. 2013. The impact of institutional pressures, top managers' posture and reverse logistics on performance – evidence from China. Int J Prod Econ. 143:132–143. doi:10.1016/j.ijpe.2012.12.021

Yin RK. 2009. Case study research: design and methods, applied social research methods series. Vol. 5. 5th ed. London: Sage.

Zhang C, Zhang N. 2010. The analysis of reverse logistics operation mode in automobile manufacturing industry – a case study basing on Jiang-Lin Corp. J Manage Case Stud. 3:59–71.

Zhang T, Chu J, Wang X, Liu X, Cui P. 2011. Development pattern and enhancing system of automotive components remanufacturing industry in China. Resour Conserv Recycl. 55:613–622. doi:10.1016/j.resconrec.2010.09.015

Zhao Q, Chen M. 2011. A comparison of ELV recycling system in China and Japan and China's strategies. Resour Conserv Recycl. 57:15–21.

Zhao X, Li Y, Flynn BB. 2013. The financial impact of product recall announcements in China. Int J Prod Econ. 142:115–123. doi:10.1016/j.ijpe.2012.10.018

Factors for implementing end-of-life product reverse logistics in the Chinese manufacturing sector

Nachiappan Subramanian[a], Angappa Gunasekaran[b], Muhammad Abdulrahman[c] and Chang Liu[d]

[a]Nottingham University Business School China, The University of Nottingham Ningbo China, Ningbo China; [b]Charlton College of Business, University of Massachusetts Dartmouth, Dartmouth, MA, USA; [c]Nottingham University Business School China, Ningbo, China; [d]Division of Economics, The University of Nottingham Ningbo China, Ningbo, China

Dedicated, skilled and relatively cheap manpower coupled with efficient manufacturing techniques has elevated China's status as the world's factory. China is now capable of producing virtually any product, from cheap toys to some of the most sophisticated goods and equipment. The resultant economic benefits and associated enormous consumption due to rise in per capita income are accompanied by an equally unprecedented negative environmental impact arising from the huge increase of end-of-life (EoL) products. This study aims to understand and prioritise EoL product reverse logistics (RL) factors from Chinese manufacturing sector perspective. Multiple case studies in five different industries within the manufacturing sector have been carried out and analytic hierarchy process (AHP) has been employed to prioritise the governing factors for the successful RL implementation in the Chinese manufacturing sector. Results indicate that Chinese firms are unlikely to embark on RL operations without external factors such as strict government legislation.

1. Introduction

Waste generated in various industries within the Chinese manufacturing sector is enormous and rising due to rapid industrialisation and the presence of 22% of world population. The industrialisation and huge population have simultaneously resulted in huge economic benefits and serious environmental pollution in most major cities of China. Waste generation in China has been estimated to be much higher than those in developed countries (Fang et al. 2007; Yuan et al. 2010). For example, recent statistics indicate 5 million tons of waste/scraped steel, 200,000 tons of non-ferrous metal, 14 million tons of waste paper, a large amount of plastic and glass waste in China have never been recycled. Waste, particularly e-waste, has become a major issue due to the high rate of electrical and electronic product production and consumption within China and the huge quantities of used electrical and electronic products shipped into China from overseas (Terazono et al. 2004; Ye et al. 2009; Streicher-Porte & Geering 2010; Chi et al. 2011). It is not surprising, therefore, that China is second in the world, after the USA, in landfilling and incineration of e-waste residues (Ma 2004; Zoeteman et al. 2010). These statistics reveal that there is a huge scope for economic recovery of valuable materials through implementing reverse logistics (RL) in the Chinese manufacturing sector. RL is a process by which a manufacturer systematically accepts previously shipped products or components from the point of consumption (or end-users) for possible reuse, remanufacture, recycle or safe disposal. RL is a major sustainable environmental management (EM) strategy because RL centres on a close-loop supply chain practice with the flow of information on products that enhance their take-back/recovery for recycling, reuse, redesign and/or remanufacturing (Haden et al. 2009; Jabbour & Puppim-de-Oliveira 2012; Junquera & Brío 2012). Thus, RL is an important process for protecting the environment and reclaiming valuable resources from end-of-life (EoL) products or wastes (Lambert et al. 2011; Abdulrahman, Gunasekaran, et al. 2014; Abdulrahman, Subramanian, et al. 2014; Hongshen & Ming 2014).

RL is well-understood and practiced in some developed countries, resulting in significant economic and environmental benefits in the practicing nations (Zhang et al. 2011; Gunasekaran & Spalanzani 2012). Most of the external and internal factors governing the successful implementation of RL have been well-addressed in developed country context (Rogers & Tibben-Lembke 2001; Daugherty et al. 2009; Gonzalez-Torre et al. 2010). Some of the key cited RL factors in these previous studies are government regulations, customer demand, entrepreneurs' policy, support of top management, stakeholder commitment, incentive systems, quality of inputs and vertical integration (Carter & Ellram 1998; Dowlatshahi 2005; Rahman & Subramanian 2012). Furthermore, a review of the literature indicates that RL studies are mostly focused on location-allocation modelling with limited focus on implementation issues (Kumar & Putnam 2008; Ilgin & Gupta 2010; Sheriff et al. 2012).

Unlike in the west, RL implementation is at an infancy stage in China (Lai & Wong 2012; Ye et al. 2013). This explains why few studies have focused on RL implementation factors in the Chinese context (Zhu et al. 2008; Lai & Wong 2012; Ye et al. 2013; Abdulrahman, Gunasekaran, et al. 2014). Most of the Chinese RL studies focus on green supply chain management (SCM) and performances (Zhu et al. 2008) and barriers to RL practices (Lai & Wong 2012; Abdulrahman, Gunasekaran, et al. 2014). For example, Zhu et al. (2008) studied the green aspects of the reverse supply chain in few Chinese industries and suggested future researchers explore motivations and barriers on why Chinese organisations do or do not implement typical green reverse supply chains. In their study, Abdulrahman, Gunasekaran, et al. (2014) empirically examined the barriers affecting RL implementation in the Chinese manufacturing industry. While the study identified the general factors affecting RL implementation in China, it did not investigate how the investigated firms prioritise RL barriers. A study by Ye et al. (2013) found the effects of three institutional pressures such as government, customers and competitor on RL practices in China. The study, however, failed to highlight firms' priorities in their RL implementation.

This study focuses on identifying key priorities of Chinese firms' RL implementation practices. Knowing firms' priorities is critical to the development and success of any RL implementation action plan by the industry as well as by government. The major contributions of this study are (1) to identify important internal and external RL factors through a comprehensive RL and sustainability literature review, (2) to develop a model for examining the key factors that motivates the Chinese manufacturers to implement RL and (3) to prioritise the identified RL factors using the analytic hierarchy process (AHP) methodology.

The rest of the article is organised as follows. We first review related literature with respect to RL implementation factors, barriers and performance outcomes. This is followed by the background of the Chinese manufacturing sectors. The next section provides the research methodology employed in this study. The following section outlines the results and discussions. The subsequent section highlights the concluding remarks of the study.

2. RL implementation factors

Few studies in the past suggested conceptual models in general to design and implement RL (Carter & Ellram 1998; Li & Tee 2012; Alfonso-Lizarazo et al. 2013). Carter and Ellram (1998) classified RL implementation factors into external and internal (regulations, customer demand and policy entrepreneurs) and noted that both the internal and external factors are not mutually exclusive. Subsequently, researchers attempted to customise the general model with additional factors such as strategic cost/benefits, strategic quality, customer service and environmental concern with respect to specific products such as EoF computers, e-waste and automotive (Dowlatshahi 2005; Ravi et al. 2005; Kumar & Putnam 2008; Rahman & Subramanian 2012). The study by Li and Tee (2012)

developed a RL model for recovery of e-wastes, taking into consideration both the formal and informal waste sectors. Alfonso-Lizarazo et al. (2013) modelled RL practice in the agro-industry sector to examine the closed-looped supply chain framework and its impact on economic profit of the firms.

These studies commonly considered the environmental, economic and legislative factors that drive RL implementation. For example, the study by Staikos and Rahimifard (2007) considered the economic factors from a cost–benefit analysis, life cycle analysis (LCA) and technical factors. Alfonso-Lizarazo et al. (2013) considered impact of RL on economic profit of the firms while Barker and Zabinsky (2011) considered the economic, integration and customer interactions through business relations. Other studies considered the corporate social responsibility (CSR) and sustainability issues in RL systems as a means of developing a complete business performance framework that measures RL performance based on the triple bottom line (3BL) approach (economic, environmental and social aspects) (Sarkis et al. 2010; Baskaran et al. 2011; Skouloudis & Evangelinos 2012; Valentinov 2013; Poveda & Lipsett 2014). Table 1 summarises the RL factors that have been applied in different sectors and in different country contexts.

Overall, a literature review revealed overwhelming focus on the electrical and electronics industry and their e-waste. For example, there are enormous studies in the Chinese context in terms of waste management and especially e-waste handling and recent developments on environmental regulations (Ma 2004; Geng & Doberstein 2008; Lau & Wang 2009; Chung & Zang 2011; Ye et al. 2013). The focus on e-waste is not surprising, given that it estimated that each year 20 to 50 million tons of e-waste are generated (Schwarzer et al. 2005; Li & Tee 2012). This suggests only limited sectors and limited products have been focused on, with other sectors such as plastic and footwear industries receiving negligible attention due to their after-effects and nature of the products.

3. Chinese manufacturing sector

Manufacturing has successfully transformed China's economy from that which was primarily agriculture based to the world's centre of manufacturing. Aided by relatively cheap, dedicated and skilled workforce, everything from toys, to cars to some of the most sophisticated electronic goods are now made in China. The significance of the manufacturing sector cannot be overemphasised as China now boasts of continual and increasing manufacturing prowess, significant cost advantage (beyond just labour cost) and worldwide market share – 5% of cameras, 30% of air conditioners and television, 25% of washing machines and 20% of refrigerators (Pinto 2005). Manufacturing sector contains very large number of firms and it is spread out throughout China (Xia & Walker 2014). The potential for generating large waste from EoL products is enormous due to production and

Table 1. Summary of RL implantation factors in various countries and sectors.

Factors	Implication	Sector	Country	Source
Legislation	Regulations or Acts passed by government agencies to ensure firms take back and reuse the products they produce	e-waste, automotive, appliances,	US, EU, Japan and China, Thailand, India	Kumar and Putnam (2008), Tan and Kumar (2006), Walker et al. (2008), Dowlatshahi (2005), Rahman and Subramanian (2012), Neto et al. (2008), Walker et al. (2008), Schwarzer et al. (2005) and Kannan et al. (2008)
		e-waste, automotive, appliances, chemical and power generation	China US, EU, Japan	Ye et al. (2013), Zhu et al. (2008), Lau and Wang (2009), Liu et al. (2006), Rahman and Subramanian (2012), Schwarzer et al. (2005) and Li and Tee, (2012).
Customer demand	Customer demand for green products	e-waste, automotive, appliances, health care, cosmetics, food retailer, chemical and power generation	Thailand, India Australia, US, EU, China, Thailand, India	Neto et al. (2008), Walker et al. (2008), Schwarzer et al. (2005), and Alfonso-Lizarazo et al. (2013)
Incentive	Benefits derived by returning products	e-waste	Australia, US, EU, Japan	Rahman and Subramanian (2012) and Kannan et al. (2008)
Strategic cost/ benefits	Non-recurring costs incurred by manufacturer for the design and implementation of a reverse supply chain system	e-waste, paper-based products, health care, cosmetics, food retailer, footwear industry	Turkey, Australia, Europe, UK, US, India	Dowlatshahi (2005), Ravi et al. (2005), Rahman and Subramanian (2012), Walker et al. (2008), Staikos and Rahimifard (2007) and Barker and Zabinsky (2011)
Environmental concern	Proactive consideration of green and sustainable issues by manufacturers	e-waste, automotive, appliances, paper-based products, health care, cosmetics, food retailer	China, Turkey, Australia, Europe, UK	Dowlatshahi (2005), Zhu et al. (2008), Lau and Wang (2009), Tan and Kumar (2006), Rahman and Subramanian (2012), Neto et al. (2008) and Alfonso-Lizarazo et al. (2013)
Resource	Possibility of using existing resources for RL or need of additional resources	e-waste, appliances	Australia, US, EU, Japan	Dowlatshahi (2005), Rahman and Subramanian (2012)
Integration and coordination	Communication, effective use of information systems	Automotive, e-waste, appliances	US, Australia, US, EU, Japan	Tan and Kumar (2006), Rahman and Subramanian (2012), Li and Tee (2012)
Volume and quality	Emphasis on quantity and nature of returned product	e-waste, paper and paper-based products, health care and automotive	Australia, Europe, US	Dowlatshahi (2005), Ravi et al. (2005), Rahman and Subramanian (2012), Li and Tee (2012)

domestic consumption. Pinto (2005) also noted that a single private Chinese company makes 40% of all microwave ovens sold in Europe. China for example is now the largest automobile producer in the world and a key market for global players in the automobile industry (PwC 2011; Amighini 2012). China's vehicle production scale reached 18.26 million vehicles in 2010, an over 30% increase from 2009's 13.79 million units (FOURIN China Automotive Intelligence). China's local automotive companies are increasingly working as part of joint ventures with leading global brands; and important trends that are likely to dominate the development of the global automotive industry over the next decade will all have China playing a key role.

Similarly China's plastic manufacturing sector employs 2.6 million workers and generated a total export value of US $14.40 billion in 2009. China's packaging market is the largest in the world and is predicted to grow to $97bn per annum by 2012 (Wood 2010). Food packaging alone accounts for 50% of the total demand for packaging, with volume growth of more than 20% being common in most food sectors. It is a similar story for China's footwear industry, with the total export value hitting US$24b in 2009. With these high-volume production and consumption in China, it is not surprising that the country is equally witnessing unsustainable development and waste generation (Hu & Lee 2010; World Bank 2013). According to the World Bank (2013) study, China's development model is based on high and intensive resource utilisation in production which is occasioned by equally high wastage and pollution. The need to move away from waste to wealth as well as towards the sustainability of China's development is the primary motivation for this study. As demonstrated above, the five industries within manufacturing sectors selected for this study are automotive, electronics, food packaging, plastic and footwear. These industries played and continue to play major roles in China's development. Identifying key RL implementation factors and prioritising them to make these firms aware of the key issues is critical to their sustainability and, by extension, the overall development of the nation.

4. Research methodology

We conducted in-depth case studies with interviews in order to explore and interpret the RL implementation factors from real-world experience, in Chinese context. We also tried to answer the question of why manufacturing companies still don't want to do full-fledged RL operations in China. The study employed case studies because it enables us to answer the 'how' questions about the contemporary set of events and 'why' questions in order to understand the scope of the problem (Barratt et al. 2011). The choice of five case studies from different industries within manufacturing sector were based on Eisenhardt (1989) argument that multiple cases are better to extend external validity and give a more objective assessment of the phenomena. In particular, four to

ten case studies are likely to create more robust and testable theory.

Case study has been carried out in five industries within manufacturing sectors such as automotive, electronics, food, plastics and leather to identify the importance of RL implementation factors and to know how well the firms are aware of RL issues. The case study used quantitative data to investigate few aspects related to external (legislation, customer demand and incentive) and internal factors (strategic cost/benefits, environmental concern, resource, integration and coordination, volume and quality) of RL implementation. We ensured that all the firms from various industries selected for our study are having quality/environmental certification. We made this as a filtering criterion for our study because if the companies have certification, then they should be knowledgeable about various best practices and about the environmental impact issues.

The case data were gathered mainly through interviews and authors on-site observations. Data collection took place during September–October 2012. Interviews were semi-structured and conducted at the respective companies' sites. We had a questionnaire with two parts. Part A consists of questions related to influence of external and internal factors with respect to successful implementation of RL. We requested the respondent to give their importance of factors for a pairwise comparison using Saaty's 9-point scale (Saaty 1980). Part B had questions related to profile of respondent and the organisation. Additional questions and clarifications were conducted through telephone calls and email exchanges with earlier respondents in each firm investigated.

However, it has to be noted that some linguistic problems were encountered; therefore translation from English to Chinese had to be done simultaneously, in order to process the interview. The responses were then transcribed and incorporated in the analysis, which gave valuable input to further evaluation of RL factor implementation. All the primary and secondary data collected were used to analyse the RL factors.

We provide a summary of the respondent characteristics and organisational characteristics in Table 2 followed by a brief description of each of the case companies.

4.1. Case companies' profile

This section provides a brief summary of the background of the Chinese manufacturing firms investigated in this study. Companies selected for our study are primarily from Zhejiang Province. The GDP growth rate of this (Zhejiang) province was 8% in 2012 (US$ 558.16 billion) and is one of the provinces with significant contribution to China's growth rate in 2012 (51.8% share of industrial sector in total economy) (Kittilaksanawong & Ren 2013). Zhejiang Province is home to dominant players in industries such as automotive, electronics, plastic, footwear and food packaging companies. Selection of case companies within each industry is based on criteria such as involvement of companies in return management, years of experience in

Table 2. Case companies' profile.

| | | | | | Respondent and company profile | | |
Organisation sector	Position in organisation	Years of experience in RL and return management	Age	Type of organisation	Number of staff in logistics and SCM	Number of staff in in RL and return management	Type of certification
Automotive company ABC	Senior manager	5	35	Joint venture	13	13	ISO 1400/1/2
Electronics company DEF	Senior manager	5	45	Private	12	11–15	ISO 9000/01/02
Food packaging company GHI	Head of unit	2	35	Joint venture	24	26	ISO 9000/01/02
Plastics company JKL	Assistant manager	2	25	Joint venture	4	4	ISO 9000/01/02
Footwear company MNO	Director	5	28	MNC	9	8	ISO 9000/01/02

return management, substantial number of staff involved in return management, process certification and the mutual acceptance of the companies to cooperate for the study.

4.1.1. Automotive company ABC

Located in Ningbo in Zhejiang Province of China, the company is a manufacturer and exporter of tool sets, tool kit, spark plug wrench, oil filter wrenches, ratchet wrenches and other automotive accessories. The company is a locally owned joint venture with nearly 40 years' of manufacturing experience. The company currently has about 15 dedicated SCM and RL management employees. The company is ISO 1400/1/2 standard certified.

4.1.2. Electronics company DEF

The company is a leading manufacturer and exporter of various lighting sensor electronics in Ningbo, in Zhejiang Province, China. Its products include sensor switches, wireless remote control door bells, smoke alarms and multifunctional wireless home security alarm systems, amongst others. The company currently has about 15 dedicated SCM and RL management employees. The company has over 20 years' experience as an exporter of specialised electronic sensor systems. It currently employs over 300 lighting specialists. The company is ISO 9000/01/02 standard and its products are manufactured under quality standard, with most products having CE, GS, UL, BSI and VDS, approval.

4.1.3. Food packaging company GHI

The company is a leading manufacturer of food and drug packaging products in Ningbo, in Zhejiang Province,

China. It specialises in food packaging pouch, medical disposable co-extrusion film, vacuum seal storage bag, films, amongst others. The company has international first-class co-extrusion film blowing production lines in a 1900-square-meter workshop that meets the GMP standard. It is a joint venture company with more than 10 years of international business experience. The company currently has more than 21 dedicated SCM and RL management employees, with all having about 3 years of experience in logistics, SCM and return management. The company is ISO 9000/01/02 standard certified.

4.1.4. Plastic company JKL

The company is established in 1997 and it specialises in designing and manufacturing moulds for local and international clients. The company is located in Ninghai in Zhejiang Province of China. This joint venture company currently has about 5 dedicated SCM and RL management employees. The company is ISO 9000/01/02 standard certified, and its moulds are manufactured to high quality certified by English, American, HASCO and D-M-E standards.

4.1.5. Footwear company MNO

The company specialises in the manufacturing and exporting of various beach slippers, flip flops, indoor slippers, children slippers, amongst others in Ningbo, in Zhejiang Province, China. The company is ISO 9000/01/02 standard certified, and about 60% of its products are exported mainly to Europe and USA. The company is a MNC and currently has about 10 dedicated SCM and RL management employees with between 4 and 7 years of experience in logistics and SCM.

4.2. AHP methodology

The AHP proposed by Saaty (1980) is very popular and has been applied in wide variety of areas including prioritising criteria, planning, selecting a best alternative, resource allocation and resolving conflicts. The AHP methodology is excellent in identifying criteria and subcriteria in a decision hierarchy and assigning rankings to the alternative options through pairwise comparison matrices (Nachiappan & Ramanathan 2008). Literature review indicates a wide-ranging applicability of AHP to real-world issues in different sectors (Pohekar & Ramachandran 2004; Subramanian & Ramanathan 2012). In RL research, Staikos and Rahimifard (2007) used AHP to develop a decision model for the footwear industry. In their study, Kannan et al. (2008) used AHP and fuzzy analytical hierarchy to create a multi-criteria decision-making model for the evaluation of collection centres for an auto tire manufacturing industry in India. Similarly, Barker and Zabinsky (2011) recently applied AHP to the evaluation of the multicriterial decision-making for RL implementation in US firms.

The application of AHP to a decision problem is based on the following steps (Zahedi 1986; Ramanathan 2006):

STEP 1: Structuring of the decision problem into a hierarchical model

It includes decomposition of the decision problem into elements according to their common characteristics and the formation of a hierarchical model having different levels. Our AHP model has three levels with goal, criteria and subcriteria as shown in Figure 1. The goal of the model is to find out from the firm's perspective the contributing factors for the successful implementation of RL. The criteria considered in the model are internal factors and external factors. The subcriteria considered for the analysis are legislation, customer demand, incentive, strategic cost/benefits, environmental concern, resource, integration and coordination and volume and quality (Rahman & Subramanian 2012).

STEP 2: Making pairwise comparisons and obtaining the judgmental matrix

In this step, the elements of a particular level are compared with respect to a specific element in the immediate upper level. First, we compared the criteria (internal and external factors) with the goal of our model – 'successful RL implementation'. Then we did compare the subcriteria with respect to our criteria. The resulting weights of the elements derived from this process are called as the local weights. The opinion of each company respondent is elicited for comparing the elements. Elements are compared pairwise, and judgments on comparative attractiveness of elements are captured using a 1–9 rating scale proposed by Saaty (1980). Usually, an element receiving higher rating is viewed as superior compared to another one that receives a lower rating. We used Expert Choice software to perform an individual pairwise comparison matrix for ranking the criteria with respect to the goal and subcrietria with respect to the criteria.

STEP 3: Local weights and consistency of comparisons

In this step, local weights of the elements are calculated using the eigenvector method (EVM). The level of inconsistency can be captured by a measure called consistency ratio (CR) (Saaty 1980). For a consistent matrix, CR = 0, and if the CR for a matrix is more than 0.1, then judgments should be elicited once again from the decision-maker till he gives more consistent judgments. We performed sensitivity analysis (a consistency index (CI)) to measure the inconsistency of each pairwise comparison (Saaty 1980; Subramoniam et al. 2013). The CI and CR of the respondent's pairwise comparison satisfies the recommended value of less than 0.1 (Saaty 1980, 2008). Global weights of the subcriteria are aggregated based on the local weights of elements of different levels. We use hierarchical aggregation rule that is available in Expert Choice software to compute the final weights of alternatives.

5. Results and discussion

The final weights obtained by AHP method for the five companies from different industries selected for our study

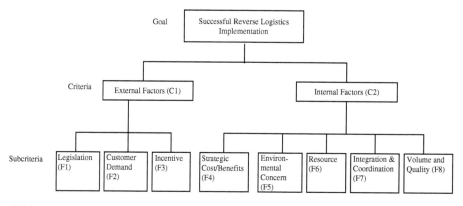

Figure 1. AHP model for successful RL implementation.

Table 3. Final weight of RL implementation factors.

Factor	Final weight				
	Automotive company ABC	Electronics company DEF	Food packaging company GHI	Plastics company JKL	Footwear company MNO
Legislation	0.59	0.62	0.60	0.50	0.50
Customer demand	0.12	0.11	0.12	0.17	0.14
Incentive	0.16	0.15	0.12	0.17	0.09
Strategic cost/benefits	0.07	0.08	0.07	0.07	0.08
Environmental concern	0.03	0.02	0.03	0.03	0.08
Resource	0.01	0.02	0.02	0.03	0.04
Integration and coordination	0.01	0.01	0.02	0.02	0.03
Volume and quality	0.00	0.00	0.03	0.02	0.03

are shown in Table 3. The results indicate that all the companies feel that RL practice will be fully implemented only with the support of external factors. The key factor the firms considered as critical for meaningful RL implementation is legislation (see Table 3). The firms believe that RL would be successful in all industries in the manufacturing sector only if there is a strong regulation and monitoring mechanism from the Chinese government. Our finding of a lack of enforceable regulations as a barrier to RL implementation in China is similar to other past studies (Lai & Wong 2012; Abdulrahman, Gunasekaran, et al. 2014).

Even in the developed parts of world, strict regulation has been identified as a major driver for RL implementation. Non-compliance with environmental regulations leads to costly legal actions, heavy penalties or outright removal from the market (Sarkis et al. 2010; Lai & Wong 2012). Additionally, the investigated firms strongly believe that informal recycling would be curbed if there is a strict government regulation and monitoring mechanism in RL implementation. According to the firms, strict government control would further encourage proper RL practices in the formal sectors. The observation is in line with recent literature which suggests that a key RL issue in China is how to set up incentives to divert waste flow from informal recyclers into formal recycling sector in order to eliminate or minimise improper recycling activities (Chi et al. 2011). The diversion of critical material source to formal recycling sector will guarantee the economic quantity of wastes required for a profitable engagement in recycling activity. Investigated companies also acknowledged their experience about steady increase of pressure from both domestic and foreign customers who are increasingly demanding for green products. They are, however, quick in pointing out that the pressures being experienced in China is little compared with what their counterparts in the developed world are experiencing. The attributed efficient recall and return handling by western firms to such pressures suggest that China has to be proactive and needs to do same as western firms to be competitive and sustainable in the future.

Our results also indicate incentives and support as the second major external factors for RL implementation in Chinese firms. All the companies investigated emphasised the importance of having some form of government supportive incentive for Chinese firms to engage in RL and also as a vital tool to encourage Chinese customers to return EoL products for recycling and/or remanufacturing. With the exception of the Footwear Company (see Table 3), the rest of the firms considered this external factor (of providing incentive to engage in RL practice) as being of a greater importance compared with customers' demand for green products. This finding may not be unconnected with the literature that suggests the upfront investment for RL systems, and infrastructure may take a long time before such investment can be paid back (Subramoniam et al. 2013). Chinese companies are ready to adopt RL to achieve green image as a business strategy and to increase their profitability. However, all the investigated firms expressed strong concern that Chinese consumers tend to consider remanufactured products to be of poor quality and will only purchase such products at ridiculously low price. Similar findings are reported in the west where consumers tend to regard remanufactured products to be of lower quality and lower market price (Dowlatshahi 2005; Kapetanopoulou & Tagaras 2011).

When compared with external factors, internal factors appear to play an insignificant role in the investigated companies (see Table 3). Results indicate that only the internal factor of strategic costs and benefits has reasonable attention from the companies studied. Table 4 shows summary results and ranking of RL factors for each sector investigated, based on the final weight scores within the sector.

The managers of the investigated companies explained that they consider RL as an integral part of business activities and would therefore only be willing to invest in RL if they see a clear prospect of making reasonable economic gains, not just the environmental benefits that are mostly highlighted by the authorities and in the media. This is surprising, given the overwhelming empirical evidence that suggests the existence of economic and environmental benefits of RL practices (Sarkis et al. 2010; Kapetanopoulou & Tagaras 2011; Kleber et al. 2011). The main issue, based on insights from our interviews, is that most of the investigated companies are either not willing to or not able to make the initial investment required for effective RL implementation. This is a more plausible

Table 4. Summary results and ranking based on final weight score of RL implementation factors.

Factor ranking	RL factor and final weight score				
	Automotive company ABC	Electronics company DEF	Food packaging company GHI	Plastics company JKL	Footwear company MNO
1	Legislation (0.59)	Legislation (0.62)	Legislation (0.60)	Legislation (0.50)	Legislation (0.50)
2	Incentive (0.16)	Incentive (0.15)	Customer demand (0.12) Incentive (0.12)	Customer demand (0.17) Incentive (0.17)	Customer demand (0.14)
3	Customer demand (0.12)	Customer demand (0.11)	Strategic cost/benefits (0.07)	Strategic cost/benefits (0.07)	Incentive (0.09)
4	Strategic cost/ benefits (0.07)	Strategic cost/ benefits (0.08)	Environmental concern (0.03); volume and quality (0.03)	Environmental concern (0.03); resource (0.03)	Strategic cost/benefits (0.08); environmental concern (0.08)
5	Environmental concern (0.03); resource (0.01); integration and coordination (0.01)	Environmental concern (0.02); resource (0.02); integration and coordination (0.01)	Resource (0.02); integration and coordination (0.02)	Integration and coordination (0.02); volume and quality (0.02)	Resource (0.04); integration/ coordination (0.03); volume and quality (0.03)

explanation, given that these companies are small and medium sized with limited financial resources as noted in the RL literature (Ravi et al. 2005; Subramoniam et al. 2013). Due to their awareness about the need for environment protection, however, the companies have expressed keenness in paying attention to environmental protection. They gave environmental concern a weightage that is next to those of strategic cost and benefit.

Since all the companies studied are in an early stage of RL, they value less the other factors such as resource reduction, integration and coordination and volume and quality of returns. These factors are weighed insignificantly compared to others such as legislation, customers' demand and incentives (see Table 3). Another possible explanation why factors such as resource reduction do not appear to be a major concern, and therefore scored very low, may be due to administrative price distortion of critical production materials which is making it possible for Chinese firms to engage in highly intensive resource utilisation in production resulting in wastage and pollution (World Bank 2013).

6. Concluding remarks

We attempted to prioritise factors that govern EoL product RL implementation among five Chinese industries within manufacturing sector. Based on the literature, we grouped RL implementation factors into external and internal. We also identified the key factors that motivate Chinese companies to implement RL practice. Our study considered different industries within manufacturing sector. Additionally, our study considered few industries such as plastics and footwear industries that have not received due attention in the RL literature before now. We used case study approach to capture the contextual RL information within the Chinese manufacturing sector. We used AHP method to prioritise the external and internal factors. Interesting finding from our study is that all companies

agree that external factors are important and they feel particularly strongly convinced that legislation is the most important factor for successful RL implementation in China. Majority of the firms (four out of five) viewed incentive factor to be more important compared with customers' demand factor for RL implementation in China. We did not see due importance to internal factors since RL implementation is at an infancy stage in Chinese companies. Despite the contributions of this study, it is not without limitations. One of the limitations of the current study is, because it is based on multiple case studies with limited sample size, there is need for caution in generalisation of its findings. Large-scale empirical study covering wider geographic area of China is needed in future to support (or disprove) our findings. Also, in future, the above study could be extended to analyse the inter-relationship among the factors considered for insights into how Chinese managers should handle such factors for successful RL implementation.

Acknowledgements

The authors would like to thank the Ningbo Science and Technology Bureau, under the Innovation Team Project (Grant No. 2011B1006) for sponsoring this research. Also the authors are grateful to the special issue editors and the anonymous reviewers for their critical and very insightful comments that have helped in improving the quality of this article.

References

Abdulrahman MD, Gunasekaran A, Subramanian N. 2014. Critical barriers in implementing reverse logistics in the Chinese Manufacturing sectors. Int J Prod Econ. 147:460–471. doi:10.1016/j.ijpe.2012.08.003.

Abdulrahman MD, Subramanian N, Liu C, Chengqi S. 2014. Viability of remanufacturing practice: a strategic decision making framework for Chinese auto-parts companies. J Clean Prod. doi:10.1016/j.jclepro.2014.02.065.

Alfonso-Lizarazo EH, Montoya-Torres JR, Gutiérrez-Franco E. 2013. Modeling reverse logistics process in the agro-industrial sector: the case of the palm oil supply chain. Appl Math Modelling. 37:9652–9664. doi:10.1016/j.apm.2013.05.015.

Amighini AA. 2012. China and India in the international fragmentation of automobile production. China Econ Rev. 23:325–341. doi:10.1016/j.chieco.2012.01.002.

Barker TJ, Zabinsky ZB. 2011. A multicriteria decision making model for reverse logistics using analytical hierarchy process. Omega. 39:558–573. doi:10.1016/j.omega.2010.12.002.

Barratt M, Choi TY, Li M. 2011. Qualitative case studies in operations management: trends, research outcomes, and future research implications. J Operations Manage. 29:329–342. doi:10.1016/j.jom.2010.06.002.

Baskaran V, Nachiappan S, Rahman S. 2011. Supplier assessment based on corporate social responsibility criteria in Indian automotive and textile industry sectors. Int J Sustain Eng. 4:359–369. doi:10.1080/19397038.2011.579360.

Carter CR, Ellram LM. 1998. Reverse logistics: a review of the literature and framework for future investigation. J Bus Log. 19:85–102.

Chi X, Streicher-Porte M, Wang MY, Reuter MA. 2011. Informal electronic waste recycling: a sector review with special focus on China. Waste Manage. 31:731–742. doi:10.1016/j.wasman.2010.11.006.

Chung S, Zhang C. 2011. An evaluation of legislative measures on electrical and electronic waste in the People's Republic of China. Waste Manage. 31:2638–2646. doi:10.1016/j.wasman.2011.07.010.

Daugherty PJ, Chen H, Mattioda D, Grawe S. 2009. Marketing/logistics relationships: influence on capabilities and performance. J Bus Log. 30:1–18. doi:10.1002/j.2158-1592.2009.tb00096.x.

Dowlatshahi S. 2005. A strategic framework for the design and implementation of remanufacturing operations in reverse logistics. Int J Prod Res. 43:3455–3480. doi:10.1080/00207540500118118.

Eisenhardt KM. 1989. Building theories from case study research. Acad Manage Rev. 14:532–550.

Fang Y, Côté RP, Qin R. 2007. Industrial sustainability in China: practice and prospects for eco-industrial development. J Environ Manage. 83:315–328. doi:10.1016/j.jenvman.2006.03.007.

FOURIN China Automotive Intelligence. 2013. [Internet]. [cited 2013 Oct 13]. Available from: http://www.fourin.com/english/img/report/CAI/CAI.pdf

Geng Y, Doberstein B. 2008. Developing the circular economy in China: challenges and opportunities for achieving 'leapfrog development'. Int J Sustain Dev World Ecol. 15:231–239. doi:10.3843/SusDev.15.3:6.

González-Torre P, Álvarez M, Sarkis J, Adenso-Díaz B. 2010. Barriers to the implementation of environmentally oriented reverse logistics: evidence from the automotive industry sector. Br J Manage. 21:889–904. doi:10.1111/j.1467-8551.2009.00655.x.

Gunasekaran A, Spalanzani A. 2012. Sustainability of manufacturing and services: investigations for research and applications. Int J Prod Econ. 140:35–47. doi:10.1016/j.ijpe.2011.05.011

Haden SSP, Oyler JD, Humphreys JH. 2009. Historical, practical, and theoretical perspectives on green management: an exploratory analysis. Manage Decis. 47:1041–1055. doi:10.1108/00251740910978287.

Hu J-L, Lee Y-C. 2008. Efficient three industrial waste abatement for regions in China. Int J Sustain Dev World Ecol. 15:132–144. doi:10.1080/13504500809469778.

Ilgin MA, Gupta SM. 2010. Environmentally conscious manufacturing and product recovery (ECMPRO): a review of the state of the art. J Environ Manage. 91:563–591. doi:10.1016/j.jenvman.2009.09.037.

Jabbour CJC, Puppim-de-Oliveira JA. 2012. Barriers to environmental management in clusters of small businesses in Brazil and Japan: from a lack of knowledge to a decline in traditional knowledge. Int J Sustain Dev World Ecol. 19:247–257. doi:10.1080/13504509.2011.634929.

Junquera B, Brío JAD. 2012. The role of environmental activity integration into the R&D department to obtain competitive advantage. Int J Sustain Dev World Ecol. 19:210–218. doi:10.1080/13504509.2011.609568.

Kannan G, Haq A, Sasikumar P. 2008. An application of the analytical hierarchy process and fuzzy analytical hierarchy process in the selection of collecting centre location for the reverse logistics multicriteria decision-making supply chain model. Int J Manag Decis Making. 9:350–365. doi:10.1504/IJMDM.2008.019360.

Kapetanopoulou P, Tagaras G. 2011. Drivers and obstacles of product recovery activities in the Greek industry. Int J Operations Prod Manage. 31:148–166. doi:10.1108/01443571111104/46.

Kittilaksanawong W, Ren Z. 2013. Innovation capability building through intermediary organizations: cases of manufacturing small- and medium-sized enterprises from China's Zhejiang province. Asian J Technol Innovation. 21:62–79. doi:10.1080/19761597.2013.819247.

Kleber R, Zanoni S, Zavanella L. 2011. On how buyback and remanufacturing strategies affect the profitability of spare parts supply chains. Int J Prod Econ. 133:135–142. doi:10.1016/j.ijpe.2010.04.020

Kumar S, Putnam V. 2008. Cradle to cradle: reverse logistics strategies and opportunities across three industry sectors. Int J Prod Econ. 115:305–315. doi:10.1016/j.ijpe.2007.11.015.

Lai K-H, Wong CWY. 2012. Green logistics management and performance: some empirical evidence from Chinese manufacturing exporters. Omega. 40:267–282. doi:10.1016/j.omega.2011.07.002.

Lambert S, Riopel D, Kader W. 2011. A reverse logistics decisions conceptual framework. Comput Ind Eng. 61:561–581. doi:10.1016/j.cie.2011.04.012.

Lau KW, Wang Y. 2009. Reverse logistics in the electronic industry of China: a case study. Supply Chain Manage Int J. 14:447–465. doi:10.1108/13598540910995228.

Li RC, Tee TJC. 2012. A reverse logistics model for recovery options of ewaste considering the integration of the formal and informal waste sectors. Procedia Integr Soc Behav Sci. 40:788–816. doi:10.1016/j.sbspro.2012.03.266.

Liu X, Tanaka M, Matsui Y. 2006. Electrical and electronic waste management in China: progress and the barriers to overcome. Waste Manage Res. 24:92–101. doi:10.1177/0734242X06062499.

Ma K. 2004. Promotion development for circular economy guiding with the scientific philosophy of development. Macro Econ Manage. 10:4–9.

Nachiappan S, Ramanathan R. 2008. Robust decision making using data envelopment analytic hierarchy process. Proceedings of the 7th WSEAS International Conference on Artificial Intelligence, Knowledge Engineering and Data bases (AIKED'08); University of Cambridge, Cambridge, p. 269–275. ISBN: 978-960-6766-41-1.

Neto JQF, Bloemhof-Ruwaard JM, van Nunen JAEE, van Heck E. 2008. Designing and evaluating sustainable logistics networks. Int J Prod Econ. 111:195–208. doi:10.1016/j.ijpe.2006.10.014.

Pinto J. 2005. Global manufacturing – The China challenge [Internet]. [cited 2013 Oct 26]. Available from: http://www.automation.com/resources-tools/articles-white-papers/articles-by-jim-pinto/global-manufacturing-150-the-china-challenge

Pohekar SD, Ramachandran M. 2004. Application of multi-criteria decision making to sustainable energy planning – a review. Renewable Sustain Energy Rev. 8:365–381. doi:10.1016/j.rser.2003.12.007.

Poveda CA, Lipsett MG. 2014. An integrated approach for sustainability assessment: the Wa-Pa-Su project sustainability rating system. Int J Sustain Dev World Ecol. 21:85–98. doi:10.1080/13504509.2013.876677.

PwC. 2011. 15th Annual Global CEO Survey: automotive industry insights [Internet]. [cited 2013 Dec 13]. Available from: http://www.pwc.com/en_GX/gx/automotive/pdf/opportunities-to-improve-financial-reporting-and-internal-controls-in-china-cas-and-c-sox.pdf

Rahman S, Subramanian N. 2012. Factors for implementing end-of-life computer recycling operations in reverse supply chains. Int J Prod Econ. 140:239–248. doi:10.1016/j.ijpe.2011.07.019.

Ramanathan R. 2006. Data envelopment analysis for weight derivation and aggregation in the analytic hierarchy process. Comput Operations Res. 33:1289–1307. doi:10.1016/j.cor.2004.09.020.

Ravi V, Shankar R, Tiwari M. 2005. Analyzing alternatives in reverse logistics for end-of-life computers: ANP and balanced scorecard approach. Comput Ind Eng. 48:327–356. doi:10.1016/j.cie.2005.01.017.

Rogers D, Tibben-Lembke R. 2001. An examination of reverse logistics practices. J Bus Log. 22:129–148. doi:10.1002/j.2158-1592.2001.tb00007.x.

Saaty TL. 1980. The analytic hierarchy process. New York: McGraw-Hill.

Saaty TL. 2008. Relative measurement and its generalization in decision making why pairwise comparisons are central in mathematics for the measurement of intangible factors-the analytic hierarchy/network process. Rev Royal Span Acad Sci Ser A Math. 102:251–318. doi:10.1007/BF03191825.

Sarkis J, Helms M, Hervani A. 2010. Reverse logistics and social sustainability. Corporate Soc Responsibility Environ Manage. 17:337–354. doi:10.1002/csr.220.

Schwarzer S, De Bono A, Guiliani G, Kluser S, Peduzzi P. 2005. E-waste, the hidden side of IT equipment's manufacturing and use. Environ Alert Bull [Internet]. [cited 2013 Dec 13]. Available from: http://archive-ouverte.unige.ch/unige:23132

Sheriff KM, Gunasekaran A, Nachiappan S. 2012. Reverse Logistics network design: a review on strategic perspective. Int J Log Syst Manage. 12:171–194. doi:10.1504/IJLSM.2012.047220.

Skouloudis A, Evangelinos K. 2012. A research design for mapping national CSR terrains. Int J Sustain Dev World Ecol. 19:130–143. doi:10.1080/13504509.2011.606338.

Staikos T, Rahimifard S. 2007. A decision-making model for waste management in the footwear industry. Int J Prod Res. 45:4403–4422. doi:10.1080/00207540701450187.

Streicher-Porte M, Geering AC. 2010. Opportunities and threats of current e-waste collection system in China: a case study from Taizhou with a focus on refrigerators, washing machines, and televisions. Environ Eng Sci. 27:29–36. doi:10.1089/ees.2009.0134.

Subramanian N, Ramanathan R. 2012. A review of applications of analytic hierarchy process in operations management. Int J Prod Econ. 138:215–241. doi:10.1016/j.ijpe.2012.03.036.

Subramoniam R, Huisingh D, Chinnam RB, Subramoniam S. 2013. Remanufacturing decision-making framework (RDMF): research validation using the analytical hierarchical process. J Clean Prod. 40:212–220. doi:10.1016/j.jclepro.2011.09.004.

Tan A, Kumar A. 2006. A decision-making model for reverse logistics in the computer industry. Int J Log Manage. 17:331–354.

Terazono A, Yoshida A, Yang JX, Moriguchi Y, Sakai S. 2004. Material cycles in Asia: especially the recycling loop between Japan and China. J Mat Cycles Waste Manage. 6:82–96.

Tian J, Chen M. 2014. Sustainable design for automotive products: dismantling and recycling of end-of-life vehicles. Waste Manage. 34:458–467. doi:10.1016/j.wasman.2013.11.005.

Valentinov V. 2013. Corporate social responsibility and sustainability: insights from Boulding and Luhmann. Int J Sustain Dev World Ecol. 20:317–324. doi:10.1080/13504509.2013.808282.

Walker H, Sisto LD, McBain D. 2008. Drivers and barriers to environmental supply chain management practices: lessons from the public and private sectors. J Purchasing Supply Manage. 14:69–85. doi:10.1016/j.pursup.2008.01.007.

Wood G. 2010. China 2012, Edge's market report on the packaging supply chain in China [Internet]. [cited 2013 Sept 29]. Available from: http://www.innventia.com/upload/Edge/Pdf/China%202012.pdf

World Bank. 2013. China 2030: building a modern, harmonious, and creative society [Internet]. Development Research Center of the State Council, the People's Republic of China; [cited 2013 Oct 30]. Available from: http://www.worldbank.org/content/dam/Worldbank/document/China-2030-complete.pdf

Xia F, Walker G. 2014. How much does owner type matter for firm performance? Manufacturing firms in China 1998–2007. Strategic Manage J. doi:10.1002/smj.2233.

Ye F, Zhao X, Prahinski C, Li Y. 2013. The impact of institutional pressures, top managers' posture and reverse logistics on performance—evidence from China. Int J Prod Econ. 143:132–143. doi:10.1016/j.ijpe.2012.12.021.

Ye J, Kayaga S, Smout I. 2009. Regulating for e-waste in China: progress and challenges. Proc ICE-Municip Eng. 162:79–85.

Yuan X, Ren L, Mu R, Ma C, Zhang K. 2010. Eco-industry and sustainability for the coal industry – a case study from YZCMG, China. Int J Sustain Dev World Ecol. 17:149–156. doi:10.1080/13504501003603215.

Zahedi F. 1986. The analytic hierarchy process – a survey of the method and its applications. Interfaces. 16:96–108. doi:10.1287/inte.16.4.96.

Zhang T, Chu J, Wang X, Liu X, Cui P. 2011. Development pattern and enhancing system of automotive components remanufacturing industry in China. Resour Conserv Recy. 55:613–622. doi:10.1016/j.resconrec.2010.09.015.

Zhu Q, Sarkis J, Lai K-H. 2008. Green supply chain management implications for "closing the loop". Transport Res E Log. 44:1–18. doi:10.1016/j.tre.2006.06.003.

Zoeteman BCJ, Krikke HR, Venselaar J. 2010. Handling WEEE waste flows: on the effectiveness of producer responsibility in a globalizing world. Int J Adv Manuf Technol. 47:415–436. doi:10.1007/s00170-009-2358-3.

Appendix. Questionnaire

Part A: AHP ranking questionnaire

Reverse logistics implementation: Determination for preference of internal over external factors of successful Reverse Logistics Implementation (Please use Saaty (1980) scale between 1.....9 as explained).

Q1: For successful implementation of Reverse Logistics according to your view which factor between internal and external is more important? And to what extent?

Internal factors preference: Determination for preference of internal factors while assessing the success of Reverse Logistics implementation (Please use Saaty (1980) scale between 1.....9 as explained).

Q2: For successful implementation of Reverse Logistics according to your view which factor (between legislation and customer demand) is more important? And to what extent?

Q3: For successful implementation of Reverse Logistics according to your view which factor (between legislation and Incentive) is more important? And to what extent?

Q4: For successful implementation of Reverse Logistics according to your view which factor (between customer demand and incentive) is more important? And to what extent?

External factors preference: Determination for preference of external factors while assessing the success of Reverse Logistics implementation (Please use Saaty (1980) scale between 1.....9 as explained).

Q5: For successful implementation of Reverse Logistics according to your view which factor (between strategic cost/benefits and environmental concern) is more important?

Q6: For successful implementation of Reverse Logistics according to your view which factor (between strategic cost/benefits and resource) is more important?

Q7: For successful implementation of Reverse Logistics according to your view which factor (between strategic cost/benefits and integration/coordination) is more important?

Q8: For successful implementation of Reverse Logistics according to your view which factor (between strategic cost/benefits and volume & quality) is more important?

Q9: For successful implementation of Reverse Logistics according to your view which factor (between environmental concern and resource) is more important?

Q10: For successful implementation of Reverse Logistics according to your view which factor (between environmental concern and integration/coordination) is more important?

Q11: For successful implementation of Reverse Logistics according to your view which factor (between environmental concern and volume & quality) is more important?

Q12: For successful implementation of Reverse Logistics according to your view which factor (between resource and integration/coordination) is more important?

Q13: For successful implementation of Reverse Logistics according to your view which factor (between resource and volume & quality) is more important?

Q14: For successful implementation of Reverse Logistics according to your view which factor (between integration & coordination and volume & quality) is more important?

Part B: Respondent and company profile

Q1: Position in the organisation

Q2: Position in the organisation

Q3: Years of experience you have in Logistics and Supply Chain Management

Q4: Years of experience you have in Reverse Logistics and return management

Q5: Age

Q6: Type of organisation

Q7: Number of staff involved in Logistics and Supply Chain functions

Q8: Number of staff involved in Reverse Logistics and return management

Q9: Types of certification your organisation registered

Social development benefits of hydroelectricity CDM projects in Brazil

Luz Fernández[a], Candela de la Sota[a], José Celio Silveira Andrade[b], Julio Lumbreras[a] and Javier Mazorra[a]

[a]Department of Industrial Chemical Engineering and Environment, Technical University of Madrid (UPM), Madrid, Spain; [b]Laboratory of Global Policy Analysis, Federal University of Bahia (UFBA), Canela, Salvador. Bahia, Brazil

In recent years, the concept of sustainable development (SD) has become increasingly recognized and important. Within organizations, SD is often portrayed as a balancing act and requires a combination of three elements to be considered: economy, environment, and society. Traditionally, organizational management research has been focused on economical and environmental fronts. However, social aspects are also important for organizations, especially those in emerging and developing countries. The goal of this article is to investigate the potential of Clean Development Mechanism (CDM) projects to deliver social benefits in Brazil's hydroelectricity sector. The investigation involved the assessment of 46 registered hydro CDM projects under the Kyoto Protocol in terms of their potential impact on the envisaged social development goals. Two case studies were also examined. Results indicate that organizations managing hydroelectric initiatives in Brazil can provide the pathway toward achieving a number of important social benefits. Successful projects were found to have good community involvement and were managed by both cooperative ventures and money-making corporations. The research also identified several challenges that are hindering hydro CDM projects from delivering more social benefits and enabled a number of recommendations to be extracted for the organizations facing these challenges.

1. Introduction

In the last 20 years, the concept of sustainable development (SD) has grown in recognition and importance, and numerous alternatives to the concept have been provided (Barkemeyer et al. 2014). Probably, the most widely stated definition of the concept is: development which 'meets the needs of the present without compromising the ability of future generations to meet their own needs' (WCED 1987). However, contest occurs in relation to what these core ideas actually 'mean'.

Previous research on how organizations have come to 'know' SD highlighted that most organizations draw on the concept of balance (Tregidga et al. 2013). Therefore, SD is portrayed as a balancing act, and it requires organizations to consider three combined elements: economy, environment, and society (i.e., the triple bottom line).

Noticeably, the economic perspective is a common realm in business. Finance managers know that a company which does not use its income to pay for its costs will soon be insolvent. From a social or environmental perspective, however, the impact may not be visible in the short term (Silvius & Schipper 2010).

Nevertheless, considerable research suggests that organizations have traditionally focused on the environmental component of SD (e.g., Rondinelli & Berry 2000). Moreover, the increase in environmental incidents has made the world aware that environmental problems affect more than just selected regions, and environmental

management (EM) has become a global concern within organizational agendas (Dale 2010). Furthermore, one of the most serious global challenges facing our societies is the need to reduce greenhouse gas (GHG) emissions (UNDP 2007; Naustdalslid 2011), and thus climate change and 'carbon management' has gradually gained prominence within the EM agendas (Kolk et al. 2008; Pinkse & Kolk 2012; Ventura et al. 2012).

Meanwhile, the social side of sustainability was not a key organizational concern and was hardly ever addressed in industry attempts at achieving SD and/or improving EM (Palmer et al. 1997). Previous research shows substantial difficulties associated with fully incorporating and operationalizing social sustainability features in various sectors (Boström 2012) and scholars argue that the concept of social sustainability has been particularly difficult to analyze, comprehend, and define (Lehtonen 2004; Littig & Grießler 2005).

From the mid-1990s, many businesses started to realize that they were ignoring the social side of the concept of sustainability and, as a result, they began to adopt practices of corporate social responsibility (Holliday et al. 2002). However, to date, the studies that explore the social side of SD within organizations in developing countries have been limited (Zeffane & Rugimbana 1995; Hopwood et al. 2005), and discussions have been dominated by US and European perspectives (Dobers et al. 2009).

This article builds on this limited body of work regarding the social pillar of sustainability in developing and emerging countries and goes beyond the broader focus on the SD goal. It also provides a narrower assessment of the delivery of social benefits in organizations implementing Clean Development Mechanism (CDM) hydroelectricity projects in Brazil. The focus on the social pillar of sustainability refers to the suitability of CDM projects to produce co-benefits that generate social development at local scale, including aspects such as job creation, income distribution, empowerment of vulnerable groups, use of local natural resources, and social acceptability. Apart from this, the article focuses on organizations implementing hydroelectricity projects in Brazil, raising important questions for other organizations implementing other CDM project types, including agroforestry, fossil fuel switch, landfill gas, and non-hydropower renewable energy CDM projects, and even projects which are not within the CDM framework.

The CDM was designed, under the United Nations Framework on Climate Change Convention (UNFCCC 2011), with two explicit and equally important goals: to assist developed countries meet their emissions reduction commitments under the Kyoto Protocol in a cost-efficient manner and to provide SD for developing countries that host the emission reduction projects. Due to this dual objective, several studies have chosen CDM to explore all the economic, environmental, and social dimensions of SD (e.g., Olsen & Fenhann 2008; UNFCCC 2011). Overall, research suggests that while the economic and environmental sides of SD are generally achieved through the CDM, it does not contribute enough to generate social benefits (Olsen 2007; Schneider 2008; Boyd et al. 2009; Subbarao & Lloyd 2011; CDMPD 2012).

Despite this general conclusion, there are meaningful evidences that show the CDM projects' potential to foster social local development (IGES 2006; Sirohi 2007; UNFCCC 2011; Crowe 2013; Karakosta et al. 2013). With the adoption of a second commitment period at the Doha conference, the CDM projects are expected to constitute an important source of international offsets during the 2013–2020 period. Consequently, new research in managing organizations to synergize efforts to reduce GHG emissions while facing social development concerns is especially relevant.

The article is structured as follows. Section 2 introduces the situation of CDM projects in Brazil. Section 3 provides an overview of the current situation of organizational management for SD. Section 4 discusses the methodology used for the project assessment, while Section 5 presents the findings from desktop and case study analysis. Finally, Section 6 discusses the results, summarizes the major arguments in this article, and suggests further areas of research.

2. Status of CDM projects in Brazil

Brazil has had a visible, proactive, and influential role in the UNFCCC 2011 negotiations. The idea of CDM as a climate change mitigation instrument was initially proposed within the context of the international negotiations of the Kyoto Protocol by the Brazilian delegation in 1997, during COP 3, in the form of a Clean Development Fund (Cole & Roberts 2011). Later, Brazil was one of the first countries to establish the legal basis required to develop projects under CDM locally by creating its Designated National Authority (DNA) by an executive order dated 7 July 1999. It was the first nation to formally designate its national authority to the CDM Executive Board. The first methodology approved under the scope of the CDM by the Executive Board was Brazilian (Landfills – Salvador, Bahia state). Later, the first project effectively registered under the CDM also was Brazilian: the Nova Gerar project (Government of Brazil 2008).

Under the UNFCCC 2011 and the resulting Marrakesh Accords, CDM projects must be approved by the host country. Its DNA issues a Letter of Approval certifying that the proposed CDM project activity assists the host country in achieving SD. To guarantee the involvement of a wide range of stakeholders and the contribution to the local SD of Brazilian CDM projects, the Brazilian DNA requires project developers to include in their domestic submissions an additional document to the Project Design Document (PDD), the so-called Annex III. The Annex III document is a description of the project's contribution to SD and should describe the project's integration into the regional economic structure and the linkages to other sectors, the potential for energy generation, or the creation of synergic effects (CIMGC 2003).

Since the first Brazilian CDM project was registered by the CDM Executive Board in November 2004, progress in CDM project development has been spectacular, and on 31 October 2013, the CDM Executive Board had registered 352 projects in the country.

Meanwhile, when the empirical research of this article began, on 30 September 2011, the CDM Executive Board had registered 194 projects that represented 6% of all CDM projects registered throughout the world (Fenhann 2011). As can be seen in Figure 1, Brazilian projects by that date focused mainly on the following areas: methane avoidance (26%), biomass energy, and hydro (23.7% each).

The distribution by state of the project activities in the Brazilian CDM market reflects the general division of the country where the south and southeast are much more developed and industrialized than the thinly populated north (Fernández et al. 2012). Figure 2 presents the geographical distribution of the CDM projects registered by the time that the research began.

Brazil's effort to reduce GHG emissions by implementing CDM projects is underscored by the fact that 65% of projects are unilateral in other words, developed without the participation of Annex I countries (Government of Brazil 2008).

Previous research regarding the Brazilian carbon market suggests that there are complex reasons behind manager's decisions to pursue CDM investments. Adding a

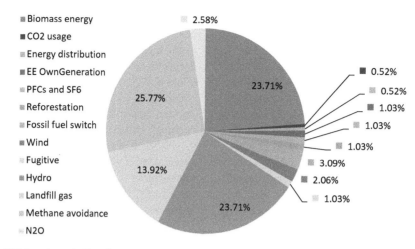

Figure 1. Registered CDM projects in Brazil.
Source: Author. Based on data from Fenhann 2011.

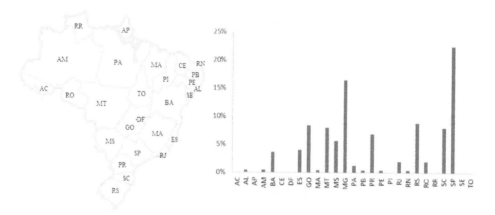

Figure 2. Geographical distributions of CDM projects in Brazil.
Source: Based on data from Fenhann 2011.

marginal increment to a project's internal rate of return appears to be one of the primary motivations followed by non-financial reputational factors (Silva-Junior 2011; de Freitas et al. 2013). To improve EM and diversify the activities of the firm are also identified as overall incentives (Silva-Junior 2011).

3. Organizational management for sustainable development

There is still no universally accepted definition of SD or an agreed basis for determining whether a specific action would contribute to SD. However, it is widely agreed that SD comprises three mutually reinforcing dimensions economic development, social development, and environmental protection (UNFCCC 2011) – and that the struggle around bringing 'meaning' to SD involves many groups, including governments, non-governmental organizations (NGOs), business organizations, and academics, all of 'which construct the meaning of the phrase in their own terms' (Eden 1994, p. 160).

Business organizations are talking about the topic of organizational management for SD since the World Commission on Environment and Development (WCED) report of 1987 (Elkington 1998). The emergence of the concept of sustainable business models was due to the desire of organizations to respect the environment and stakeholders because otherwise organizations need to make amendments to compensate their actions (Hawken 1993). However, SD innovation is often difficult and risky (Hall & Vredenburg 2003), and a change in the paradigm of their strategies is necessary to operationalize the concept of sustainability in business models, from maximizing profit (Stormer 2003) to also integrate social and environmental concerns (Robinson 2004).

In spite of difficulties, many organizations have revised their business models (Hall & Vredenburg 2003), and there are articles that present the results of empirical studies of making sustainable practices in business from different sectors. For instance, Hall and Vredenburg (2003) performed a field research of more than 40 companies from various industrial settings in some developed and emerging countries, including aerospace, agriculture, chemicals, forestry, retailing, and the energy sector, to explore some of the underlying characteristics of innovation dynamics to achieve SD.

To obtain the aims of SD, there are three basic variables available for business organizations (Baumgartner & Zielowski 2004): organizational structure, formal management instruments, and organizational culture. Within the organizational structure responsibilities, tasks and procedures for SD have to be defined. Formal management instruments are, for example, the standards for EM like ISO 14,001, the European EMAS scheme, or other standards for quality management. Useful instruments for these purposes can be 'balanced scorecard' (Kaplan & Norton 1992), 'sustainability balanced scorecard' (Figge et al. 2002), and 'life cycle assessment' (UNEP-SETAC Life Cycle Initiative 2009).

Benefits of managing for SD have been rather explored in the companies' world, mainly on financial performance. Some studies have concluded that aligning organizations with SD is the key to business competitiveness and provides the opportunity to gain operative and strategic advantages and increase the reputation of both internal and external stakeholders (Tregidga et al. 2013). Nevertheless, literature review has revealed that there is a general lack of studies about issues concerning management for SD in other types of organizations different to companies, like governments, NGOs, or academics groups, although there are some exceptions, as the studies made by Beringer and Adomßent (2008) and Castro and Jabbour (2013), which analyze the contributions made by Higher Education Institutions for Sustainable Development.

In the last few years, there are many organizations that have focused on the environmental component of SD (Rondinelli & Berry 2000) and taken into account the aspects of EM in their organizational culture and structure. EM is defined as 'the organization-wide process of applying innovation to achieve sustainability, waste reduction, social responsibility, and a competitive advantage via continuous learning and development, and by embracing environmental goals and strategies that are fully integrated with the goals and strategies of the organization' (Haden et al. 2009, p. 12). But, as Jabbour et al. (2008) said, improving environmental conditions is fallacious without the real involvement of companies in this process. What is defended is the development of a socio-environmental perspective which aims at using resources efficiently, and conciliating economic growth, technological advances, and ecological limitations. However, traditionally, the social side of sustainability has not been widely considered within organizational concerns, and it has been hardly addressed in industry attempts at achieving SD and/or improving EM (Palmer et al. 1997).

Even in our days, literature about management for SD is much more reduced in organizations of developing and emerging countries (Dobers et al. 2009). This may be due to the fact that while organizations in developed countries have traditionally operated in a regulated environment, with numerous laws and regulations which governed their activities and make their directors accountable to a broader range of stakeholders (Deloitte 1992), organizations in developing and emerging countries faced constraints such as weaknesses in public administration and management or a lack of overall planning mechanisms (Zeffane & Rugimbana 1995). Hence, the existence of theoretical and practical understanding of how organizations can be managed in developing and emerging countries could be very important in order to contribute to achieve a really SD (Nelson & Prescott 2008).

Examples of identified organization management for social development benefits are the Bottom of the Pyramid (BOP) settings, which present potential ideal opportunities to connect business with sustainability in the developing world (Matos & Silvestre 2013). Also, corporate social responsibility practices have been previously highlighted to suppose a twist toward social sustainability in developing countries with weak institutional environment (Dobers et al. 2009).

Other examples of management practices can be found in the following sectors: (i) the manufacture organizations including social and environmental considerations in supply chains to reduce impacts and social exclusion (Hall & Matos 2010); (ii) the firms that have developed the ability to become socially embedded to create more total values (social and economic) and have a greater positive impact in a social context (Sanchez et al. 2006); (iii) the social enterprises which lead to SD through innovative approaches and creative thinking (Azmat 2013); and (iv) the efforts made by organizations to achieve a sustainable tourism development thanks to a better stakeholder engagement (Kent et al. 2012; Doiron & Weissenberger 2014).

In addition, good practices for social benefits in developing and emerging countries could also be found in some organizations which have implemented CDM projects under the Kyoto Protocol (Sutter 2003; Olsen & Fenhann 2008; Gangale & Mengolini 2011; Fernández et al. 2012; Karakosta et al. 2012, 2013; Crowe 2013).

However, further research is needed to understand how organizations can create value in developing and emerging countries through balancing economic, ecological and overall social elements, promoting equitable relationships amongst stakeholders (Boons & Lüdeke-Freund 2013).

4. Methodology

4.1. Project selection and sample size

The CDM has continued to evolve since the first registered projects in 2005. In order to reflect the most comprehensive social development benefits, all hydroelectricity projects registered in Brazil before the start of this research, October 2011, were selected as project sample. Hydroelectricity projects were chosen for three main reasons: (i) hydroelectric power plants produce over 80% of the country's electric energy (Government of Brazil 2012);

(ii) more than 25% of the CDM registered in Brazil by October 2011 were hydro projects (see Figure 1); and (iii) there are numerous different types of organizations directly related with the hydroelectric sector in Brazil.

Identifying the hydro CDM was relatively straightforward, as CDM registered projects are publically available and classified by host country in the CDM pipeline of the UNEP Risoe Centre (Fenhann 2011).Thus, the final database consisted of 46 hydroelectricity CDM projects.

As part of the research, 2 of the 46 projects were further investigated as case studies. The first case study is a small hydroelectric plant implemented by a local company in the state of Santa Catarina, in southern Brazil. The second one is a large hydropower plant, implemented by the Brazilian multinational Grupo Votorantim in the state of Bahia, in the north-east of the country (see Table 1 for case study project details).

This selection was done based on theoretical and not statistical reasons. Eisenhardt (1989) suggested that case studies *may be chosen to provide examples of polar types.* Thus, as it can be seen in Table 1, the two hydro projects were selected based on their intrinsic differences.

The case study research combined data collection through archival sources (e.g., PDD, memories of RSC of the companies, and webs of the companies), on-site observations, and interviews. A triangulation was applied by multiple data collection methods, which provides stronger substantiation of constructs and hypotheses (Stake 1995).

Interviewees were selected to gather a range of different perspectives and are listed in Table 1. In this way, it was sought to include for each project at least one representative from the following stakeholders: (i) project manager; (ii) local employee; and (iii) local authority. In addition, it was required to include at least two representatives of the local communities (e.g., head or communities or representatives of community base organizations or non-profit local organizations). Finally, 15 people were interviewed during the research.

It is important to take into consideration that hydroelectric enterprises have often proved to be social and environmentally unsustainable, both on an international and on a Brazilian level (Bermann 2007). However, the two projects are further studied because both of them placed an emphasis on social sustainability, although in a very different way and using different management practices.

4.2. Development of social indicators

Sustainability assessments and indicators aim to produce and communicate information needed for evidence-based policymaking, strategic planning, or learning (Lyytimäki et al. 2013).

In the absence of an appropriate ready-made set of social indicators to use for CDM project assessment, a number of methodologies that focus on assessing SD benefits from the CDM projects were analyzed for this study (Begg et al. 2003; Rezende & Merlin 2003; Sutter 2003; Sutter & Parreño 2007; Olsen & Fenhann 2008; Subbarao & Lloyd 2011; UNFCCC 2011; Fernández et al. 2012; Ventura et al. 2012). Eventually, the proposed indicators of the sustainability and empowerment model (S&E), as detailed by Fernández et al. (2012), were adapted and aggregated to create the indicators (see Table 2).

4.3. Analyzing CDM projects documents for the delivery of social development benefits

To assess CDM projects for the delivery of social development benefits, a desktop analysis of each individual project was conducted utilizing both the PDD and the Annex III document. As explained earlier, Brazil requests the so-called Annex III documents as part of their domestic submission of the CDM projects. To use these documents, allowed for a consistent means of assessment across all projects, with documentation publicly available

Table 1. Case study projects.

CDM project title	Location	Project type and subtype	Type of implementing organization	Scale	Activity description	Stakeholders' involved for the case study
Alto Benedito Novo Small Hydroelectric Project	Santa Catarina (South Brazil)	Hydro; Run of river	Cooperative	Small	Construction of small hydroelectric plant (renewable electricity generation)	1 project manager, 2 local workers, 2 members of a local cooperative, 2 local authorities
Votorantim's Hydropower Plant with existing reservoir 'Pedra do Cavalo' CDM Project	Bahia (North Brazil)	Hydro; Existing dam	Brazilian Multinational company	Large	Construction of electric substations, fabrication, and installation of turbines and generator	1 project manager, 2 company executives, 1 local worker, 1 local authority, 3 members of local cooperatives

Table 2. Proposed indicators to assess social development benefits at the local level in Brazil.

Indicator grouping	Indicator subsets
Financial benefits for the local economy	I1. Enhancement of local tourism I2. Equitable share of revenue from the CERs (with funds reaching the local communities) I3. Support for local entrepreneurial activity I4. Local or community cost savings
Local employment generation	I5. Local jobs generation
Investment in local infrastructure and basic services	I6. Building/ improved local infrastructure (e.g., roads or public buildings) I7. Access to clean and affordable energy
Development/diffusion of local/imported technology	I8. Development, use, improvement and/or diffusion of a new local or international technology I9. Collaboration with local universities or research centers for the development, use, or diffusion of a new local or international technology
Engagement of local population and generation of social capital	I10. Adequate mitigation measures of stakeholder concerns proposed by the project developer I11. Positive stakeholder perception of the project's contribution to the generation of improvements in the living conditions I12. Promotion of social harmony and social cohesion (e.g., by the creation/ promotion of new associations or cooperatives) I13. Increased awareness of environmental issues I14. Professional training of local workers I15. Migration reduction
Empowerment of vulnerable groups	I16. Vulnerable groups (women, indigenous, children, and people with disabilities) are intentionally included in processes, stakeholder participation, revenue sharing, and other project activities
Labor conditions improved	I17. Improvements in working conditions
Promotion of education	I18. Improving accessibility to educational resources (e.g., donating resources for local education and or increased funding for local education)
Promotion of health	I19. Reducing exposure to factors that impact health and safety (e.g., non-potable water, smoke), and/or changes that improve lifestyles. I20. Improving health service delivery in the community (e.g., by funding vaccination campaigns and or/ health and safety campaigns, buying equipment or supplies for hospitals, and so on)
Sustainable use of natural resources improved	I21. Avoiding deforestation, forest degradation, and land erosion I22. Enhancement of local biodiversity I23. Decreased pressure on natural resources I24. Promoting waste management (including reutilization and recycling)
Environmental pollution and risks reduced	I25. Reducing odor and noise pollution I26. Reducing the risk of landslides I27. Reducing the risk of fire and explosions
Improved air, soil, and/or water quality	I28. Reducing air pollutants other than GHG I29. Enhancement of water quality I30. Improvement of soil recovery/fertility

and accessible through www.cdmpipeline.org (UNFCCC 2011) website or through the CIMGC website.

Each CDM project was assessed against the indicators of Table 2, with the ultimate goal of discovering whether there were any explicit indications in the official project documents, that social development benefits would be delivered if any, to the organization itself or the local community where the CDM project is implemented.

Given the difficulty of providing an objective assessment of each indicator based on the information available at documentary level, no numerical scoring was provided during the desktop review. The decision to make for each of the SD criteria is 'positive contribution', 'no contribution', or 'negative contribution'.

However, this desktop approach presents significant limitations. Assessing the statements from various sections of the documents could involve some subjectivity because different analysts and assessment procedures may assign different indicators to a given social benefit. Intersubjective testing with a second analyst coding the same documents to check for deflected analytical results, although recommendable, was not possible due to the lack of resources. Hence, a single analyst assessed and assigned indicators for all projects. This solution was previously adopted in other studies based on a desktop analysis of PDD (e.g., UNFCCC 2011; Subbarao & Lloyd 2011).

In addition, a case study analysis of two registered CDM projects was carried out based on the findings from site visit information and actual data.

4.4. Case study analysis

To complement the desktop analysis and in order to assess the actual ground level social development impacts, detailed case studies of two registered CDM hydroelectricity projects with actual field data were carried out. The case studies allowed gathering additional information based on field observations and on relevant stakeholders' understanding of the variables that govern successful social development benefits. As Matos and Silvestre (2013) stated, case studies are an ideal way to investigate sustainability issues because they allow the identification and analysis of insights from the diversity of stakeholders involved and the complexity of their relations.

The same set of indicators and the assessment criteria used earlier to assess the 46 registered hydro CDM projects was applied whilst assessing the social development benefits from the case study projects. Thus, during the on-the-ground research, semi-structured qualitative interviews were used, and the interview protocol was based on the indicators in Table 2.

As respondents from the organization (such as project developers, company managers, or technical advisors) may wish to overvalue the benefits to provide a better image, a balanced number of stakeholders were chosen for each of the case studies. Interviews were carried out with 15 stakeholders, seven in Alto Benedito Novo Small Hydroelectric Project and eight in Votorantim's Hydropower Plant, including directors, technical advisors, managers, employees, and representatives of the local communities (see Table 1). Additional data were captured to provide context and nuance to the corresponding data and conclusions from the perspective of different stakeholders. Combining the results of the desktop review with the case study analysis increased the credibility and validity of the results through cross verification and provided a more detailed and balanced picture of the situation (Yin 2008). In CDM research, the combination of both techniques is increasingly being used (e.g., Subbarao & Lloyd 2011).

5. Results

The results of the desktop and the case studies are presented separately in this chapter. First, the quantitative results from the desktop analysis of the social development benefits generated by the organizations are shown.

Second, qualitative results of case studies are analyzed and triangulated with information from the desktop study.

5.1. Findings from desktop analysis

The initial objective in the analysis of the hydro CDM projects was to analyze how the organizations are delivering social development benefits. These social benefits can be achieved in both, the own organizations and the nearby communities.

Figure 3 presents the indicator groupings and the number of projects that impact on each of them. The results show that the social development benefits most frequently claimed by the organizations implementing hydroelectricity CDM projects are *Local employment generation, Engagement of local population and generation of social capital, Development/diffusion of local/imported technology* and *Invest in local infrastructure*.

In addition, *Financial benefits for the local economy* and *Sustainable use of natural resources improved* are also claimed by almost half of the analyzed projects.

Such beneficial positive claims far exceed those of *Empowerment of vulnerable groups, Labour conditions improved* and *Promotion of education and health*.

Overall, these results correlate with other studies where the local employment is the most prominent social benefit of CDM projects (e.g., Olsen & Fenhann 2008; Subbarao & Lloyd 2011; UNFCCC 2011). Table 3 contains a summary of the results based on the most frequently claimed indicator groupings.

Although the results presented above correspond to the information presented in both PDD and Annex III, it is important to point out that some aspects are specifically requested to be included in these documents. Actually, Annex III documents are almost a 'checklist' whereby project developers argue that their projects meet the prescribed criteria of job creation, improvement of working conditions, training, and income distribution (Cole & Roberts 2011). Thus, indicators directly linked with Annex III requirements are those that are most claimed within their corresponding groupings (Fernández et al.

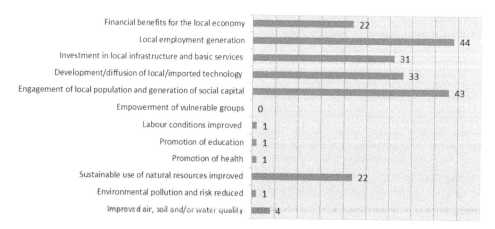

Figure 3. Social SD benefits obtained from the desktop analysis.

Table 3. Most frequently claimed social indicator grouping from the desktop analysis.

Social SD indicator groupings	Social SD indicator grouping in desktop analysis results
Financial benefits for the local economy	Results from the desktop analysis reveal that 22 of the 46 assessed projects have produced financial benefits for the local economy. In particular, around 40% of the projects have impacted on the indicator 'Support for local entrepreneurial activity'. These results were obtained due to the fact that hydro projects made use of the immediately and cheaply available local resources, which in turn appeared to have an economic impact on the community.
Local employment generation	PDD and Annex III information indicates that 44 of the 46 projects have contributed to the generation of local employment. Nevertheless, it is important to highlight that this indicator grouping encompasses both temporary and long-term jobs, as well as skilled and un-skilled jobs, because reviewed documents do not make any distinction between them. It is necessary for a deeper analysis to quantify each type of job created.
Engagement of local population and generation of social capital	Almost all the hydro projects examined (43 of 46) have had a marked influence in terms of engagement of local population and generation of social capital. 76% of organizations are being effectively used to increase environmental awareness (Indicator 13), and 36% have developed activities for the professional training of local workers (I.14). However, only 14% have implemented adequate mitigation measures of stakeholder concerns (I.10) and 17% of organizations have had a positive stakeholder perception in terms of the project's contribution to improve their living conditions (I.11).
Development/diffusion of local/ imported technology	Findings show that 69% of organizations have developed, used, and/or improved a new local or international technology (I.8) for the community through their projects. Surprisingly, the collaboration of the organizations with local universities or research centers (I.9) was found to be very low. Only one of the 46 revised projects have included this aspect, despite the potential of this type of collaborations to enable sustainable development at the local level.
Invest in local infrastructure and basic services	31 projects have contributed to better infrastructures and/or clean affordable energy for the community population. This may be due to the fact that hydropower plants have provided (in 63% of the assessed projects) to improve the access to clean and affordable energy (I.7).
Sustainable use of natural resources improved	Given its nature, hydropower plants are a type of project through which organizations can enhance improvements in the use of water as a local resource to generate electricity. But, beyond this aspect, little impacts have been produced on the local resources. Only 8% of the projects have contributed to enhance the local biodiversity (I.22), and any initiative has been found to decrease the pressure on natural resources (I.23).

2012). The case study projects were used to make a comparison between the social developmental benefits assumed in the PDDs against the actual benefits delivered on the ground.

5.2. Findings from case study analysis

The main findings of both case studies are presented separately, and then a systematization of the results has been elaborated to allow an automatic comparison.

5.2.1. Alto Benedito Novo Small Hydroelectric project, Santa Catarina, Brazil

The 'Alto Benedito Novo Small Hydroelectric Project' is registered as a CDM project since 2007. This is a small hydroelectric plant with installed capacity of 15 MW, located in the Benedito River, Santa Catarina State, Brazil. The purpose of the project's activity is to dispatch renewable electricity to the members of an agricultural cooperative, which is part of the company responsible for the project, CEESAM Geradora S/A. The project includes the exportation of the energy surplus to the

interconnected grid, offsetting thermal generation with renewable electricity generation. Since the project consists of a run-of-river hydropower plant, it presents significantly less negative environmental impacts than large hydropower facilities, mainly because the project does not have a flooded area.

The results of the interviews show that most of the social impacts generated by the project are economical. Thanks to an agreement between CEESAM Geradora S/A and the municipality, the price of energy in the city of Benedito Novo is lower than the price in nearby communities. This price decrease has forested major business development and led to new business. In addition, the company has hired local staff for the operation, management, and repair services of the ifacility.

In addition, CEESAM Geradora S/A makes periodic donations of school supplies to the schools in the area, and with the money expected from the sale of carbon credits (when the project was visited in November 2011 the company still had not received any credit), it plans to invest in computers for those schools, which would help to improve local children's education. The selection of the materials to be donated to the schools is done taking into account the opinions of different stakeholders of the school community.

The technology used for the project has been developed by the local company itself. Furthermore, there have been workshops with several stakeholders to explain the basis of the technology, and thanks to them, other small hydropower plants have been developed in the nearby communities.

Given its nature, the project contributes to the better use of local natural resources. However, it cannot be said that there is a direct contribution aimed at improving local environmental conditions. In relation to this, the representative of the company stated during an interview that reforestation activities are designed to be implemented when they get the money from the sale of carbon credits. It is important to highlight that the project has a clear environmental benefit due to the reduction of GHG which, in the absence of the project, would go into the atmosphere from power generation through fossil fuels. However, indicators designed for this study consider only benefits at local level, not the overall benefits produced.

Therefore, in general terms, CEESAM Geradora S/A relates to a sustainable business model where economic, environmental, and social values are created through the local and clean production of electricity.

5.2.2. Votorantim's Hydropower Plant with existing reservoir 'Pedra do Cavalo' CDM project

Votorantim's Hydropower Plant with existing reservoir 'Pedra do Cavalo' was registered as a CDM project in 2006. The project included the construction of electric substations and the installation of turbines and generators in a dam built in 1985, with the main objective of supplying the city of Salvador with water. The plant has an installed electric capacity of 162 MW and is located in the towns of São Félix and Cachoeira, in the state of Bahía, north-east of Brazil. The plant is owned by Votorantim Cimentos Ltda. and is administered by Votorantim Energia Ltda. Both are subsidiaries of the GrupoVotorantim, a Brazilian multinational company, which operates in several sectors such as finance, energy, siderurgy, steel, paper, etc. The Grupo Votorantim is present in over 20 countries and is one of the largest Brazilian industrial conglomerates.

It is very important to clarify that, as the power plant was implemented in an existing reservoir, the Votarantim's Hydropower CDM project adds a new function to the reservoir without resulting in additional environmental impacts. That is why the present assessment doesn't take into account issues associated with projects flooding large areas, such as additional GHG emissions from biomass decomposition, inequitable land loss, and forced relocations of neighboring populations.

Thanks to the project, an important number of direct jobs were created during the construction phase. In addition, indirect jobs were generated for the maintenance of the facility. It was found that the community was involved in all phases of the project. Votorantim carried out several public hearings with fishers, NGOs, public institutions, and private companies. The company also organized several visits to the plant so that stakeholders could understand the project.

A percentage of the money from the sale of carbon credits is destined to the Votorantim Institute, an organization established to underpin Votorantim Group's commitment with the communities in the aim of strengthening corporate and human capital. One of the activities carried out by the Institute is the investment in different business projects in the neighboring communities of hydropower plant 'Pedra do Cavalo'. The income generation programs implemented by Votorantim could be a successful model for these kinds of programs.

In the same manner as the previous case, the impacts resulting from the reduction of GHG emissions are not considered as local benefits, and the major environmental benefit is the improvement in the use of natural resources. However, the company implements environmental recuperation programs such as recovery of degraded areas, management of aquatic ecosystems, monitoring of water quality and fish fauna, and environmental education program.

Findings suggest that the community experience of the Votorantim Institute plays a key role in the success of its activities.

5.2.3. Systematization of case study results

The selected cases illustrate differences in context and organizational innovation approaches toward the incorporation of social sustainability in business models. However, despite the differences between the two organizations, both projects appeared to be relatively successful in terms of delivering the envisaged social development benefits to the local community as indicated in the PDD and Annex III.

Votorantim's case is an example of a large project managed by a multinational company that act to further the interests of others (including groups or societies of which they are part) to ultimately serve their own self-interest. However, the research highlighted that the social benefits of the project were implemented by a different organization. In fact, the ultimate objective of this so-called Votorantim Institute is precisely, to define corporate social responsibility practices to promote SD benefits within the local communities.

On the other hand, the important social benefits of the Alto Benedito Novo Small Hydroelectric Power Plant are due to its intrinsic characteristics: small project managed by a local company which is closely linked to the community.

Both companies have been able to manage their projects while maintaining its purpose and its structure, but in alignment with the needs of the communities in which they operate.

Table 4. Systematization of the results from case study analysis.

Identified practices/benefits	Alto Benedito Novo Small Hydroelectric Project	Votorantim's Hydropower Plant with existing reservoir 'Pedra do Cavalo' Project
Practices		
Community-based projects	Yes	No
Local stakeholder participation	Yes	Yes
Involvement of a foundation/NGO or a community-based organization.	Yes	Yes
Incentivized project developer (committed to SD and fight against poverty)	Yes	Yes
Project developer with good corporate social responsibility practices	No	Yes
Benefits		
Financial benefits for the local economy	Yes	Yes
Local employment generation	Yes	Yes
Investment in local infrastructure and basic services	Yes	Yes
Development/diffusion of local/imported technology	Yes	No
Engagement of local population and generation of social capital	Yes	Yes
Empowerment of vulnerable groups	No	No
Labor conditions improved	No	No
Promotion of education	Limited	No
Promotion of health	No	No
Sustainable use of natural resources improved	Yes	Yes
Environmental pollution and risks reduced	No	No
Improved air, soil, and/or water quality	No	No

Table 4 shows a systematization of the results from case study analysis, indicating the main differences and similarities between the two projects analyzed and the principal social benefits generated by each one.

6. Discussion and conclusions

The combined desktop and case study results of this research suggest that organizations managing hydroelectric initiatives in Brazil under the CDM are able to offer a pathway toward achieving a number of important social benefits. These social benefits were mainly found related to employment generation and revitalization of the local economy.

However, the research also identified that projects often failed to deliver significant or substantial long-term development benefits beyond the economic benefits on a local and regional scale. Thus, most of the assessed projects have not had any impact on the promotion of health or education, or contributed to the empowerment of vulnerable groups, such as women or children. These findings agree with previous studies about hydro CDM projects in Brazil and other developing countries (e.g., Cole & Roberts 2011).

The two projects for the case study analysis were chosen because, despite their differences, both of them were found to emphasize social sustainability although in a very different way and using different management practices. This allowed us to break down differences and similarities, and to systematize lessons learnt from two organizations that have defined their added values in concert with social sustainability in a different way.

Alto Benedito Novo is a small hydroplant managed by a local enterprise whose main activity is strongly linked with the social benefits for the community. Results from this case study allow us to understand how hydro projects can enhance the development of micro-enterprises as well as the revitalization of local economies. On the other hand, Pedra do Cavalo is a hydroelectric dam managed by a big Brazilian company, whose main activity barely provides direct social benefits and which has reinforced these social aspects as a part of its corporate social responsibility. The latter is an example of an alternative management procedure aiming to switch from community assistance to community development through the corporate social responsibility practices of the company. Both initiatives demonstrated to be beneficial in terms of raising community environmental awareness.

Overall, results suggest that the main shared strength is that social benefits are achieved by entities interested in local sustainability (i.e., a local cooperative and a foundation), resulting in a crucial effort to involve local stakeholders. We conclude that this involvement, albeit obtained in different ways, is a key aspect in achieving real social sustainable benefits for people and climate. This agrees with previous findings from other renewable energy CDM developing country studies (e.g., Cole & Roberts 2011; Subbarao & Lloyd 2011).

Furthermore, the research identified several challenges that are hindering the hydro CDM projects to deliver more social benefits and enabled a number of recommendations to be extracted for the organizations to face those challenges:

(1) To promote the participation of a diverse number of local stakeholder groups, which provide better opportunities to learn and obtain innovative solutions.

(2) To encourage the collaboration and communication between different stakeholders and the organizations to coordinate sustainability efforts. When stakeholders collaborate and work in partnership, the chances of finding creative solutions are higher. At this point, cooperatives and NGOs should play an important role.

(3) To find effective mechanisms and spaces which facilitate active stakeholders' participation where they express their advice.

(4) To promote technologies which enable the sustainable use of natural resources to be improved, environmental impacts to be reduced, and the decrease of community dependency on external resources.

(5) To include both learning and skill building as part of the stakeholder relations process. It enhances the empowerment of the communities and increases their autonomy.

(6) To take into account, specifically, the particular needs of some vulnerable groups such as women and children. This prevents the contribution to increase iniquity and injustice.

(7) To strengthen the role played by local, regional, and national governments, which can implement monitoring mechanisms, tax exemptions, and other incentives to SD-oriented organizations.

(8) To raise awareness about the importance of SD.

The limitations of this work are linked to interviewees' ability to articulate facts and opinions and the small sample size of the case study. As earlier explained, to minimize such limitations, a variety of stakeholders were surveyed, and the information was triangulated with other references. Nonetheless, this research did not determine conclusively how organizations can be managed to meet the social development needs of local communities. Instead, it nuances the question to hydro projects in Brazil and calls for additional research to further evaluate practices to foster social benefits being implemented by organizations in developing countries both within and outside the CDM framework.

References

Azmat F. 2013. Sustainable development in developing countries: the role of social entrepreneurs. Int J Sust Dev World Ecol. 36:293–304.

Barkemeyer R, Holt D, Preuss L, Tsang S. 2014. What happened to the 'development' in sustainable development? business guidelines two decades after Brundtland. Sust Dev. 22:15–32. doi:10.1002/sd.521.

Baumgartner RJ, Zielowski C. 2004. Organizational culture toward sustainable development. In: Hosni Y, Smith R, Khalil T., editors. New directions in technology management: changing collaboration between government, industry and university. Proceedings of the 13th International Conference on Management of Technology; 2004 Apr 3–7; Washington (DC).

Begg K, Parkinson S, vd Horst D, Wilkinson R, Theuri D, Gitonga S, Mathenga M, Amissah-Arthur H, Atugba S, Ackon S. 2003. Encouraging CDM energy projects to aid poverty alleviation. In: Final report of project R8037 under the DFID KAR programme. Surrey: Centre for Environmental Strategy, University of Surrey.

Beringer A, Adomßent M. 2008. Sustainable university research and development: inspecting sustainability in higher education research. Environ Educ Res. 14:607–623. doi:10.1080/13504620802464866.

Bermann C. 2007. Impasses e controvérsias da hidreletricidade. Estud Av. 21:139–153. doi:10.1590/S0103-40142007000100011.

Boons FAA, Lüdeke-Freund F. 2013. Business models for sustainable innovation: state of the art and steps towards a research agenda. J Clean Prod. 45:9–19. doi:10.1016/j.jclepro.2012.07.007.

Boström M. 2012. The problematic social dimension of sustainable development: the case of the forest stewardship council. Int J Sust Dev World Ecol. 19:3–15. doi:10.1080/13504509.2011.582891.

Boyd E, Hultman N, Roberts JT, Corbera E, Cole J, Bozmoski A, Ebeling J, Tippman R, Manna P, Brown K, Liverman DM. 2009. Reforming the CDM for sustainable development: lessons learned and policy futures. Environ Sci Policy. 12:820–831. doi:10.1016/j.envsci.2009.06.007.

Castro R, Jabbour CJC. 2013. Evaluating sustainability of an Indian university. J Clean Prod. 61:54–58. doi:10.1016/j.jclepro.2013.02.033.

Clean Development Mechanism Policy Dialogue [CDMPD]. 2012. Climate change, carbon markets and the CDM: a call to action. Luxembourg: Report of the high-level panel on the CDM policy dialogue.

Cole J, Roberts JT. 2011. Lost opportunities? A comparative assessment of social development elements of six hydroelectricity CDM projects in Brazil and Peru. Clim Dev. 3:361–379. doi:10.1080/17565529.2011.623831.

Comissão Interministerial de Mudança Global do Clima, [CIMGC]. 2003. Resolução no 1 de 11 de setembro de 2003 [Internet]. [cited 2011 Sep 15]. Available from: http://www.mct.gov.br/upd_blob/0008/8694.pdf

Crowe TL. 2013. The potential of the CDM to deliver pro-poor benefits. Clim Policy. 13:58–79. doi:10.1080/14693062.2012.709080.

Dale VH. 2010. Environmental management welcomes a new face and reinforces its focus on science-based stewardship. Environ Manage. 45:1243–1243. doi:10.1007/s00267-010-9505-3.

Deloitte T. 1992. Business strategy for sustainable development: leadership and accountability for the 90s international institute for sustainable development. Darby: Diane Publishing Company.

Dobers P, Halme M. 2009. Editorial corporate social responsibility and developing countries. Corp Soc Responsib Environ Mgmt. 16:237–249. doi:10.1002/csr.212.

Doiron S, Weissenberger S. 2014. Sustainable dive tourism: social and environmental impacts – the case of Roatan, Honduras. Tourism Manag Perspect. 10:19–26. doi:10.1016/j.tmp.2013.12.003.

Eden S. 1994. Using sustainable development : the business case. Global Environ Change. 4:160–167. doi:10.1016/0959-3780(94)90050-7.

Eisenhardt KM. 1989. Building theories from case study research. Acad Manage Rev. 14:532–550.

Elkington J. 1998. Cannibals with forks: the triple bottom line of 21st century business. Gabriola Island, BC: New Society Publishers.

Fenhann J. 2011. CDM/JI Pipeline Analysis and Database [Internet]. Roskilde: UNEP Risoe. [cited 2011 Dec 1]. Available from: http://cdmpipeline.org/

Fernández L, Mileni-Bogo J, Lumbreras J, Andrade JC. 2012. Exploring co-benefits of clean development mechanism projects: lessons learned from Santa Catarina, Brazil. Int J Clim Change: Impacts Responses. 3:121–142.

Figge F, Hahn T, Schaltegger S, Wagner M. 2002. The sustainability balanced scorecard, linking sustainability management to business strategy. Bus Strat Env. 11:269–284. doi:10.1002/bse.339.

de Freitas ARP, de Abreu MCS, Albuquerque AM. 2013. Implicações Estratégicas de Projetos de Mecanismos de Desenvolvimento Limpo em Empresas de Energia Renovável. Sistemas & Gestão. 8:334–345.

Gangale F, Mengolini A. 2011. CDM contribution to RES penetration in the power generation sector of China and India. Int J Sust Dev World Ecol. 18:283–290. doi:10.1080/13504509.2011.553354.

Government of Brazil. 2008. Brazil's contribution to prevent climate change. White Paper, MREIMCT/MMA/MMEIMDIC. Brasilia: Government of Brazil.

Government of Brazil. 2012. Balanço Energético Nacional. Resultados Preliminares. Ano base 2011 [Internet]. [cited 2011 Dec 12]. Available from: https://ben.epe.gov.br/downloads/S%C3%ADntese%20do%20Relat%C3%B3rio%20Final_2012_Web.pdf

Haden SS, Oyler JD, Humphreys JH. 2009. Historical, practical, and theoretical perspectives on green management: an exploratory analysis. Manag Decis. 47:1041–1055. doi:10.1108/00251740910978287.

Hall J, Matos S. 2010. Incorporating impoverished communities in sustainable supply chains. Int J Phys Distribution Logistics Manag. 40:124–147. doi:10.1108/09600031011020368.

Hall J, Vredenburg H. 2003. The challenges of innovating for sustainable development. Sloan Manage Rev. 45:61–68.

Hawken P. 1993. The ecology of commerce. A declaration of sustainability. Canada: HarperCollins.

Holliday CO, Schmidheiny S, Watts P. 2002. Walking the talk: the business case for sustainable development. Greenleaf, Sheffield: Berrett-koehler Publishers.

Hopwood B, Mellor M, O'Brien G. 2005. Sustainable development: mapping different approaches. Sust Dev. 13:38–52. doi:10.1002/sd.244.

Institute for Global Environmental Strategies [IGES]. 2006. Clean development mechanism for poverty reduction in Asia and the Pacific. Paper presented at: IGES-UNDP Regional Workshop, Developing a Regional Strategy in the Asia Pacific Region; 2006 Mar 30–31; Bangkok. Available from: www.iges.or.jp/en/cdm/pdf/regional/activity_regional01/Background.pdf.

Jabbour CJC, Santos FCA, Nagano MS. 2008. Environmental management system and human resource practices: is there a link between them in four Brazilian companies? J Clean Prod. 16:1922–1925. doi:10.1016/j.jclepro.2008.02.004.

Kaplan RS, Norton DP. 1992. The balanced scorecard. measures that drive performance. Harvard Bus Rev. January–February. 71–79.

Karakosta C, Doukas H, Psarras J. 2012. Carbon market and technology transfer: statistical analysis for exploring implications. Int J Sust Dev World Ecol. 19:311–320. doi:10.1080/13504509.2011.644638.

Karakosta C, Marinakis V, Letsou P, Psarras J. 2013. Does the CDM offer sustainable development benefits or not? Int J Sust Dev World Ecol. 20:1–8. doi:10.1080/13504509.2012.752768.

Kent K, Sinclair AJ, Diduck A. 2012. Stakeholder engagement in sustainable adventure tourism development in the Nanda Devi Biosphere Reserve, India. Int J Sust Dev World Ecol. 19:89–100. doi:10.1080/13504509.2011.595544.

Kolk A, Levy D, Pinkse J. 2008. Corporate responses in an emerging climate regime: the institutionalization and commensuration of carbon disclosure. Eur Accounting Rev. 17:719–745. doi:10.1080/09638180802489121.

Lehtonen M. 2004. The environmental–social interface of sustainable development: capabilities, social capital, institutions. Ecol Econ. 49:199–214. doi:10.1016/j.ecolecon.2004.03.019.

Littig B, Grießler E. 2005. Social sustainability: a catchword between political pragmatism and social theory. Int J Sust Dev. 8:65–79. doi:10.1504/IJSD.2005.007375.

Lyytimäki J, Tapio P, Varho V, Söderman T. 2013. The use, nonuse and misuse of indicators in sustainability assessment and communication. Int J Sust Dev World Ecol. 20:385–393. doi:10.1080/13504509.2013.834524.

Matos S, Silvestre BS. 2013. Managing stakeholder relations when developing sustainable business models: the case of the Brazilian energy sector. J Clean Prod. 45:61–73. doi:10.1016/j.jclepro.2012.04.023.

Naustdalslid J. 2011. Climate change–the challenge of translating scientific knowledge into action. Int J Sust Dev World Ecol. 18:243–252. doi:10.1080/13504509.2011.572303.

Nelson J, Prescott D. 2008. Business and the millennium development goals: a framework for action. London: International Business leaders Forum and UNDP.

Olsen KH. 2007. The clean development mechanism's contribution to sustainable development: a review of the literature. Clim Change. 84:59–73. doi:10.1007/s10584-007-9267-y.

Olsen KH, Fenhann J. 2008. Sustainable development benefits of clean development mechanism projects. A new methodology for sustainability assessment based on text analysis of the project design documents submitted for validation. Energ Policy. 36:2819–2830. doi:10.1016/j.enpol.2008.02.039.

Palmer J, Cooper I, van der Vorst R. 1997. Mapping out fuzzy buzzwords-who sits where on sustainability and sustainable development. Sustainable Dev. 5:87–93. doi:10.1002/(SICI)1099-1719(199708)5:2<87::AID-SD70>3.0.CO;2-Z.

Pinkse J, Kolk A. 2012. Addressing the climate change – sustainable development nexus: the role of multistakeholder partnerships. Bus Soc. 51:176–210. doi:10.1177/0007650311427426.

Rezende D, Merlin S. 2003. Social carbon: adding value to sustainable development. instituto ecológica. São Pulo: Peirópolis.

Robinson J. 2004. Squaring the circle? some thoughts on the idea of sustainable development. Ecol Econ. 48:369–384. doi:10.1016/j.ecolecon.2003.10.017.

Rondinelli DA, Berry MA. 2000. Environmental citizenship in multinational corporations: social responsibility and sustainable development. Eur Manag J. 18:70–84. doi:10.1016/S0263-2373(99)00070-5.

Sanchez P, Ricart JE, Rodríguez MA. 2006. Influential factors in becoming socially embedded in low-income markets. Green Manag Int. 51:19–38.

Schneider L. 2008. A clean development mechanism (CDM) with atmospheric benefits for A post-2012 climate regime. Discussion paper [Internet]. Berlin: World Wildlife Fund. [cited 2011 Dec 15]. Available from: http://www.oeko.de/oekodoc/779/2008-227-en.pdf

Silva-Junior AC. 2011. Projetos de mecanismo de desenvolvimento limpo (MDL): promotores de transferência de tecnologia e tecnologias mais limpas no brasil. Salvador de Bahía: Faculdade Politécnica, Universidade Federal da Bahia.

Silvius AG, Schipper R 2010. A maturity model for integrating sustainability in projects and project management. Paper presented at: 24th World Congress of the International Project Management Association; Istanbul.

Sirohi S. 2007. CDM: is it a 'win-win' strategy for rural poverty alleviation in India?. Clim Change. 84:91–110. doi:10.1007/s10584-007-9271-2.

Stake RE. 1995. The art of case study research. Thousand Oaks (CA): Sage.

Stormer F. 2003. Making the shift: moving from 'ethics pays' to an inter-systems model of business. J Bus Ethics. 44:279–289.

Subbarao S, Lloyd B. 2011. Can the clean development mechanism (CDM) deliver? Energ Pol. 39:1600–1611. doi:10.1016/j.enpol.2010.12.036.

Sutter C. 2003. Sustainability check-up for CDM projects: how to assess the sustainability of international projects under the Kyoto Protocol. Berlin: Wissenschaftlicher Verlag.

Sutter C, Parreño JC. 2007. Does the current clean development mechanism (CDM) deliver its sustainable development claim? An analysis of officially registered CDM projects. Clim Change. 84:75–90. doi:10.1007/s10584-007-9269-9.

Tregidga H, Kearins K, Milne M. 2013. The politics of knowing 'organizational sustainable development'. Organ Environ. 26:102–129. doi:10.1177/1086026612474957.

UNDP. 2007. Human development report 2007/8. fighting climate change: human solidarity in a divided world. New York (NY): Palgrave Macmillan.

UNEP-SETAC Life Cycle Initiative. 2009. Guidelines for social life cycle assessment of products. United Nations Environment Programme. ISBN: 978-92-807-3021-0

United Nations Framework Convention on Climate Change [UNFCCC]. 2011. Benefits of the Clean Development Mechanism [Internet]. ISBN 92-9219-086-5. Bonn: UNFCCC. [cited 2011 Dec 15]. Available from: http://cdm.unfccc.int/about/dev_ben/pg1.pdf

Ventura AC, Fernandez L, Andrade JCS, Lumbreras J. 2012. The human side of social technology for climate change mitigation and human development: the case of efficient stoves in Brazil. Inl J Environ Sust Dev. 11:375–393.

World Commission on Environment and Development [WCED]. 1987. Our common future. Oxford: Oxford University Press.

Yin RK. 2008. Case study research: design and methods. Thousand Oaks (CA): Sage.

Zeffane R, Rugimbana R. 1995. Management in the less-developed countries: a review of pertinent issues, challenges and responses. Leadersh Organ Dev J. 16:26–36. doi:10.1108/01437739510098003.

Sustainable development in the BRICS countries: an efficiency analysis by data envelopment

Naja Brandão Santana[a], Daisy Aparecida do Nascimento Rebelatto[a], Ana Elisa Périco[b] and Enzo Barberio Mariano[c]

[a]Production Engineering Department, University of São Paulo, São Carlos, SP, Brazil; [b]Economics Department, State University of São Paulo, Araraquara, SP, Brazil; [c]Production Engineering Department, State University of São Paulo, Bauru, SP, Brazil

There is much concern about the social and environmental impacts caused by the economic growth of nations. Thus, to evaluate the socio-economic performance of nations, economists have increasingly addressed matters related to social welfare and the environment. It is within the scope of this context that this work discusses the performance of countries in the BRICS group regarding sustainable development. The objective of this study regards evaluating the efficiency of these countries in transforming productive resources and technological innovation into sustainable development. The proposed objective was achieved by using econometric tools as well as the data envelopment analysis method to then create economic, environmental, and social efficiency rankings for the BRICS countries, which enabled to carry out comparative analyses on the sustainable development of those countries. The results of such assessments can be of interest for more specific scientific explorations.

1. Introduction

The socio-environmental impacts generated by the economic growth of countries have brought about increasing concerns in society. Such concerns can be seen in the various means of communication, and this signals the need for more responsible actions by the human race.

In the 1970s, in the work of Meadows et al. (1972) – The Limits to Growth – it was reported that the current development model was incompatible with the preservation of the environment. In other words, if developing countries started to consume the same level of resources as the developed countries, the planet would soon be in a catastrophic situation.

The fact is that economic growth, in most cases, is accompanied by the excessive use of natural resources and negative environmental and social impacts, such as, for instance, income inequality, exploitation of manual labor, and toxic gas emissions.

Thus, to evaluate the socio-economic performance of nations, economists have increasingly addressed matters related to social welfare and the environment. The progress of a nation, traditionally measured by economic indicators such as gross domestic product (GDP), needs new assessment modes.

Given the criticisms regarding the usefulness of GDP as a performance indicator of nations, the human development index (HDI) was created by the United Nations Program for Development to translate not only the economic aspect of various countries, but also issues related to the quality of life of populations. In addition to HDI, another example is the Gini coefficient, which according to Olmedo et al. (2009) is one of the inequality indicators used in studies about social development. Furthermore, life expectancy at birth, according to Sen (1998), is a decisive indicator to verify the full success of a society, a simple indicator that represents the overall health of a community and also the situation of its development.

However, it should be pointed out that these indicators do not account for the environmental impacts caused by human actions. In light of these circumstances, the concept of sustainable development was intentionally undertaken in this paper.

The literature points out that sustainable development is a multidimensional concept and that, in order to evaluate a system, the economic, social, and environmental aspects should be taken into account in an integrated manner (Pope et al. 2004). Seen from this perspective, evaluating the sustainable development of regions requires using other indicators, a measure to inform environmental performance, as for instance carbon dioxide emissions (CO_2).

It is worth noting that the discussion included in this work initiated in the idea of progress from the concept of economic growth to the concept of development and, more specifically, to the concept of sustainable development. Thus, considering the theoretical aspects of these concepts, the focus of this paper is to discuss the performance of the countries in the BRICS group with regards to sustainable development, in order to compare their efficiency in transforming productive resources and technological innovation into sustainable development, within a period of 8 years (2000–2007).

The proposed objective was achieved by using econometric tools as well as the data envelopment analysis (DEA) method to then create economic, environmental, and social efficiency rankings for the BRICS countries, which enabled to carry out comparative analyses on the sustainable development of those countries. The results of such assessments can be of interest for more specific scientific explorations.

2. Economic growth and de-growth/human and sustainable development

The core discussion contained in this work originated from the evolution of the economic growth concept in the human development concept and later in the sustainable development concept. Thus, while economic growth can be defined as the increase in production and per capita income, Sen (1999) defines human development as the process of expanding the freedoms enjoyed by people, such as economic, social, and political liberty, by expanding their ability to perform activities that are freely chosen and valued. According to Mariano and Rebelatto (2013), the product of human development, with its multidimensional nature, is quality of life, whereby to obtain a set of indicators that could encompass all the desires of an individual, which tend to be increasingly broader, is a very difficult task.

According to Cracolici et al. (2009), Ranis et al. (2000), and Suri et al. (2011), the increase in GDP per capita is a fundamental prerequisite to improve the quality of life of the population. On the other hand, economic growth can also result in poor development, producing social inequalities, unemployment, poverty, and environmental deterioration (Sachs 2001). Thus, it can be stated that it is not economic growth itself, but its quality that determines the well-being of the population, as good growth is that which reduces extreme poverty, decreases inequalities, and is capable of self-sustainment (Lopes et al. 2008).

In short, economic growth is a necessary condition, but not a sufficient condition for achieving a full and happy life for all (Ranis et al. 2000; Sachs 2001; Mariano & Rebelatto 2013). The relationship between economic wealth and quality of life was closely examined and systematized by Suri et al. (2011), and the efficiency in this relationship was determined by Morais and Camanho (2011) in cities of Europe and by Mariano and Rebelatto (2013) in 101 countries of the world.

Going a bit further, we arrive at the idea of sustainable development, which according to the definition conveyed in the Brundtland report, consists of promoting economic growth, with the ensuing satisfaction of the interests and needs of the current generations, without having to compromise the needs of future generations (World Commission on Environment and Development 1987). According to Fredericks (2012), this definition implies,

above all, an ethical question, which can be better understood by the following excerpt:

> Dominant normative elements of the sustainability movement include the assumption that humans should take responsibility for their actions; that ecosystems, human societies, and sometimes individual species or entities are worthy of being sustained; and that equity or justice between people living today, between those presently alive and future generations, and potentially between humans and other biota are valuable. (Fredericks 2012, p. 2)

It is worth noting that the term sustainable development was first discussed by the World Conservation Union in the document entitled World Conservation Strategy, which states that 'for development to be sustainable, the aspects relating to the social and ecological scope as well as the economic factors must be considered, including the living and nonliving resources and the short- and long-term advantages of alternative actions' (International Union for Conservation of Nature and Natural Resources – IUCN 1980). In this context, Dittmar (2014) asserts that most countries, at least from the 1992 United Nations summit in Rio, have been adopting policies for sustainable development with the purpose of combining economic growth with social development and environmental protection.

Thus, Pope et al. (2004) express sustainability as a multidimensional concept in which the economic, social, and environmental aspects should be considered and integrated, which are called the three pillars of sustainability or Triple Bottom Line.

In fact, it should be noted that the positive integration of the three pillars of sustainability is needed to facilitate the achievement of sustainable development. Nonetheless, the integration of economic, environmental, and social dimensions is also frequently associated with conflicts between these aspects that tend to hinder the achievement of sustainable development (Hansmann et al. 2012).

The study by Kaivo-oja et al. (2013) indicated that the three dimensions of sustainability are far from being positively correlated. On the contrary, the authors argue, for example, that there is strong negative correlation between human well-being and environmental well-being. This finding is problematic, since it contradicts the three pillar's definition of sustainability presented in the Brundtland report of the World Commission on Environment (Kaivo-Oja et al. 2013). With regards to this, Bebbington and Larrinnaga (2014) argue that the familiar definition of sustainable development, presented in the Brundtland report, owing to its radical nature, can be appreciated only in the context of its creation, since this definition denotes that human development problems cannot be separated from environmental problems.

Further, to some scholars, sustainability cannot be achieved by a high level of economic growth, but rather seeking a lower level of production and consumption. So the idea of sustainable de-growth emerges, in other words, the scale reduction of production and consumption in the pursuit of social well-being and improved environmental conditions. In the papers published by researchers in this field, such as Hueting (2010), Alier et al. (2010), Schneider et al. (2010), Trainer (2012), and Whitehead (2013), there are warnings to the risks of continued growth of countries at such pace, which will inevitably result in the planet not being able to withstand such a load of resource consumption, in addition to the production of waste and greenhouse gas emissions. All of this reaffirms the statements made by Meadows et al. (2004) on the limits to growth.

In this regard, considering the economic and environmental dimensions, Kaivo-oja et al. (2013) show the opposite, since, according to them, the trade-off relationship between economic and environmental development has decreased, and according to the authors, this trend is positive from the point of view of sustainability.

3. BRICS

It can be observed that the old order of international politics is dying; the system has been transformed from a unipolar to a multipolar system. The change of the North American power, perceived from the 2008 financial crisis, has occurred alongside a growing trend of regionalization in the global political economy, and the rise of BRICS is a clear illustration of this trend (Öniş & Kutlay 2013).

In their study, Dolgikh and Kokin (2009) report that the term 'BRIC' refers to the four emerging countries (Brazil, Russia, India, and China), whose economies indicate rapid growth trends. According to these authors, the BRIC acronym first appeared in November 2001 in a report entitled 'Building Better Global Economic BRICs', whose authorship was attributed to Jim O'Neill, an economist at Goldman Sachs investment bank. In that report, O'Neill (2001) reported that in the 10 years that followed, the weight of the BRIC countries – especially China – on the worldwide GDP would grow significantly, and this aroused interest about the impact of fiscal and monetary policies of these countries on the global economy.

However, according to Armijo (2007) and Dolgikh and Kokin (2009), it was in 2003, after the research report from Goldman Sachs was published, 'Dreaming with BRICs: the path to 2050', that the BRIC acronym was proclaimed as a part that assessed the perspective of economic growth of the BRIC countries and of their population. Wilson and Purushothaman (2003) highlighted in the report 'Dreaming with BRICs: the path to 2050' that in 2050 Brazil, Russia, India, and China would play a larger force and a new role in the world economy.

Amorim (2010) stated that the consolidation of the BRIC concept came about only because in the years following the release of the 2003 report, a significant economic growth was observed for the BRIC countries, higher than initially projected. To Amorim (2010), this economic growth encouraged Goldman Sachs bank to prepare another report, entitled 'BRICs and Beyond'. In

this report's analysis, O'Neill (2007) presented some updated prognosis for the BRIC countries, acknowledging that the economic growth in these countries had been faster than originally forecasted.

In the data collection conducted by Yao et al. (2009), Brazil, Russia, India, and China collectively account for 28.9% of the world's land area and 43.2% of the world population. Therefore, Amorim (2010) warned that the BRIC group holds considerable land areas, abundant diversity and amounts of natural and energy resources, important technological development, and accelerated economic growth.

In 2011, the former BRIC acronym had a letter added, becoming BRICS, where S refers to South Africa. In August 2010, O'Neill claimed that South Africa could be considered the next country to join the BRIC group. In early 2011, at the invitation of the founding member countries, South Africa officially became part of the group of countries with the greatest growth potential.

Although these countries are presented as a block with similar characteristics, it should be pointed out that they also have economic, social, and cultural differences, which can be perceived with regards to population, territorial size, climate, religion, history, and so on. Moreover, according to Jacobs and Van Rossem (2013), the idea of grouping the BRICS countries based only on their economic growth perspectives has been questioned; they state that the overall strength of a country depends on factors that go beyond GDP, such as military and political resources. The authors warn that policy makers should be careful when extrapolating economic potential to actual power in the global system, since power is a multidimensional and relational phenomenon.

3.1. Economic growth of BRICS

For a more in-depth study on the economic growth of the BRICS countries, it is advisable to return to O'Neill (2001), who compared the GDP growth of the G7 countries with the GDP growth of the BRIC countries. According to O'Neill (2001), the initial prediction indicated that in 2001 and 2002, the GDP growth in the G7 countries would be low. However, China's GDP growth would be high, and Russia and India would have a higher real GDP growth than the G7 countries. In this analysis, Brazil was the only country in the group that would undergo low growth, similar to that of the G7 today.

In a later work, Wilson and Purushothaman (2003) reported that in the next 50 years, the BRIC economies together would become the biggest global economies. Moreover, according to Tseng (2009), Goldman Sachs projected that in less than 40 years, the combined GDP of these four economies would collectively exceed that of the G6 group.

To verify the proposed estimates regarding the economic growth of the BRIC countries, Wilson and Purushothaman (2003) developed a different analysis to project this long-term growth, based on econometric research for several countries. Thus, the authors used the econometric model of Levine and Renelt to explain the average GDP growth over the next 30 years, as a function of initial income per capita, investment rates, population growth, and the number of secondary school enrollment.

Although the technique used in the Levine and Renelt model was different from that used in their projections, Wilson and Purushothaman (2003) showed similar results, corroborating earlier projections.

A possible alternative to confirm the theory defined by O'Neill (2001) and Wilson and Purushothaman (2003) is to present the work of Yao et al. (2009), who used the argument that in 2005 the BRIC countries generated about 27% of global GDP. According to these authors, the high economic growth potential of these countries could be attributed to their fertile lands and rich natural resources, including a large available and low cost workforce, combined with the high rate of foreign direct investment.

To reinforce the argument used by Yao et al. (2009), Dolgikh and Kokin (2009) presented results from a study conducted in 2008 by the Research Grant Thornton International, which for the first time calculated an index of fast-growing markets. The results showed that the BRIC countries are among the five high economic growth countries. What was observed, according to the authors, was that all BRIC countries had rapid economic growth; however, China stood out as the country with the most dynamic economic growth among the countries analyzed.

Among the statistical studies that confirmed the significant economic growth of the BRIC group, Yao et al. (2009) pointed out that crude oil production achieved by the group accounted for 20.6% of the world's oil production in 2004. Moreover, these authors observed that foreign direct investment provided the BRIC countries the capital needed for economic development.

In the search for other factors that could contribute to economic growth, Lawson et al. (2006) found that infrastructure is vital to growth while it plays an important role to solve income inequality. Based on their observations, the authors listed some important points in terms of the infrastructure of the BRIC countries: (1) significant growth in mobile telephony; (2) intense electricity consumption; (3) greater access to basic sanitation; (4) increased access to water sources, along with urbanization; (5) increased number of infrastructure projects.

A brief analysis of this information shows that BRICS countries have shown an economic growth trend, which can be seen by how these countries behave in the international market or by the advances in infrastructure that tend to bring socio-economic progress.

However, in spite of the aforementioned, over the years, there has been a slowdown in the economic growth of the BRICS group. In the work entitled 'Broken BRICs: why the rest stopped rising', Sharma (2012) states that the extravagant predictions about the BRICS group have been toppled, since the observed economic growth has slowed sharply. According to the author, it is possible that the new global economic order is more similar to the earlier one

than what most observers expect, and there will be economic growth for emerging countries; however, this will occur slowly and different from the experts' forecasts.

3.2. Social and environmental development of BRICS

According to May (2008), the argument used for looking into the accelerated growth rates of BRIC countries is the ability to lift millions of people out of absolute poverty. However, the author also found that in this path, the trend is that desirable economic growth is accompanied by unsustainable levels of consumption. The author highlighted that the pursuit of rapid growth could bring as a consequence the future scarcity of natural resources, which according to him is contradictory to sustainability, since the pressures weighing on the systems that support life are significant.

Thus, Plotnikova (2011) indicates that the economic growth of BRICS must be based on sustainable development, seeking to provide qualitative improvements to their systems, in view of the great responsibility to promote sustainable development in light of the projected economic growth potential.

In terms of population, Lastres et al. (2007) pointed out that the population representativeness of the BRIC group, in terms of world population, can be considered a challenge. These authors also added that the challenges seen in large populations relate primarily to infrastructure, health, and education services. In addition to these, the authors reported there are other problems related to population issues, such as unemployment and high income distribution inequality.

To validate all of these issues related to the population problems of BRICS countries, the projections of Wilson and Purushothaman (2003) indicated that despite their rapid economic growth, the populations of these countries are still, and will remain until 2050, likely to be poorer on average than the G6 population.

Lastres et al. (2007) analyzed the HDI and noted that in the 1990–2002 period, the four countries that made up the BRIC group at that time were in the medium human development category (HDI between 0.5 and 0.8). However, according to the authors, the analysis allowed to assert that over that period the country had a slight and continuous HDI improvement, becoming the highlight of progress because of India. According to Lastres et al. (2007), India's HDI evolved from 0.297 in 1990 to 0.595 in 2002, despite its significant population growth.

To complement the previous information on the HDI of the BRIC countries, we turn to May (2008) to state that, as a whole, these countries have an average index of 0.708. Thus, the BRIC group was ranked in the 'low-medium' classification of countries in terms of development.

As stated by May (2008), the BRIC countries are culturally heterogeneous, with religious, ethnic, and racial diversity. However, as explained by the author, the BRIC countries have similar aspirations to achieve human development and improved quality of life, although some invest more than others in education, health, and infrastructure.

With regards to the environment, May (2008) noted that annual CO_2 emissions of the BRIC countries account for approximately two thirds of the global average. The author also reported on the ecological footprints of these countries, which are considered heavy and involve considerable costs due to the damage caused by the inability of the ecosystems to provide services. However, Lawson et al. (2007) presented evidence that urbanization and industrialization are particularly responsible for environmental degradation, also including agricultural-related activities as a significant source of pressure on the environment. According to these authors, atmospheric pollution is a growing problem and a predictable growth consequence of the BRIC countries, given their current high energy intensity phase.

Thus, it can be acknowledged, as did Tamazian et al. (2009), that over the past few years, the BRIC economies have experienced episodes that have contributed to increased CO_2 levels, which implies adverse consequences to global mitigation strategies concerning this dire trend. In this way, looking for solutions regarding the problem of greenhouse gas emissions, May (2008) identified some alternative behavior options to consider the accelerated growth of the BRIC countries sustainable:

> [...] (i) allow the scarcity resulting from excessive growth to signal the correct use of the remaining resource reserves through the price system or (ii) invest heavily in education and technological innovation to separate development from resource exhaustion. The position of ecological economics is that there needs to be a third option: (iii) seek a path to stability, initially ensuring a better income distribution so that everyone can benefit from a sustainable economy. (May 2008, p. 4)

According to May (2008), the aforementioned behavioral options do not repudiate the actions that take advantage of market opportunities or investments in human capital and technological innovation. The goal, according to the author, is the need for caution with rapid growth due to the imminent uncertainties of their effects.

To justify the negative consequences that the accelerated economic growth of the BRIC countries has brought to the world, in their work, Pao and Tsai (2010) presented the Environmental Kuznets Curve hypothesis for the BRIC countries. Based on the work of these authors, it was concluded that increased environmental pollution occurs together with economic growth; however, it stabilizes and begins to decrease after a certain level of income per capita. In addition to these authors, Tamazian et al. (2009) also conducted studies on the adequacy of the Environmental Kuznets Curve for BRIC countries and concluded that economic development would reduce environmental degradation after high economic growth.

Moreover, according to Plotnikova (2011), though the BRICS (1) have negative scale impact on a global ecosystem, (2) show level of ecological efficiency of economic

systems at a low enough level, and (3) have the need and duty of global scale to strengthen a transition policy to ecological-oriented models of economic development, this group of countries could collectively represent the world leader of sustainable development direction driving.

It bears repeating that the rising levels of environmental pollution cannot be considered normal, as well as the exploitation of natural resources resulting from economic growth. The technological innovation initiatives, when properly assimilated, represent a promising path to reduce these detrimental trends that plunder the planet, as they may find productive alternatives that could minimize the social–environmental damage across the globe.

In terms of environmental protection, we resorted to the Kyoto Protocol, a Protocol that took effect in February 2005 with the goal of reducing Greenhouse Gas (GHG) emissions and mitigating the negative impacts of global warming. Two groups of countries were created to implement this protocol: (1) 'Annex I', developed countries accountable for the current GHG levels, requiring them to reduce their emissions, and (2) 'Non-Annex I', developing countries, large emitters but not required to reduce their emissions (United Nations 1998).

Thus, with regards to the member countries of the BRICS group, it was perceived that the only 'Annex I' country is Russia, and therefore, it committed to reduce its GHG emissions between 2008 and 2012; however, the other members of the BRICS countries (South Africa, Brazil, China, and India) are 'Non-Annex I', since they are considered developing countries and therefore are not obliged to commit to emissions reduction targets, though little by little they are adopting voluntary actions.

4. Method

The main objective in this work is to compare the efficiency of the BRICS countries in transforming productive resources and technological innovation into sustainable development. For this, the DEA technique was used, that is an Operational Research method, developed by Charnes et al. (1978), which through the empirical construction of a piecewise-linear boundary aims to determine the productive efficiency of a set of DMUs – Decision Making Units (Mariano & Rebelatto 2013).

Three DEA applications were performed, each referring to one of the sustainability dimensions: economic, environmental, and social. The initial proposal of this work predicts the presence of four variables for each analysis (economic, environmental, and social), three input variables, and one output variable. Applying the criteria proposed by Nunamaker (1985) that the number of units analyzed should be at least three times the sum of inputs and outputs used, the number of units analyzed should be at least 12. To perform this DEA processing step, the software Frontier Analyst Professional was used in the three subdivided applications.

The data collection and analysis considered the period that begun in 2000 up to 2007. To determine this, the criterion used was the availability of data and the history of the object of study (the BRICS group), that only began to be widespread in the international market in 2001. Thus, 2000 was set as the starting point for the analysis period, that is, one year prior to the creation and dissemination of the BRIC term.

According to the classification proposed by Lyytimäki et al. (2013), the three sustainability indicators generated in this work from the efficiency calculated using DEA can be classified as strategic long-term usage, since they allow identifying long-term priority and strategic action areas for the BRICS countries. Taking the work of Lyytimäki et al. (2013) as a reference, great care was taken in choosing the indicators in order to avoid the risks cited by the authors.

As the goal of the present study is to compare the efficiency of the BRICS countries in transforming productive resources and technological innovation into sustainable development, the variables selected seek to portray such issues in order to develop the analysis model. The Cobb–Douglas production function was used as a reference in this choice. Thus, with respect to the input variables, the variable chosen was the 'Gross Fixed Capital Formation' to represent the capital variable, of the original Cobb–Douglas production function; the variable 'employed population' to represent the work variable, also from the original Cobb–Douglas production function; and the 'R&D spending' to represent the countries' technological innovation, chosen based on the work of Ruffoni et al. (2004).

It is important to mention that the use of the variable R&D spending had a 1-year lag since the return for this type of spending needs a period of time to materialize. Therefore, the analysis period was adjusted by excluding the year 2000, thereby including seven periods (2001–2007) and no longer eight periods.

In the set of output variables, the 'GDP' variable was chosen to specify the countries' economic development, and this variable was chosen based on its use in studies that evaluate the sustainability of regions, as for instance in the works of Shi et al. (2004) and Zhen et al. (2009).

The second output variable chosen to translate the countries' environmental development was the 'CO$_2$ emission' indicator. This indicator has been constantly used in studies evaluating the environmental sustainability of regions, as for example in Lee and Huang (2007), Tamazian et al. (2009), Zhen et al. (2009), Boggia and Cortina (2010), Pao and Tsai (2010), and others. Furthermore, the use of 'CO$_2$ emission' was chosen as a variable for environmental development based on the Environmental Kuznets Curve (Grossman & Krueger 1991) that shows the relationship between a country's pollution and GDP per capita. Thus, as CO$_2$ is the main

greenhouse gas responsible for intensifying the greenhouse effect, the emission of this pollutant was then adopted to conduct the work described herein.

It should be noted that output variables that relate to waste and pollutants are termed 'undesirable outputs' that need to be reduced to improve the countries' performance; thus, the variable CO$_2$ emission fits in this category (Seiford & Zhu 2002). To solve this question, in this work, the method used to treat the variable CO$_2$ emission was to multiply each undesirable output by '−1'. As the DEA analysis does not allow using negative values, the value obtained by multiplying by '−1' was added to a set translation vector, ensuring that the values achieved would become positive.

And the third output variable chosen, which represents social development, was 'life expectancy at birth'. This variable was chosen based on its use in works such as in Mahlberg and Obersteiner (2001), Despotis (2005), Ramanathan (2006), Lee and Huang (2007), Zhen et al. (2009), Mariano and Rebelatto (2013), and also in the work of Sen (1998), which pointed to life expectancy as a decisive indicator to measure the success and progress of a society. In this context, and according to Gisbertt and Palleja (2006), life expectancy at birth is one of the most commonly used indicators for international comparisons.

The variables were validated by the multiple regression technique and correlation analysis, inspired by the stepwise method. The basic feature of the multiple regression technique is to identify the relationships between variables, determining the theoretical model for the three proposed analyzes (economic, environmental, and social). The stepwise method is one of the first procedures suggested by Norman and Stoker (1991) to conduct the validation of pre-selected variables and uses the correlation analysis, starting from an initial pair of the highest correlation. The result analysis achieved with the validation by linear regression and stepwise method determined how each DEA application should be conducted, that is, which inputs and outputs would be examined in the economic, social, and environment applications. Table 1 summarizes the variables used.

4.1. DEA's models and tools

The DEA has basically three options regarding the orientation of the models, input orientation, output orientation, and input–output orientation. Specifically, in this work, the use of the input orientation or doubly oriented model is considered unfavorable because the countries analyzed did not seek to reduce their inputs. As one of the objectives is to increase the countries' outputs, in other words, increase

Table 1. Variables used.

Application	Type of efficiency	Input	Output
1	Economic	Gross fixed capital formation; employed population, and R&D expenditure	GDP
2	Environmental	Gross fixed capital formation and expenditure on R&D	CO$_2$ emission
3	Social	Gross fixed capital formation; employed population and R&D expenditure	Life expectancy

$$Min \sum_{j=1}^{n} v_j \cdot x_{j0} - w$$

Subject to:

$$\sum_{i=1}^{m} u_i \cdot y_{i0} = 1$$

$$\sum_{i=1}^{m} u_i \cdot y_{ik} - \sum_{j=1}^{n} v_j \cdot x_{jk} + w \leq 0, \quad for\ k = 1, 2, ..., h$$

w without restriction of signal

Figure 1.   Output-oriented DEA-BCC model.

Notes: Wherein x_{jk} represents the amount of input j of DMU k; y_{ik} represents the amount of output i of DMU k; x_{j0} represents the amount of input j of the DMU under analysis; y_{i0} represents the amount of output i of the DMU under analysis; v_j represents the weight of input j for the DMU under analysis; u_i represents the weight of output i for the DMU under analysis; w represents the scale factor; m represents the number of outputs analyzed; n represents the number of inputs analyzed; and h represents the number of DMUs analyzed.

the BRICS group's sustainable development, the DEA model with output orientation was chosen.

The DEA model to be selected regards the relationship established between input and output, that is, the type of return to scale. In this work, the BCC model was used, which means that the outputs increase or decrease at a different rate than the inputs, respecting the issue regarding the size of the units analyzed. That means that input reductions or increases do not generate changes in the outputs in the same proportion. Figure 1 presents the output-oriented DEA-BCC model.

In general, the DEA analysis can show similar scores between efficient units, since it does not take into account factors such as the balance between variables, prior information about the weights, attributing zero weights, and others (Mariano & Rebelatto 2013). Based on this understanding, it was necessary to develop methods to differentiate these units. The research was conducted using the inverted frontier method, consisting of the following steps:

(1) Switch the place of inputs and outputs
(2) Solve the resulting model
(3) Calculate the composite index, considering the classical and inverted frontiers (Leta et al. 2005).

According to Leta et al. (2005), the composite index is calculated from the arithmetic mean between the classical

frontier index ($E_{classical}$) and the inverted frontier index subtracted from one ($1 - E_{inverted}$). To obtain values between 0 and 1, the composite index results must be standardized. According to the composite index, the most efficient DMU will be that which can show a good performance in its strong points, which is evaluated by the standard efficiency level, not showing a very bad performance in its weak points, which is measured by the efficiency obtained in the inverted frontier subtracted from one (Leta et al. 2005).

In this study, each country at a specific time was considered as a separate unit. According to Cooper et al. (2000), time-dependent analysis of DEA is known as 'window analysis', a technique that considers units of time as if it were a separate unit. The window analysis is a process similar to the moving average, where each time a new unit enters another unit exits, usually the first one that entered in the previous analysis. Cooper et al. (2000) used the following relationship to calculate the number of windows and their amplitude.

$$W = k - p + 1 \qquad (1)$$

$$p = \frac{k + 1}{2} \qquad (2)$$

wherein

W = number of windows; k = number of years and p = window amplitude.

In the work reported herein, the analysis period corresponded to 7 years ($k = 7$). Thus, the calculations determined that the number of windows for DEA would be four and the window amplitude would also be four.

5.   Results

The present study focuses on the efficiency analysis of the BRICS group to transform productive resources and technological innovation into sustainable development through the DEA. Thus, through the analysis window, the efficiency indexes of the countries studied in each window and also a total average efficiency index for each application (economic, social, and environmental) were obtained and are presented below.

The economic efficiency indices for each of the four windows constructed are shown in Table 2. It was observed

Table 2.   Efficiency results of windows, economical application.

Mean efficiency	Window				
	1 (2001–2004)	2 (2002–2005)	3 (2003–2006)	4 (2004–2007)	Mean total
South Africa	0.67	0.65	0.65	0.65	0.66
Brazil	0.98	0.98	0.99	0.99	0.98
China	0.67	0.65	0.65	0.65	0.65
India	0.49	0.48	0.49	0.51	0.49
Russia	0.54	0.52	0.50	0.50	0.51

Table 3. Efficiency results of windows, environmental applications.

Mean efficiency	Window				
	1 (2001–2004)	2 (2002–2005)	3 (2003–2006)	4 (2004–2007)	Mean total
South Africa	0.99	0.99	0.99	0.99	0.99
Brazil	0.88	0.90	0.91	0.93	0.90
China	0.28	0.23	0.18	0.14	0.21
India	0.80	0.81	0.81	0.81	0.81
Russia	0.76	0.77	0.79	0.80	0.78

Table 4. Efficiency results of windows, social applications.

Mean efficiency	Window				
	1 (2001–2004)	2 (2002–2005)	3 (2003–2006)	4 (2004–2007)	Mean total
South Africa	0.81	0.79	0.75	0.69	0.76
Brazil	0.97	0.99	0.99	0.99	0.99
China	0.57	0.57	0.56	0.55	0.56
India	0.51	0.50	0.49	0.48	0.49
Russia	0.86	0.88	0.90	0.92	0.89

that of the BRICS countries, Brazil had the highest average economic efficiency, followed by South Africa, China, Russia, and India, in descending order of efficiency.

In turn, Table 3 shows the efficiency indices of the DEA environmental application. It should be highlighted that China was classified as the country with the lowest environmental efficiency, with an average efficiency ratio of 21%, well below the average of the group of countries studied.

Finally, Table 4 shows the results of the DEA social application. As noted, with regards to the average social efficiency, Brazil leads with almost 100% of efficiency; followed by Russia, South Africa, China, and India, in order of decreasing efficiency.

The DEA results are explained in two tables, which are the basis to analyze the results. Table 5, the first table, summarizes the efficiency ranking of each country in each of the pillars of sustainability analyzed.

Table 6 was built to respond to the issues that would probably emerge from the results shown in Table 5, which shows the data referring to 2007, the input and output variables used in the DEA, for each country.

The idea of presenting only the data for 2007 was based on the fact that, in most cases, year to year stable data behavior was observed; therefore, it was decided to present the data from the most recent analysis years.

After the DEA analysis results were shown, the discussion for each individual country began.

5.1. China

Going back to the information shown in Table 6, it was noticed that China was the country of the BRICS group with the highest fixed capital, with the largest manual labor and highest investment in technological innovation. However, the economic application of DEA showed an average efficiency ratio of 65%.

Over the past three decades, China has shown rapid economic growth, going from a planned economy to a market economy through the reforms adopted in 1978 (World Bank 2011c). According to the World Bank (2011c), China currently holds the second highest world economy position and is expected to reach the first position, overtaking the United States (Wilson & Purushothaman 2003).

However, despite its comfortable economic position when compared to other BRICS countries, the analysis in this study revealed that China failed to efficiently transform its high inputs into GDP outputs, although this country presented the highest GDP in the BRICS group.

With regards to the environmental aspect, it was observed that China has the highest CO_2 levels among the BRICS countries. It therefore makes sense that this country was ranked the least efficient of the group.

In the literature consulted, we cite the work of Armijo (2007), who reports that the lack of natural resources and

Table 5. Mean efficiency ranking of BRICS, from 2001–2007.

	Economic application	Environmental application	Social application
South Africa	2nd	1st	3rd
Brazil	1st	2nd	1st
China	3rd	5th	4th
India	5th	3rd	5th
Russia	4th	4th	2nd

Table 6. Input and output, 2007.

	Gross fixed capital formation[a]	Population employed[b]	R&D[c]	Gross domestic product[d]	CO_2 emission[e]	Life expectancy[f]
South Africa	38,298,311,187	13,887,854	3,975,582	178,644,321,362	433,172	51.43
Brazil	138,994,881,914	89,950,866	16,420,804	815,703,390,474	368,015	72.16
China	930,624,500,534	740,235,780	84,043,907	2,456,684,033,218	6,533,018	72.94
India	245,751,962,059	423,228,908	21,393,437	773,393,372,039	1,611,042	63.39
Russia	100,484,784,168	71,473,738	19,630,811	410,505,209,128	1,536,099	67.50

Sources: UNESCO and World Bank. [a]Gross fixed capital formation (constant 2000, US$); [b]Labor force – Unemployment; [c]Gross domestic expenditure on R&D (constant 2005, US$); [d]Gross domestic product (constant 2000, US$); [e]$CO_2$ emissions (kt); [f]Life expectancy at birth, total (years).

environmental pollution represents two factors that tend to limit China's economic progress. Another author, May (2008), added that this could result in a bigger ecological footprint that this country could bear. Moreover, as Grumbine (2007) pointed out, China's energy production composition (dependent on power plants and coal) and its consumption are troubling aspects of this country's accelerated economic growth. According to the Central Intelligence Agency, CIA (2012a), air pollution, water scarcity and pollution, deforestation, soil erosion, desertification, and the trade of endangered species are the highlighted issues regarding China's environment.

Analyzing China's efficiency with regards to its social aspect, the data inserted in the economic and environmental analyses is reiterated. That is, despite having the highest input values in the group analyzed, China's average social efficiency is only 56%.

It is surprising to note that this occurred despite the country's highest life expectancy in the group, which is of 72.9 years. This served to demonstrate that China has the potential to achieve greater life expectancy, given the inputs considered. However, the high life expectancy is not positive in all aspects. The aging Chinese population can be considered a limiting factor to the projected economic growth, since the trend is a decrease in the working population, due to increased longevity and also due to the nationally promoted one-child policy (Qiao 2006).

China's poverty reduction coupled to economic growth observed in the last three decades was, according to the World Bank (2011c), globally acknowledged. As Dolgikh and Kokin (2009) state, China is the country with the lowest unemployment rate and the highest capacity to generate employment of the BRICS countries. Notwithstanding, according to the World Bank (2011c), poverty reduction remains this country's major challenge, since coupled to its economic rise, rural–urban migration, social inequality, and rapid urbanization also ensued. Furthermore, the per capita income in China is below the world average (CIA 2012a).

5.2. India

Returning to the data presented in Table 6, India is the second ranking country in fixed capital, manual labor, and investment in technological innovation. However, its mean

efficiency ratios show that the country has not been efficient in its use of high inputs to create its outputs.

In terms of the economic aspect of the BRICS group, India was the country that had the lowest average efficiency, 49%. Thus, it was concluded that this country can achieve, by optimizing the use of its high inputs, higher GDP levels, while also achieving better economic efficiency levels.

According to Nassif (2006), India's economic growth was evidenced between 1985 and 1990, when policy measures were adopted by the government in order to end the protectionist scenario of an inefficient industry that showed little ability to compete in the global market. Thereafter, the growth of India's economy was observed, one of the fastest growing economies, particularly based on the expansion of information technology services, according to Vieira and Veríssimo (2009). However, as reported by the CIA (2012b), the marks of former autarchic policies remain, as well as inadequate physical infrastructures, persisting high inflation, high interest rates, and the little progress of economic reforms, all of which tend to limit the country's economic growth.

The environmental analysis showed that India achieved an average efficiency ratio of 81%. However, it is plausible to declare that this rate could be higher if the use of its gross fixed capital formation inputs and R&D investments are optimized in order to reduce the levels of CO_2 emission, whose current rate is the second highest in the group studied.

Furthermore, the productive sector's excessive dependence on coal has required, according to May (2008), investments in renewable energy sources and also in alternative energy to lower the CO_2 emission levels.

Analyzing India's social aspect, it was found that the country's average efficiency ratio of 49% was the lowest in the BRICS group. This is because in spite of the fact the country holds the second to last place in input levels (after China), India ranks second to last in life expectancy, of 63.4 years.

India's economic growth brought, according to May (2008), certain social benefits, for example, the increase in per capita income, increased life expectancy and literacy rate, and also a drop in the number of people living below the poverty line. On the other hand, the World Bank (2011d) reported that poverty remains to be India's main challenge, one-third of the world's poor population. Income disparity was observed, and most of the population has not benefited from the country's economic growth; moreover, there are limited non-agricultural employment opportunities and poor access to basic education, some of the factors indicated by the CIA (2012b).

It is assumed that some factors may be related to India's low efficiency in the current analysis. One of these concerns the need to liberalize trade, and other factors are related to rural–urban migration, education, environment, and infrastructure, in addition to the permanent popular conflicts that must also be considered within the Indian context (Armijo 2007; Poddar & Yi 2007).

5.3. Brazil

Brazil was the country of the BRICS group that showed median input levels, while achieving higher efficiency rates than the other countries in the group. In the economic analysis, Brazil ranked the most efficient, with an average efficiency of 98%. That is, despite not having high levels of fixed capital, labor, and technological innovation, the country had the second highest GDP of the group and the highest economic efficiency.

Brazil, whose economy leads in South America, is a country which, according to the CIA (2012c), is characterized by having good agricultural, mining, manufacturing, and service sectors. Leme (2006) reports that the measures adopted, with emphasis on macroeconomic stability aiming to increase the country's economic growth, resulted in reduced inflation and public debt. Thus, although in recent decades Brazil has presented the lowest GDP growth rate of the BRICS countries, Vieira and Veríssimo (2009) attributed this performance to the measures implemented to cool the economy and curb inflation. In this study, Brazil stood out as the most efficient country in the economic application. Thus, we can assume that if Brazil increases its inputs, while maintaining its economic policy, it can achieve higher GDP output values.

The environmental analysis of Brazil made it clear once again that it is possible to do more with less. Despite its median input levels, the country managed to stand out as the country that emitted less CO_2 levels and achieved an average efficiency ratio of 90%. This was not the highest efficiency index of the group, which belongs to South Africa, but it was a satisfactory efficiency value.

The World Bank (2011b) pointed out that, while the country has made progress in reducing forest deforestation and has become one of the leaders in climate negotiations – pledging on a voluntary basis to further reduce greenhouse gas emissions – Brazil has faced challenges to combine the benefits from agricultural growth, environmental protection, and sustainable development. Deforestation of the Amazon region, the illegal wildlife trade, soil degradation, water pollution, and oil spills represent some of the other problems related to the Brazilian environment (CIA 2012c).

In the social aspect, Brazil stood out in the BRICS group with the highest efficiency level, which was 99%. This is because, despite having median inputs, the country had the second highest life expectancy of the group, of around 72.16 years.

With regard to Brazil's social aspect, some observations are made. According to May (2008), because of Brazil's colonial legacy, it is considered one of the most unequal countries in the world, although there has been a decrease in income inequality and has also achieved the lowest unemployment rate in its history, of about 4.7% in December 2011, according to the data from the CIA (2012c). On the other hand, the stable economic growth policy has benefited the low-income population with improved social welfare, despite the social disparities still observed. In addition, there have been innovative social programs that seek inclusive economic growth, which resulted in a reduction of social inequality, as for instance the Social Assistance *Bolsa Família* Program (World Bank 2011b).

5.4. Russia

With regard to Russia's input and output levels, the country fell within the median level category in the group. Considering its inputs, this country showed a great similarity with Brazil, which also showed median input levels.

However, the data obtained in the economic analysis showed that Russia achieved a low level of average efficiency (51%). This is because when compared with the other BRICS countries, the country had a low GDP value.

According to the CIA (2012d), Russia has undergone significant changes with the collapse of the Soviet Union, as the country is no longer an isolated global economy, and became a market-based economy, meaning that it is globally inserted. Thus, authors such as Macfarquhar (2007) recognized that, despite the deep economic depression that occurred during the 1990s, since 1999, Russia has had a rapid expansion. According to the opinion of other authors, such as Vieira and Veríssimo (2009), this economic growth was achieved on account of the high oil prices, the production growth of industries and services, and also by stimulating the domestic market. However, Russia has not yet achieved its best economic phase, since the vulnerability of its economy is mainly attributed to the fact that it focuses exclusively on the exploitation of natural resources, which tends to limit its economic growth (Armijo 2007).

In the environmental analysis, Russia obtained an average efficiency ratio of 78%. This index is due to the country's CO_2 emission levels, which are very high when compared with their median input levels.

According to Armijo (2007) and Dolgikh and Kokin (2009), Russia's intense economic growth was supported by the exploitation of energy resources. Thus, caution and attention are required for the environmental problems facing the country, regarding its energy matrix that is significantly dependent on fossil fuels. This causes the

CO_2 emission level per capita to be similar to the largest world emitters and the largest among the BRICS countries, according to May (2008). Deforestation, erosion and soil contamination, water contamination, and the lack of efficiency in municipal solid waste management are, according to the CIA (2012d), some of the other environmental problems facing the country.

In the social aspect, Russia obtained an average efficiency index of 89%. This ratio was considered good, since it classified Russia in second place for the social analysis efficiency. This ranking was achieved due to the fact that, despite the country's median input levels, of the BRICS group, Russia ranks third in life expectancy, 67.5 years.

According to the World Bank (2011e), there were gains in the living conditions of the Russian population since the turn of the century, with strong growth in employment, wages, and income for most of the population. Moreover, between 1999 and 2003, a significant decline in poverty was observed, placing the country in first place in GDP per capita of the BRICS group (UNDP 2006; Dolgikh & Kokin 2009). All these factors may have contributed to Russia achieving second place in social efficiency, as reported in this study.

However, in conclusion, it can be assumed that this country can do more with their inputs to maximize their outputs and therefore achieve a higher efficiency level. In addition, there is the vulnerability of the Russian economy, which is mainly due to the concentrated exploitation of natural resources. This also seems to be hindering development, insofar as it can result in a de-industrialization process and a consequent currency devaluation (Armijo 2007).

5.5. *South Africa*

South Africa is undoubtedly the BRICS country that showed the lowest levels of inputs and outputs.

One of the initiatives of the South African government was launching a strategic plan for the period of 2009–2014, choosing priorities such as more inclusive economic growth, infrastructure, rural development, food security, agrarian reform, education, crime reduction, improved public services, sustainable management of resources, and their proper use, among other factors (World Bank 2011a).

However, the economic analysis for this country showed an average efficiency index of 66%. This was due to their low levels of inputs and also low GDP output.

The fact is that little by little the country has gained prominence in the international economic scenario, becoming more active in events such as meetings of the International Monetary Fund and G20 (19 largest economies plus the European Union). However, South Africa still suffers from the influences of its complex history of oppression and violence (World Bank 2011a). According to reports from the CIA (2012e), it can be admitted that

South Africa's outdated infrastructure also tends to limit its economic growth.

With regards to the environmental analysis, it was observed that South Africa is considered the most efficient country in the group, with an average efficiency ratio of 99%. It is not difficult to find the answer to this high level of efficiency, since South Africa is the country with the lowest levels of inputs, and it is possible that due to this it has the lowest level of CO_2 emissions of the BRICS group.

Socially, South Africa achieved an average efficiency index of 76%. The low input levels resulted in a low output level for life expectancy (51.4 years). This country had the lowest life expectancy of the BRICS group, much lower than the group average. However, it should be noted that the low life expectancy in this country may be due to the numerous cases of HIV and tuberculosis, violence, and other problems inherited from the apartheid regime (World Bank 2011a). In addition to the low life expectancy, unemployment was also taken into consideration by the CIA (2012e), a serious problem for the country's social development.

Thus, it is reasonable to say that despite South Africa's position as a leader in the sub-regional and continental levels, the country continues to have significant income and wealth differences. The economic growth observed in the country's post-apartheid resulted in increasing social inequality and also high unemployment rates and the limited access of the poor population to basic services, which are some of the problems this country faces (World Bank 2011a).

6. Conclusions

The international economic scenario has demonstrated a new dynamics with respect to the accelerated economic growth of some countries to the detriment of others; countries that in the past were considered unshakable economic powers are currently losing ground to those which in the past showed no prominence whatsoever. On the other hand, the emerging countries deserve recognition, formerly called underdeveloped countries, but which are currently gaining space in the international economic arena, as for instance the countries that make up the BRICS group.

What is observed is that the current world order and its requirements demonstrate that the way to grow is no longer considered sustainable, in other words, economic growth measured by GDP should no longer be the only performance parameter of nations. The constant battles for diligence and attention to social and environmental issues have demanded a new behavior from countries in order to ensure sustainability.

Therefore, this work sought to determine the efficiency of the BRICS countries with regards to transforming productive resources and technological innovation into sustainable development. The efficiency ratings in the three DEA applications (economic, environmental, and social)

brought to light some results that can be of interest for more specific scientific explorations.

Among the findings, the main highlight of the BRICS group was Brazil, whose results suggest that GDP growth may be the result of a more humane production mode, with a simultaneous increase in income distribution and environmental attention. It should be emphasized that the DEA is an analysis technique for relative efficiency, thus the focus on Brazil only refers to a comparative analysis within the BRICS group.

On the other hand, the development of this work helps to reflect on China's productive mode, which despite having the highest GDP of the group, was, surprisingly, the third of the group in economic efficiency because its inputs are very high. This suggests that China should work more efficiently in order to reduce its inputs to continue its high economic growth in the long term. In addition, the high levels of CO_2 emissions, the predatory productive mode adopted by the country long ago, and its social problems were highlighted.

With regard to India, it was highlighted that this country is in a scenario of little progress in economic reforms and also a compromised social scenario due to poverty. Thus, India has serious social issues that may be impacting its economic efficiency. Therefore, it is suggested that India should primarily address the problem of poverty in their society through social programs, as was observed in Brazil in recent years.

As for Russia, it can be emphasized that despite its economic improvement after the recession of the 1990s, the country is still affected by the vulnerability of its economy. Additionally, it is the largest CO_2 emitter per capita of the BRICS group, and its economy depends on the exploitation of natural resources. Thus, it is suggested that Russia should invest in sustainable technology to jointly solve their economic and environmental problems. However, since the turn of the century, this country has seen social gains.

Finally, South Africa is a country that emits low levels of CO_2 when compared with other BRICS countries, and this is because their production levels are also low. Moreover, the country shows significant improvement in its social setting, despite the persistence of problems inherited from the Apartheid era. As shown earlier, South Africa joined the BRICS group by presenting economic growth potential. However, its economy is still smaller than that of other countries in the group. Therefore, the great challenge for this country is to grow, maintaining their low CO_2 levels and social improvements.

The goal of the comparative study of the BRICS countries' efficiency to transform productive resources and technological innovation into sustainable development had no intention to bring definitive conclusions. Nevertheless, this work has enabled the construction of an interesting comparison chart between the BRICS countries, and this analysis could be replicated for other groups of countries in different situations from those observed in the BRICS group.

We believe this study represents an initial step for performing new analysis works on the subject. It is reasonable to assume that adding other variables, or even replacing some variables, new and relevant results can be achieved. Furthermore, implementing other research methods, with new tools, could also be helpful to attain results that could be compared with the results that were achieved in the present work.

References

Alier JM, Pascual U, Vivien FD, Zaccai E. 2010. Sustainable degrowth: mapping the context, criticisms and future prospects of an emergent paradigm. Ecol Econ. 69:1741–1747. doi:10.1016/j.ecolecon.2010.04.017.

Amorim C. 2010. Existe realmente o BRIC? [Is there really BRIC?] Revista Economia Exterior. 52nd ed. Espanha: Estudios de Política Exterior SA.

Armijo LE. 2007. The BRICS countries (Brazil, Russia, India, and China) as analytical category: mirage or insight? Asian Perspect. 31:7–42.

Bebbington J, Larrinaga C. 2014. Accounting and sustainable development: an exploration. Account Org Soc. doi:10.1016/j.aos.2014.01.003.

Boggia A, Cortina C. 2010. Measuring sustainable development using a multi-criteria model: a case study. J Environ Manage. 91:2301–2306. doi:10.1016/j.jenvman.2010.06.009.

[CIA] Central Intelligence Agency. 2012a. [Internet]. [cited 2012 Apr]. Available from: https://www.cia.gov/library/publications/the-world-factbook/geos/ch.html

[CIA] Central Intelligence Agency. 2012b. [Internet]. [cited 2012 Apr]. Available from: https://www.cia.gov/library/publications/the-world-factbook/geos/in.html

[CIA] Central Intelligence Agency. 2012c. [Internet]. [cited 2012 Apr]. Available from: https://www.cia.gov/library/publications/the-world-factbook/geos/br.html

[CIA] Central Intelligence Agency. 2012d. [Internet]. [cited 2012 Apr]. Available from: https://www.cia.gov/library/publications/the-world-factbook/geos/rs.html

[CIA] Central Intelligence Agency. 2012e. [Internet]. [cited 2012 Apr]. Available from: https://www.cia.gov/library/publications/the-world-factbook/geos/sf.html

Charnes A, Cooper WW, Rhodes E. 1978. Measuring the efficiency of decision-making units. Eur J Oper Res. 2:429–444. doi:10.1016/0377-2217(78)90138-8.

Cooper WW, Seiford LM, Tone K. 2000. Data development analysis: a comprehensive text with models, applications, references and DEA-solver software. London: Kluwer Academic Publishers.

Cracolici MF, Cuffaro M, Nijkamp P. 2010. The measurement of economic, social and environmental performance of countries: a novel approach. Soc Indicators Res. 95:339–356. doi:10.1007/s11205-009-9464-3.

Despotis DK. 2005. A reassessment of the human development index via data envelopment analysis. J Oper Res Soc. 56:969–980. doi:10.1057/palgrave.jors.2601927.

Dittmar M. 2014. Development towards sustainability: how to judge past and proposed policies? Sci Total Environ. 472:282–288. doi:10.1016/j.scitotenv.2013.11.020.

Dolgikh E, Kokin S. 2009. The Chinese economy and the other BRIC countries: the comparative analysis. Paper presented at: International Conference on Management Science & Engineering; Moscow

Fredericks SE. 2012. Justice in sustainability indicators and indexes. Int J Sust Dev World Ecol. 19:490–499. doi:10.1080/13504509.2012.714807.

Gisbertt FJG, Pallejá RP. 2006. Esperanza de vida en España a lo largo del siglo XX: las tablas de mortalidad del Instituto Nacional de Estadística. Documentos de trabajo, Fundación BBVA [Internet]. Available from: http://www.fbbva.es/TLFU/dat/DT_2006_11.pdf

Grossman GM, Krueger AB. 1991. Environmental impacts of a North American free trade agreement [working paper no. 3914]. National Bureau of Economic Research. Cambridge (MA): MIT Press.

Grumbine RE. 2007. China's emergence and the prospects for global sustainability. Bioscience. 57:249–255. doi:10.1641/B570308.

Hansmann R, Mieg HA, Frischknecht P. 2012. Principal sustainability components: empirical analysis of synergies between the three pillars of sustainability. Int J Sust Dev World Ecol. 19:451–459. doi:10.1080/13504509.2012.696220.

Hueting R. 2010. Why environmental sustainability can most probably not be attained with growing production. J Cleaner Prod. 18:525–530. doi:10.1016/j.jclepro.2009.04.003.

[IUCN] International Union for Conservation of Nature and Natural Resources. (1980). World conservation strategy: living resource conservation for sustainable development [Internet; cited 2013 Mar 9]. Available from: http://www.data.iucn.org/dbtw-wpd/edocs/WCS-004.pdf

Jacobs LM, Van Rossem R. 2013. The BRIC phantom: a comparative analysis of the BRICs as a category of rising powers. J Policy Model. doi:10.1016/j.jpolmod.2013.10.008.

Kaivo-oja J, Panula-Ontto J, Vehmas J, Luukkanen J. 2013. Relationships of the dimensions of sustainability as measured by the sustainable society index framework. Int J Sust Dev World Ecol. doi:10.1080/13504509.2013.860056.

Lastres HMM, Cassiolato J, Matos M, Szapiro M, Zucoloto G, Koeller P. 2007. Estudo comparativo dos sistemas nacionais de inovação no Brazil, Russia, India e South Africa (BRICS). RedeSist. 2nd ed. Rio de Janeiro: Redesist. Available from: http://brics.redesist.ie.ufrj.br/Projeto%20BRICS.pdf

Lawson S, Heacock D, Stupnytska A. 2006. BRICs and beyond. New York (NY): Goldman Sachs Economic Research Group. Chapter 9, Building the BRICs: infrastructure opportunities; p. 115–120.

Lawson S, Heacock D, Stupnytska A. 2007. BRICs and beyond. New York (NY): Goldman Sachs Economic Research Group. Chapter 8, Why the BRICs dream should be green; p. 109–114.

Lee YJ, Huang CM. 2007. Sustainability index for Taipei. Environ Impact Assess Rev. 27:505–521. doi:10.1016/j.eiar.2006.12.005.

Leme P. 2006. BRICs and beyond. New York (NY): Goldman Sachs Economic Research Group. Chapter 5, The 'B' in BRICs: unlocking Brazil's growth potential; p. 73–84.

Leta FR, Soares de Mello JCCB, Gomes E, Ângulo-Meza L. 2005. Métodos de melhora de ordenação em DEA aplicados à avaliação estática de tornos mecânicos. [Methods of improvement of order in DEA applied to static evaluation of lathes]. Investigação Operacional. 25:229–242.

Lopes R, Thomas V, Wang Y. 2008. The quality of growth: fiscal policies for better results [IEG working paper]. Washington (DC): IEG IEG-World Bank.

Lyytimäki J, Tapio P, Varho V., Söderman T. 2013. The use, non-use and misuse of indicators in sustainability assessment and communication. Int J Sust Dev World Ecol. 20:385–393. doi:10.1080/13504509.2013.834524.

MacFarquhar R. 2007. BRICs and beyond. New York (NY): Goldman Sachs Economic Research Group. Chapter 2, Russia: a smooth political transition; p. 27–43.

Mahlberg B, Obersteiner M. 2001. Remeasuring the HDI by data envelopment analysis [Interim Report IR-01-069].

International Institute for Applied Systems Analysis (IIASA). Laxenburg.

Mariano EB, Rebelatto DAN. 2013. Transformation of wealth produced into quality of life: analysis of the social efficiency of nation-states with the DEA's triple index approach. J Oper Res Soc. doi:10.1057/jors.2013.132.

May PH. 2008. Como superar as contradições entre crescimento e sustentabilidade? Inovações institucionais nos BRICS. In: Dupas G, editor. Meio ambiente e crescimento econômico: Tensões estruturais. São Paulo: Ed. UNESP; p. 229–264.

Meadows DH, Meadows DI, Randers J, Behrens WW III. 1972. The limits to growth. New York (NY): Universe Books.

Meadows DH, Randers J, Meadows DL. 2004. Limits to growth: the 30-year update. White River Junction (VT): Chelsea Green.

Morais P, Camanho AS. 2011. Evaluation of performance of European cities with the aim to promote quality of life improvements. Omega. 39:398–409. doi:10.1016/j.omega.2010.09.003.

Nassif A. 2006. A economia indiana no período 1950–2004 – Da estagnação ao crescimento acelerado: lições para o Brazil? [Texto para Discussão, no. 107]. Rio de Janeiro: BNDES. Available from: http://www.bndes.gov.br/SiteBNDES/export/sites/default/bndes_pt/Galerias/Arquivos/conhecimento/td/td-107.pdf

Norman M, Stoker B. 1991. Data envelopment analysis: the assessment of performance. Chichester: Wiley.

Nunamaker TR. 1985. Using data envelopment analysis to measure the efficiency of non-profit organizations: a critical evaluation. Managerial Decis Econ. 6:50–58. doi:10.1002/mde.4090060109.

Olmedo LJI, Martín EB, Gallardo EMP. 2009. Tres medidas complementarias de desigualdad [Three complementary measures of inequality]. Estadística Española. 51:363–394.

O'Neill J. 2001. Building better global economic BRICs [global economics paper, no. 66]. New York (NY): Goldman Sachs Economic Research Group. Available from: http://www.content.gs.com/japan/ideas/brics/building-better-pdf.pdf

O'Neill J. 2007. BRICs and beyond. New York (NY): Goldman Sachs Economic Research Group. Chapter 12, Current Answers (and questions) about BRICs and the N-11; p. 151–158.

ÖNİŞ Z, Kutlay M. 2013. Rising powers in a changing global order: the political economy of Turkey in the age of BRICs. Third World Q. 34:1409–1426. doi:10.1080/01436597.2013.831541.

Pao HT, Tsai CM. 2010. CO_2 emissions, energy consumption and economic growth in BRIC countries. Energy Policy. 38:7850–7860. doi:10.1016/j.enpol.2010.08.045.

Plotnikova GA. 2011. BRIC-countries potential and state policy of sustainable development. Paper presented at: XVIII International Conference on Management Science & Engineering; 2011 Sep 13–15; Roma.

Poddar T, Yi E. 2007. BRICs and beyond. New York (NY): Goldman Sachs Economic Research Group. Chapter 1, India's rising growth potential; p. 9–25.

Pope J, Annandale D, Saunders AM. 2004. Conceptualising sustainability assessment. Environ Impact Assess Rev. 24:595–616. doi:10.1016/j.eiar.2004.03.001.

Qiao HH. 2006. BRICs and beyond. New York (NY): Goldman Sachs Economic Research Group. Chapter 3, Will China grow old before getting rich?; p. 45–57.

Ramanathan R. 2006. Evaluating the comparative performance of countries of the Middle East and North Africa: a DEA application. Socio Econ Plann Sci. 40:156–167. doi:10.1016/j.seps.2004.10.002.

Ranis G, Stewart F, Ramirez A. 2000. Economic growth and human development. World Dev. 28:197–219. doi:10.1016/S0305-750X(99)00131-X.

Ruffoni J, Zawislak PA, Lacerda JS. 2004. Uma análise comparativa entre indicadores de desenvolvimento tecnológico e de crescimento econômico para grupo de países. Paper presented at: XXIII Simpósio de Gestão da Inovação Tecnológica; 19 a 22 de outubro de 2004; Curitiba.

Sachs I. 2001. Repensando o crescimento econômico e o progresso social: o âmbito da política. In: Arbix G, Zilbovicius M, Abramovay R. (Orgs.), editors. Razões e ficções do desenvolvimento. São Paulo: Editora Unesp/Edusp.

Schneider F, Kallis G, Alie JM. 2010. Crisis or opportunity? Economic degrowth for social equity and ecological sustainability. Introduction to this special issue. J Cleaner Prod. 18:511–518. doi:10.1016/j.jclepro.2010.01.014.

Seiford LM, Zhu J. 2002. Modeling undesirable factors in efficiency evaluation. Eur J Oper Res. 142:16–20. doi:10.1016/S0377-2217(01)00293-4.

Sen A. 1998. Mortality as an indicator of economic success and failure. Econ J. 108:1–25. doi:10.1111/1468-0297.00270.

Sen A. 1999. Development as a freedom. 1st ed. Oxford: Oxford University Press.

Sharma R. 2012. Broken BRICs: why the rest stopped rising. Foreign Aff. 91:2–7.

Shi C, Hutchinson SM, Xu S. 2004. Evaluation of coastal zone sustainability: an integrated approach applied in Shanghai Municipality and Chong Ming Island. J Environ Manage. 71:335–344. doi:10.1016/j.jenvman.2004.03.009.

Suri T, Boozer MA, Ranis G, Stewart F. 2011. Paths to success: the relationship between human development and economic growth. World Dev. 39:506–522. doi:10.1016/j.worlddev.2010.08.020.

Tamazian A, Chousa JP, Vadlamannati KC. 2009. Does higher economic and financial development lead to environmental degradation: evidence from BRIC countries. Energy Policy. 37:246–253. doi:10.1016/j.enpol.2008.08.025.

Trainer T. 2012. De-growth: do you realise what it means? Futures. 44:590–599. doi:10.1016/j.futures.2012.03.020.

Tseng CY. 2009. Technological innovation in the BRIC economies: a comparative study based on patent citation data demonstrates the premium these countries place on innovation. Res Technol Manage. 52:29–35.

United Nations. 1998. Kyoto protocol to the United Nations framework convention on climate change [Internet]. [cited 2012 Jun]. Available from: http://unfccc.int/resource/docs/convkp/kpeng.pdf

[UNDP] United Nations Program for Development. 2006. Human development report. Beyond scarcity: power, poverty and the global water crisis. New York (NY): United Nations Development Programme (UNDP).

Vieira FV, Veríssimo MP. 2009. Crescimento econômico em economias emergentes selecionadas: Brasil, Rússia, Índia, China (BRIC) e África do Sul. Economia e Sociedade. 18:513–546. doi:10.1590/S0104-06182009000300004.

Whitehead M. 2013. Editorial: degrowth or regrowth? Environ Value. 22:141–145. doi:10.3197/096327113X13581561725077.

Wilson D, Purushothaman R. 2003. Dreaming with BRICs: the path to 2050 [global economics paper, no. 99] [Internet]. New York (NY): Goldman Sachs Economic Research Group. Available from: http://www.goldmansachs.com/our-thinking/archive/archive-pdfs/brics-dream.pdf

World Bank. 2011a. [Internet]. [cited 2011 Jul]. Available from: http://web.worldbank.org/WBSITE/EXTERNAL/COUNTRIES/AFRICAEXT/SOUTHAFRICAEXTN/0,menuPK:368086~pagePK:141132~piPK:141107~theSitePK:368057,00.html

World Bank. 2011b. [Internet]. [cited 2011 Jul]. Available from: http://web.worldbank.org/WBSITE/EXTERNAL/COUNTRIES/LACEXT/BRAZILEXTN/0,contentMDK:20189430~pagePK:141137~piPK:141127~theSitePK:322341,00.html

World Bank. 2011c. [Internet]. [cited 2011 Jul]. Available from: http://www.worldbank.org/en/country/china/overview

World Bank. 2011d. [Internet]. [cited 2011 Jul]. Available from: http://www.worldbank.org.in/WBSITE/EXTERNAL/COUNTRIES/SOUTHASIAEXT/INDIAEXTN/0,contentMDK:20195738~pagePK:141137~piPK:141127~theSitePK:295584,00.html

World Bank. 2011e. [Internet]. [cited 2011 Jul]. Available from: http://web.worldbank.org/WBSITE/EXTERNAL/COUNTRIES/ECAEXT/RUSSIANFEDERATIONEXTN/0,contentMDK:21054807~menuPK:517666~pagePK:1497618~piPK:217854~theSitePK:305600,00.html

World Commission on Environment and Development. 1987. Our common future (Brundtland report). Oxford: Oxford University Press.

Yao X, Watanabe C, Li Y. 2009. Institutional structure of sustainable development in BRICs: focusing on ICT utilization. Technol Soc. 31:9–28. doi:10.1016/j.techsoc.2008.10.013.

Zhen L, Cao S, Wei Y, Dilly O, Liu X, Li F, Koenig H, Tscherning K, Helming K. 2009. Comparison of sustainability issues in two sensitive areas of China. Environ Sci Policy. 12:1153–1167. doi:10.1016/j.envsci.2009.03.002.

Social learning for sustainability: supporting sustainable business in Brazil regarding multiple social actors, relationships and interests

Marcia Juliana d'Angelo and Janette Brunstein

Center for Applied Social Sciences, Universidade Presbiteriana Mackenzie, São Paulo, Brazil

Finding solutions for complex environmental, economic and social issues in organisations relies on coordinated actions among several social actors that are involved in the sustainable development web and demands that they learn new business methods. In this scenario, which involves multiple social actors, relationships, contexts and interests, social learning has emerged as a hybrid approach to resolving complex environmental and social problems. Such an approach marks a different situation for organisations whose focus is not only on supporting such problem resolution but also on transforming such crises into opportunities to generate sustainable products and services. Thus, this study discusses how one of the largest companies in Latin America's chemical segment formed a network with 23 social actors and is socially learning to deal with the dialectic between return on investments for its shareholders and benefits for its stakeholders. Research was conducted based on Boje's narrative analysis. The data was built through interviews, informal conversations, textual and audio-visual documents and non-participant observation. This paper discusses the concept and describes the social learning process for sustainability (in this case, for sustainable agriculture) from the viewpoint of a for-profit organisation. In this manner, this study contributes to strengthening the connection between social learning and sustainability.

1. Introduction

Social learning for sustainability has emerged as a hybrid approach to the resolution of complex social and environmental problems (Kilvington 2007, 2010). Such an approach is a different reality for organisations focused not only on merely resolving these problems but also on creating opportunities for the generation of sustainable and lucrative products and services. Thus, this paper presents a case study to discuss the central theme of how an organisation and its network of multiple social actors in Brazil are socially learning to deal with the dialectic between return on investment for shareholders and benefits to its other audiences of interest.

Glasser (2007, p. 56) recognised that 'there is as yet no widely accepted, clear and coherent interpretation of social learning. It goes without saying that there is also no lucid, well-developed social learning for sustainability paradigm'. The authors of the Stockholm Environment Institute (SEI) Project Report on Social Learning and Sustainability from the SEI (Swartling et al. 2011) agree that social learning is defined in various ways and recognise that, while having a single definition may be problematic, an equally challenging goal for scholars of this theme is adherence to a consensual definition of social learning.

Another reflection of the SEI Project Report (Swartling et al. 2011, p. 11) is that 'using social learning synonymously with other terms or with fields of research is problematic'. The authors argue that 'if social learning is everything, it loses its meaningfulness'. They add that 'striving for terminological specificity and conceptual clarity is a worthwhile goal, as is having terms that are accessible to individuals working in a diverse array of fields'.

Besides the difficulty of defining this construct, the SEI Project Report identified three other relevant issues emerging in the social learning debate. The first refers to creating social processes and spaces that foster interactions promoting dialogue regarding the relations between learning and variables such as confidence, communication and social capital, and also between learning and collaborative and participative processes. The second issue refers to the comparability of cases investigated in studies about social learning, which presents a great challenge for scholars due to the wide variety of research; is it possible to have strong, significant comparisons? Can results be aggregated over the course of cases in the absence of similar methods and epistemologies? The third issue emphasises the need to deepen the conceptual discernment of social learning.

Despite these difficulties, researchers who participated in the SEI Project Report acknowledge the importance of strengthening the connection between social learning and sustainability since attaining sustainable trajectories requires learning quickly as well as learning to avoid unsustainable behaviours:

We need to improve our understanding of the ways in which learning can benefit society and the environment.

What kinds of learning would help individuals, groups, organizations and society achieve better results? Learning is central to adaptation as actions are changed in response to feedback. Learning also has a pivotal role to play in transformations, where systems' trajectories need to be questioned critically and possibly altered. This often requires making difficult decisions in the arena of 'hard politics'. What tradeoffs are critical to sustainability? The foregoing takes learning into the domain of social change, where establishing values and creating innovative institutions are required for sustainability. (Swartling et al. 2011, p. 11)

This being so, it is an opportune moment for studies in this field. Traditionally, research on social learning for sustainability has been more geared towards ecosystems management and natural resources, resolution of environmental problems, dealing with climate change and fostering environmental learning, as shown in the SEI Project Report (Swartling et al. 2011). However, few studies, in Brazil and the international literature, have examined social learning for sustainability from the perspective of for-profit organisations. This study intends to make its contribution to filling this gap by investigating how the process of social learning for sustainability, undertaken at a for-profit organisation located in Brazil (the chemical company[1]), considered one of the largest companies in Latin America's chemical segment, favours negotiation among its network of multiple social actors in the quest for balanced interests.

The main objective of this study is to present a case study to discuss the social learning for sustainability experiences of the chemical company, to analyse how its network of multiple social actors are engaged in discourse and action whilst still considering the company's need to engage in sustainable business. At the end, we intend to present the implications of this process to arrive at a better understanding of the meaning of social learning in a for-profit organisation.

The study's specific objectives are:

(1) To identify and map the social learning for sustainability elements in a large scale for-profit organisation's sustainable business programme.
(2) To describe and analyse the organisational spaces and environments that favour social learning.
(3) To discuss the concept of social learning for sustainability in the context of a for-based organisation located in Brazil.

To meet these objectives, we selected the Programme for Environmental Compliance and Education, in the town of Bebedouro, in the state of São Paulo. In addition, this programme was created in 1984 to promote the recovery of the native forests on the banks of the Paraíba do Sul River, in the town of Guaratinguetá, in the state of São Paulo. This initiative was triggered by Brazilian environmental legislation and evolved that included environmental education and consultancy actions for the development of sustainable agriculture. The environmental compliance programme guides and supports rural producers in the recovery and restoration of permanent preservation areas, aiming to protect biodiversity. The environmental actions include activities in public schools, teacher training and raising young people's awareness of the 'importance of sustainability' (Foundation 2011, p. 12).

This case is emblematic for studying social learning for sustainability because, despite being based on a single organisation's viewpoint, it covers a successful experience that includes fundamental elements for studying a social learning process, which are:

- a multiplicity of social actors: rural producers, students, teachers and parents that constitute this programme's relationship network, along with a cooperative, a foundation for the promotion of sustainable development, agricultural technicians, a university, a financial institution, government (municipal and federal), social entrepreneurship organisations and financing agents, totalling 23 social actors, all involved in a web of multiple interests, contexts and relationships;
- a solid and lasting initiative over the course of almost 30 years (1984–2014), which saw numerous changes in the Brazilian environmental legislation together with generations of government and corporate administrations;
- the resolution of conflicts between rural landowners, civil society, government and the organisation itself;
- a process of educating new generations in schools and local communities.

Over these 30 years, this programme has not lost strength; on the contrary, it has been expanded to other towns, growth that has allowed a consistent social learning process to be observed. Figure 1 shows the programme's main indicators.

We hope that this study contributes to strengthening the connection between social learning and sustainability, an undertaking recommended by social learning for sustainability theorists for the advancement of these study fields (Swartling et al. 2011). In the corporate world, we hope this work can help other organisations find elements that help them to construct their own social learning narratives and stories over the course of or as part of their value chain.

2. In search of a new social learning for sustainability process in business administration

Social learning theory was not originally intended to deal with the management of ecosystems, governance, climate change and environmental education. Rather, it was conceived to discuss and understand individual learning in distinct social contexts. However, from its first formulation 'the term social learning conceals great diversity', according to Parson and Clark (1995, p. 429):

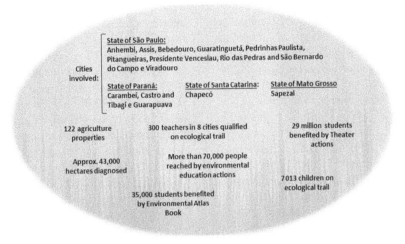

Figure 1.   Indicators of the Programme for Environmental Compliance and Education.

Source: Foundation (2011), The Chemical Company (2013).

That many researches describe the phenomena they are examining as 'social learning' does not necessarily indicate a common theoretical perspective, disciplinary heritage, or even language, concepts, and research methods of a half-dozen major disciplines; they focus on individuals, groups, formal organizations, professional communities, or entire societies; they use different definitions of learning, of what it means for learning to be 'social' and of theory. The deepest difference is that for some, social learning, means learning by individuals that takes place in social settings and/or is socially conditioned; for others it means learning by social aggregates.

Other applications of the social learning concept are mentioned by Glasser (2007), for example, in the transmission of culture (Boyd & Richerson 1985); in human behavioural and psychological problems (Bandura 1977; Rosenthal & Zimmerman 1978; Gardner & Stern 1996); in political and planning research (Heclo 1974; Friedmann & Abonyi 1976; Robinson 2003); in management and organisational change theory (Mckenzie-Mohr & Smith 1999; Wegner 1999); in the provision of human services (Goldstein 1981); in environmental politics (Webler et al. 1995; Fiorino 2001) and currently in environmental and natural resource management (Lee 1995; Leeuwis & Pybyrn 2002; Keen et al. 2005). To this last application, we add authors Pahl-Wostl

(2002), Pahl-Wostl et al. (2007) and Kilvington (2007, 2010) and in the theory of strategic group identity, we add Peteraf and Shanley (1997).

In an effort to understand the process of social learning for sustainability in business administration within this broad diversity of applications, this study provides to a theoretical review that reflects how the concept of social learning psychology on the individual level was appropriated by the field of collective sustainability learning in organisations. Four relationship axes exist between these constructs, as shown in Figure 2.

The original proposal of social learning theory – axis I – was developed in the 1970s by Albert Bandura, a social behaviourist, to describe how individuals learn and alter their behaviours within a social context. It combines elements of behavioural and cognitive theories, suggesting that observational learning and reciprocal interactions between environmental, behavioural and cognitive factors impact individual decision-making. It postulates that social actors model their behaviours on the references of others so that they can vicariously learn about uncertain environments. Learning vicariously means that, when one watches other individuals performing a task, expectations about one's own capacities increase. In this process, an

Figure 2.   Relationships between the social learning concept and other constructs.

Source: The authors.

individual learns a behavioural trait by observing that of other individuals (Bandura 1977). This study came to be considered as the sociocognitive theory of individual learning. Social cognition consists of an approach to understanding human social behaviour through investigation of the mental process of individuals interacting with others (Godoi & Freitas 2008). It tries to understand how aspects of social knowledge affect the attitudes and behaviours of individuals in diverse social situations and how to bring about changes in their knowledge (Tenbrunsel et al. 2004 apud Godoi & Freitas 2008). Summing up, according to Bandura (1977), human behaviour is explained via the influences of behavioural, cognitive and environmental structures. That is, the locus of learning is the social interactions between the individuals and environment.

The transfer of social learning theory to the organisational learning sphere – axis II – was possible because the authors who consider the sociocognitive perspective in organisational learning, such as Antonacopoulou and Chiva (2007), Elkjaer (2001, 2003) and Defillippi and Ornstein (2003), base themselves on the premises that (1) individuals learn via social interaction within a sociocultural context; (2) organisations recognise the organisational context in the learning process and (3) knowledge is generated on the basis of interpersonal relations and interpretations developed during daily organisational practices (Godoi & Freitas 2008).

Elkjaer (2003) uses social theory to show that learning results from daily life experiences, and therefore organisational learning can be based on social learning theory. Thus, his organisational learning proposal, whose presuppositions are principally based on Dewey's studies, is anchored upon a three-element structure. The content of organisational learning relates to an individual's effort to become a practitioner of some activity, area or thematic, since learning is a way of being and becoming part of an organisation's social world. The learning process is necessarily attached to the participation and interaction of individuals within the organisation. Thus, 'learning' is present in all places and all daily practices of the organisation. However, as Dewey says (Elkjaer 2001), mere participation in daily organisational practices does not create learning, as an individual learns through the reorganisation and reconstruction of his experience. This experience, in turn, is based on changes that imply reflection upon earlier actions to anticipate future consequences. It can thus be said that the third element of his proposal, the relationship between the individual and organisation, derives from the participation and interaction of individuals in organisational processes. Individuals are part of the organisational practice and this relationship is jointly woven and takes context into consideration. Such an understanding of context is twofold: (1) both individual and context are historically produced and (2) context is constructed as individuals interact in the organisation's social processes.

The connection between the social learning theory and sustainability field – axis III – was also possible because,

although Bandura's (1977) social learning theory was developed to explain individual behaviour, it can also be applied to understanding how collective learning occurs (Glasser 2007). Thus, some researchers share the interest in approaching social learning as a means to an end (Kilvington 2010). This end is seen as a sustainable future (Keen et al. 2005). 'It is to address complex problems resistant to solution which require the presence of multiple disciplines and perspectives and a fundamental change in social and institutional impediments' (Dale 1989 apud Kilvington 2010, p. 40).

To Keen et al. (2005, p. 262), social learning in environmental management essentially refers to change management. It concerns 'processes that allow us to share our understandings and better negotiate social change in such a way that diverse viewpoints are taken into consideration'. That is, 'the more we construct our knowledge matrix through sharing understandings, the more insights we can gain'. To these authors, social learning is

> The collective action and reflection that occurs among different individuals and groups as they work to improve the management of human and environmental interrelations. Social learning for improved human interrelations with the environment must ultimately include us all, because we are all part of the same system and each of us will inevitably experience the consequences of these change processes. (Keen et al. 2005, p. 4)

Based on a transdisciplinary approach, Keen et al. (2005) define five interlinked elements that form the foundation of social learning: (1) reflection and reflexivity; (2) system orientation and system thinking; (3) integration and synthesis; (4) negotiation and collaboration and (5) participation and engagement. Their approach also rests on three agendas to support the collective action needed for environmental management: learning partnerships; learning platforms and learning values and ethics.

Social learning is also a means to a sustainable future in studies by Kilvington (2010, p. 54), who suggests that 'in the arena of environmental management and sustainable development, social learning has emerged as an approach to complex problem solving similar to, and sharing common elements of, adaptive management or collaborative management'. That is, the concept of social learning emerges as a link between the concepts of adaptive management and collaborative learning, suggesting a holistic approach. It relates to the challenge of building capacity for social learning in situations of complex environmental management. Kilvington (2010, p. 300) concludes that

> It is important to understand social learning not as a model for 'how things should be done' but rather as a set of premises or conditions, the management of which is important to the ability of groups of stakeholders to find their way through complex problems where each share some knowledge, and towards which each need to take some action. The ideas that make up social learning are fundamentally about improving the basis for learning and

adaptation. There are no set steps to be followed, nor does it prescribe any particular starting position. Rather these ideas can be applied to improve the situation from 'where you are now'.

In the HarmoniCOP – Harmonizing Collaborative Planning Cooperation Project, which involves several social actors to manage hydrographic basins in various European regions – social learning is also being discussed as a means, a process and an output to reach sustainable results. The input is the context (the governance system together with physical system or natural environment). The activities are performed via relational practices (involvement of actors and management of problematics), and the outcomes are the technical and relational qualities established among the actors involved in the process. Thus, social learning is understood as 'learning together to manage together', since not all social actors involved possess the necessary resources to act satisfactorily individually (HarmoniCOP 2005, p. 2). Social learning means that all stakeholders learn to manage the questions in which they are interested. It is based on dialogue and contains elements that range from the recognition of interdependencies among stakeholders to the composition of arrangements that promote the implementation of solutions, also covering cognitions, attitudes, abilities and joint actions amongst all those involved. Social learning for sustainability presupposes dialogues in which the goal is not to 'win' the debate but reach a consensus (HarmoniCOP 2005).

Finally, the connection between social learning, sustainability and organisations – axis IV – springs from the proposal for multiple actor collaboration by Bouwen and Taillieu (2004), who understand social learning as closely linked to organisation learning in collaborative projects related to natural resource matters and involving multiple actors. This proposal covers six elements – context, participation, social learning processes, relational practices, recognition of social identities and stakeholder interdependency and generated knowledge – and is based on the social constructivism paradigm, whose learning locus is sited in social relationships and not simply in people's minds (cognitivist approach). That is, knowledge and reality are constructed via social interactions. According to these authors:

> In our definition of social learning we want to include also the social organizational learning that takes place at the systemic or cultural level during joint practices and experiences when stakeholders meet in common actions and conversations on different levels of activity. It can be considered as learning how to participate and learning how to get involved with other stakeholders, to get desirable social outcomes in terms of joint project work or development of common attitudes. (Bouwen and Taillieu 2004, p. 141)

Dessie et al. (2012, p. 265) are more specific, suggesting that the role of social learning, in particular, for soil conservation,

> Opens a new space for communicative action, which allows actors to go beyond the conventional linear interaction and knowledge transfer. Actors can create an inter-subjective understanding of soil conservation problems and solutions through a more communicative form of interaction. Moreover, social learning also creates space for the emergence of new actors, such as farmers' organizations, which encourage more collective action in the adoption of soil conservation measures.

3. Methodology

To understand a business experience that reveals this collective learning for the sustainability process, in consonance with the last axis, we proceeded to a qualitative study, based on the narratives and stories that comprise the chemical company's Programme for Environmental Compliance and Education. According to Boje (2008, p. 1), storytelling organisations are defined as a 'collective storytelling system in which the performance of stories is a key part of members' sense making and a means to allow them to supplement individual memories with institutional memory'. That is, how people and organisations reveal the meaning of their experiences via a narrative or story. For him, 'every workplace, school, government office or local religious group is a Storytelling Organization' (Boje 2008, p. 4).

Boje (2008) prefers the term 'storying' to 'storytelling', since 'telling' stories is limited to oral expression. His contribution lies precisely in the interrelationships of narrating and storying processes by juxtaposing different mediums of expression: oral, textual, visual, architectonic and gestural.

Therefore, to understand the relationship of the story network involved in the Programme for Environmental Compliance and Education in the town of Bebedouro, we chose a study methodology offering a paradigmatic approach aligned to a postmodern conception, as such an approach enables us to best understand fragmented local stories and narratives. Boje (2001, p. 6) recommends an antenarrative analysis methodology for dealing with 'the prevalence of fragmented and polyphonic storytelling in complex organisations'.

Our interest lay in finding out these social actors' stories and analysing how the actors were constructing and perceiving the Bebedouro region's reality. To study this wide relationship network, we followed the assumptions of social constructivism, whose main principle posits that reality is socially constructed and the locus of learning lies in social relationships and not simply in people's minds. Thus, this research focuses on interactions and dialogues amongst the multiple social actors involved in the Programme for Environmental Compliance and Education.

The data was collected via 19 semi-structured interviews, informal conversations occurring in person or by telephone; documents (such as reports, books, presentations, sites, information for the press and videos) provided by the social actors; and non-participant observation in activities with students and teachers. To interpret and discuss these data, we adopted a combination of eight options of Boje's (2001) antenarrative analysis: deconstruction, grand narrative, microstoria, story network, intertextuality, causality, plot and theme.

We started with an analysis of the story or antenarrative network, where each story is understood as constituting nodes. These nodes can be people, organisations, places, groups, histories, categories, contexts and so on. Links among these nodes can be analytical or virtual, representing the intensity of relationships through several lines, according to Boje (2001). 'An antenarrative analysis traces the storytelling behaviour in the organizing situation and the organization is seen as a storytelling system in which stories are the medium of exchange' (Boje 2001, p. 10). The analysis focuses on the complex and dynamic relationships between identified nodes. It does not focus only on the map, once the antenarrative 'territory is messier than the map' (Boje 2001, p. 65).

Figure 3 illustrates the story network map of the Programme for Environmental Compliance and Education in the town of Bebedouro, where 25 nodes were identified (the programme's 23 social actors and Guaratinguetá experience and its economic history). These nodes were organised into five groups – the organisation (the chemical company), clients, partners, Bebedouro community and government. The stories were also seen as contexts, as in the case of the

Guaratinguetá experience, whose historical context launches the narratives. Then, the stories were seen as connections linked by lines that show the direction of each relationship. These connections generated 20 direct and indirect relationships that formed four narratives and 10 stories, which were connected in time sequence to other stories, past, present and future.

Table 1 shows these relationships and the most recurring analysis in this study to understand these stories and narratives.

The data interpretation process was complemented by the analysis of deconstruction, microstoria, grand narrative and intertextuality. As each actor told the story solely within his or her own context, without mentioning the programme's beginning; deconstructing the narratives and stories was necessary to understand them from these multiple viewpoints. The order of the deconstructed narratives and stories is shown in Table 1.

Thus, we used microstoria analysis together with an understanding of local stories and knowledge by tracing the experiences of local social actors and their social relationships. Simultaneously, we analysed the grand narratives to understand how they are resisted in various ways by local stories in this business experience. In addition, we considered intertextuality among different mediums of expression texts (the documental material available) to

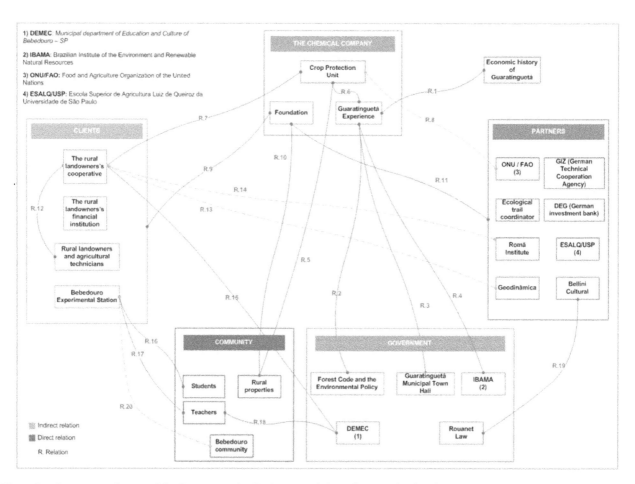

Figure 3.   Story network map of the Programme for Environmental Compliance and Education.
Source: The authors.

Table 1. Relationships amongst several actors of the Programme for Environmental Compliance and Education in the town of Bebedouro (São Paulo).

Narratives (N)		Stories (s)	Main social actors	Relationship number and direction	Main antenarrative analysis options used
N.1: The relationship between the experience of The Chemical Company industrial complex in Guaratinguetá in the recovery of ciliary forests and the Programme	s.1	The reasons for the devastation of ciliary forests in the Paraíba Valley	• Guaratinguetá experience • Its economic history	R.1 (Direct)	Causality
	s.2	What does Brazilian environmental legislation say about the protection of native forest?	• Guaratinguetá experience • Brazilian environmental legislation (government)	R.2 (Direct)	Theme
	s.3	The recovery of ciliary forests in the Paraíba Valley	• Guaratinguetá experience • IBAMA • Town of Guaratinguetá	R.3 R.4 (Direct)	Theme
N.2: The Chemical Company's contribution to sustainability in agriculture – the relationship between The Chemical Company Crop Protection Unit and the Programme	s.4	The meaning attributed to sustainability by The Chemical Company Crop Protection Unit	• Rural properties • Crop Protection Unit • Cooperative	R.5 R.6 R.7	Theme
	s.5	The sustainable business development strategy	• ONU • FAO	(Direct) R.8 (Indirect)	Theme
N.3: The relationship between the Foundation and the Programme	s.6	The reasons for the creation of The Chemical Company's Foundation	• The Foundation • Crop Protection Unit's clients	R.9 R.10	Causality + Theme
	s.7	The Foundation's activity focus	• Rural producers		
	s.8	Technical cooperation between Brazil and Germany	• The Foundation's partners • Financing agents	R.11 (Direct)	
N.4: The experience of the town of Bebedouro, SP with the Programme	s.9	First, the Bebedouro experience in the environmental compliance aspect	• Cooperative • Social entrepreneurship organisations • Students • Teachers • Bebedouro Community • Municipal department of Education and Culture of Bebedouro • Guaratinguetá Municipal Town Hall	R.12 to R.20 (Direct), except R.13, R.14, R.20 which are indirect	Plot + Theme
	s.10	Second, the Bebedouro experience in the environmental education aspect			

Source: The authors.

link the 'web of complex inter-relationships ensnaring each story's historicity and situational context between other stories' (Boje 2001, p. 91).

4. Presentation and discussion of results

For each story, in addition to presenting the report, the social learning for the sustainability process developed in the Programme for Environmental Compliance and Education was reflected upon. These reflections involved

identifying the voices in the stories, what was being learned, how it was learned and, last, the social learning elements. Table 2 presents a summary of the reflections on the process of social learning towards sustainable agriculture at the chemical company.

On the basis of these reflections, all the elements were gathered in Figure 4, which sums up the process of social learning for sustainable agriculture in the chemical company in Brazil. It takes the nested systems form, as recommended by Keen et al. (2005), showing that all elements,

Table 2. Summary of the reflections on the process of social learning for sustainability towards sustainable agriculture from the viewpoint of a for-profit organisation.

Identified elements of social learning for sustainability	Stories	Goals of the identified elements of social learning	Participating voices	What was learned?
Narrative 1: Relationship between The Chemical Company industrial complex in Guaratinguetá in the recovery of ciliary forests and the Programme				
Recognising environmental problems and conflicts • Recognising the conflicts of interests • Recognising the multiple social actors involved in these conflicts • Recognising the need to resolve an environmental problem	Story 1: The reasons for the devastation of ciliary forests in the Paraiba Valley	Understanding the dynamics of the natural forest, its level of devastation and the impacts	1. Nature 2. The Chemical Company (landowner) 3. Guaratinguetá Municipal Town Hall 4. IBAMA 5. Government, through environmental legislation 6. Paraiba Valley community 7. Remaining Guaratinguetá community	• How to begin building a dialogue with the local reality impacted by the environmental problem • How to identify the causes and consequences of an environmental problem
Re-learning a new way of reconciling interests	Story 2: What does Brazilian environmental legislation say about the protection of native forest?	Directing and standardising the adoption of safe environmental practices with long-lasting results	Same as above	• The procedures required to preserve the environment
Understanding the surroundings, causes and consequences of the environmental problem	Story 1: The reasons for the devastation of ciliary forests in the Paraiba Valley	Proposing viable solutions	Same as above	• Development of a shared perception of the problem and of what environmental practices and procedures should be followed • Proposal and implementation of a viable plan for ciliary forest recovery
Developing competencies for ciliary forest recovery	Story 3: The recovery of ciliary forests in the Paraiba Valley	• Solving an environmental problem • Having access to specialised knowledge	Same as above	• How to recover ciliary forests in degraded areas • How to interrupt loss of diversity in the region • How to meet the requirements of Brazilian environmental legislation • How to encourage the development of reforestation models • How to encourage the performance of similar initiatives

(Continued)

Table 2. (Continued).

Identified elements of social learning for sustainability	Stories	Goals of the identified elements of social learning	Participating voices	What was learned?
Narrative 2: The Chemical Company's contribution to sustainability in agriculture: Relationship between The Chemical Company Crop Protection Unit and the Programme				
Transforming environmental crises into opportunities for sustainable business in a network of social actors	Story 4: The meaning attributed to sustainability by The Chemical Company Crop Protection Unit	Learning to deal with the dialectic between return on investments for shareholders and the	1. The Chemical Company Agro – Crop Protection Unit	• How to connect a business unit's core business with sustainability
Formulating a strategy for developing sustainable business in a network of social actors	Story 5: The sustainable business development strategy	search for benefits for its other interested parties	2. Rural landowners (indirect clients of this business unit)	• To replicate this experience for its clients and contribute to sustainable agriculture
			3. Cooperative (direct client of this business unit)	• To help its clients develop sustainable business
				• To benefit farmers, with the support and guidance of ciliary forest restoration on their rural properties
Narrative 3: The relationship between The Chemical Company's Foundation and the Programme				
Structuring an implementation and management model for the sustainable business strategy	Story 6: The reasons for the creation of The Chemical Company's Foundation	Supporting the Crop Protection Unit in the implementation of its business strategy	1. The Chemical Company	How to adequately prepare for implementation
• Formulating a system-oriented model	Story 7: The Foundation's activity focus		2. Government	To seek and share the necessary resources via strategic partnerships
• Forming strong strategic partnerships	Story 8: Technical cooperation between Brazil and Germany		3. Partners	
• Sharing human, technological, financial and informational resources			4. Clients	
• Raising awareness and qualifying social actors			5. Community	
• Using diverse spaces that favour social learning				
Narrative 4: The experience of the town of Bebedouro – SP with the Programme				
Coordinating for complex implementation of a strategy for supporting sustainable business in a network of social actors	Story 9: First, the Bebedouro experience in the environmental compliance aspect	• Establishing relationships with social actors	1. The Chemical Company	• How to resolve conflicts
Coordinating involving multiple	Story 10: Second, the Bebedouro experience in the environmental education aspect	• Recognising the social identities of each actor and accommodating the differences in competencies, interests and power relations in compliance with this programme's goals	2. Government	• How to ensure engagement, participation, collaboration and negotiation
• Social actors			3. Partners	
• Interests			4. Clients	
• Contexts			5. Community	
• Social learning spaces				
• Partnerships				
• Conflicts of interests				
• Power relationships				

Source: The authors.

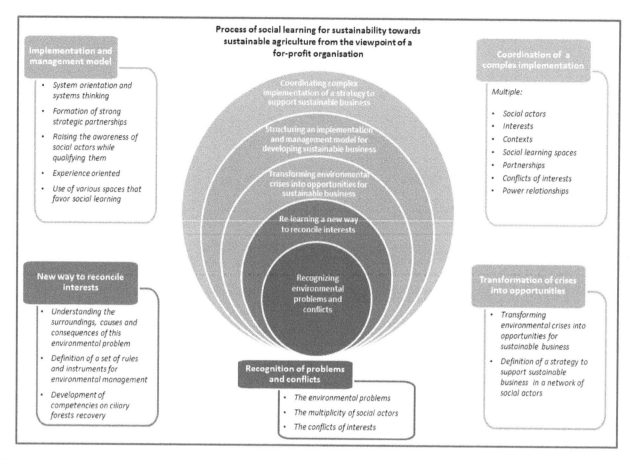

Figure 4.   Process of social learning for sustainability towards sustainable agriculture from the viewpoint of a for-profit organisation.
Source: The authors.

such as the dimensions of sustainability, are jointly constructed, being integrated and, at times, inseparable.

4.1   Recognising environmental problems and conflicts as a starting point for social learning for the sustainability process

The Programme for Environmental Compliance and Education was launched in 1984 and sprung from the need to resolve a complex environmental problem: the devastation of ciliary forests (native forest) on the banks of the Paraíba River, in the town of Guaratinguetá. The soil degradation was caused by use of the land for sugarcane and coffee crops and, later, for dairy farming, by rural landowners since the eighteenth century, whose only concern was quick enrichment. The environmental impact from this business model helped remove the natural plant cover and expose the soil to the effects of strong tropical rain, which results in soil and water loss. Water erosion, a natural process that occurs on a geological time scale, tends to be accelerated by anthropic action, to the point where its effects are made visible by the formation of ravines and gullies and by the silting and eutrophication of streams, rivers and lakes (Silva et al. 2011).

Thus, in the case of the lands acquired by the chemical company, conflicts of interest led to:

- land being used with no ecological and environmental science by rural landowners from the eighteenth century (**landowners × nature**);
- landowners' noncompliance with environmental legislation, in force in Brazil since 1934, in permanent protection and legal reservation areas (**landowners × government**);
- consequences for Guaratinguetá communities, particularly for the Paraíba Valley community, such as floods, fires, erosion, water shortages, high temperatures and alterations in seasons, as well as degraded areas being revegetated by grassy species and isolated arboreal native species as well as by some species that indicate highly acidified soils, such as satintail, flatsedge and signalgrass (**landowners × community**).

These conflicts of interest involved the natural environmental and six social actors with different interests:

(1) Nature: to be environmentally recovered in terms of fauna, flora, soil, hydric system and so on;
(2) The chemical company (landowner) in Guaratinguetá: to comply with environmental legislation, at least at the official statement level;

(3) The government, on the municipal sphere (Guaratinguetá Municipal Town Hall): to ensure compliance with environmental legislation;

(4) The government, in the federal sphere (Brazilian Institute of the Environment and Renewable Natural Resources, IBAMA): to also ensure compliance with environmental legislation;

(5) The government in the federal sphere again, via environmental legislation, the Forest Code and the Environmental Policy: to provide guidelines for the standardisation of safe environmental practices and with lasting results;

(6) The Paraíba Valley community and the remaining Guaratinguetá community: to increase the percentage of native forest in the urban area, recompose degraded areas susceptible to erosion and stabilise slopes, thus preventing erosion and landslides.

As below, all the elements involved in the experience of ciliary forest recomposition in Guaratinguetá – environmental problems, conflicts of interests and multiplicity of social actors – presuppose a social learning process such as that proposed by the HarmoniCOP Project (2005, p. 2), whose concept is to 'learn together to manage together'. It refers to the involvement and collaboration of diverse social actors to propose viable solutions to a common problem, including conflict resolution and reaching consensus regarding which solution is technically and financially viable to implement without, however, requiring less effort.

4.2 Re-learning a new way to reconcile interests between landowners and other social actors of the Programme

To deal with the conflicts listed above, an element that played a determining role in the chemical company's process of social learning for sustainability: the *definition of a set of rules and instruments for environmental management* to direct and standardise the adoption of safe and long-lasting environmental practices, here represented by environmental legislation, more specifically, by the Forest Code and the Environmental Policy. In fact, Brazilian environmental legislation has a direct and very strong link with this programme, since one of its great priority goals is compliance with the Brazilian Forest Code.

These laws form a set of regulatory command and control instruments, through the specific public power that establishes the standards and monitors environmental quality, regulating activities and applying sanctions and penalties via legislation and norms (Leal 1998). The main characteristic of this regulatory policy is not to give landowners a choice, given their responsibility for the devastation of forests and other vegetation; they must follow the imposed rule or submit to penalties in legal or administrative actions. They are not free to select and promote adjustments simply when it is convenient for them. For this reason, a coercive power relationship exists between the government and rural landowners, as the Brazilian state has the means to make the law stand and curb practices that can degrade the environment.

As stated in the HarmoniCOP Project (2005), the government does not need to abandon its power and will always have a special role and unique resources as a regulatory power. Nor should it abandon its responsibilities, as it is a relevant actor in the process of social learning. The more the government shares responsibilities, the more it increases its effectiveness and power. In the Programme for Environmental Compliance and Education, through this set of regulatory command and control instruments, rural producers are oriented as to the necessary procedures for environmental preservation, particularly in permanent protection and legal reservation areas. Thus, principally by force of law, the chemical company, the Municipal Urban Services and Agriculture Office of the Town of Guaratinguetá and, later, IBAMA, undertook actions to find a viable solution for the environmental problem of ciliary forest devastation.

Another element present in this social learning process was an *understanding of the surroundings, causes and consequences of this environmental problem*. That is, actors shared a perception of the problem and what environmental practices and procedures should be followed by the chemical company and government bodies, which relates to Bouwen's and Taillieu's (2004) assumptions that social learning can also be revealed through collaboration among multiple actors. Thus, these actors proposed and implemented a viable plan for ciliary forest recovery, followed by development and critical evaluation of solutions. Decision-making was based on arrangements to promote action implementation (each social actor had well-defined attributes). In other words, they learned by doing, living and experiencing.

Thus, over the course of 23 years (1984–2007), a positive consequence of this process of social learning for sustainability was the *development of a body of knowledge, abilities and attitudes* surrounding the following three elements: (1) how to recover ciliary forests in degraded areas and how to interrupt loss of diversity in the region; (2) how to meet the requirements of Brazilian environmental legislation and (3) how to encourage the development of reforestation models as well as the execution of similar initiatives, using species of easy dissemination to repopulate the area. This body of knowledge, abilities and attitudes is also a desirable result, becoming a self-reinforcing dynamic in social learning for sustainability, as proposed by the HarmoniCOP Project (2005). In this way, the development of competencies for ciliary forest recovery within the organisation, that is, the land it owns, results from social learning for sustainability at the chemical company via its relationships with the natural environment, government and Guaratinguetá community.

The Guaratinguetá experience is close to what Bouwen and Taillieu (2004) understand as a process of circulatory knowledge construction, since the experience involved different actors in a participatory manner, that is, in essentially relational processes: the creation, development and sharing of knowledge.

4.3 Transforming environmental crises into opportunities for sustainable business in a network of social actors

The chemical company's experience in Guaratinguetá could have been limited to the region, with its only fruit being the Semente do Amanhã (Tomorrow's Seed) Project, which inserted environmental education into the town's municipal school syllabus and transformed the recovered area into an open-air classroom. However, this trajectory was altered when the chemical company Agro Crop Protection Unit gave sustainability the meaning of sustainable agricultural production by constructing its sustainability identity on the basis of value aggregation for the rural producer's harvest. In addition, within the alternatives available for sustainable agriculture, this unit chose to seek a balance between production and biodiversity, that is, to interrupt biodiversity loss and guarantee good quality harvests for rural producers.

Through the experience of ciliary forest recovery, in 2007, the managers of the Crop Protection Unit arrived at new learning: replicating this experience for their clients and contributing to sustainable agriculture. This process is known as reflexivity, according to Keen et al. (2005) and leads to social change. Thus, this business unit strategically decided to support its clients in the development of sustainable business – that is, business that is economically viable and consonant with the social and environmental demands of the sustainable development paradigm – as part of its strategy of winning the loyalty of large clients.

Based on the successful Guaratinguetá experience, the chemical company Agro Crop Protection Unit began to benefit farmers, supporting and guiding ciliary forest restoration on their rural properties by integrating the Cooperate Commitment Project – Client Management Relationship programme – targeting cooperatives aligned with the chemical company Agro Crop Protection Unit guidelines. Although no costs were imposed for agricultural producers, financial resources for this Project were provided on the basis of reciprocity between the chemical company Agro Crop Protection Unit and its clients. The greater the client's participation in the unit's business, the more resources were available for the Programme for Environmental Compliance and Education, and vice versa. As the manager of the cooperative's technical farming department said, 'If the cooperative moves away from the chemical company, if it buys fewer the chemical company products, it will have fewer resources in this Cooperate Project and the investment will have to be reduced. So it's a two-way street'.

In other words, this business unit decided to support the development of sustainable business in one element of its value chain, specifically, in the primary activities of sales and marketing, and defined a sustainable business strategy on the basis of competencies developed by the

ciliary forest recovery organisation. On the contrary, this programme would have been one more socio-environmental action for the organisation, with no return for its business. For this reason, the *definition of strategy for supporting sustainable business* is a necessary element for social learning towards sustainable agriculture to occur in this organisation.

To operationalise this business strategy, the chemical company managers undertook certain actions as follows:

- transferring the management of the programme to the Foundation;
- expanding the programme to cover environmental education and
- changing the name from Paraíba do Sul River Ciliary Forest Recomposition programme to Programme for Environmental Compliance and Education.

With the transfer of this programme's strategic management to the Foundation, the Crop Protection Unit does not lose its focus on developing new businesses and selling, and furthermore has the Foundation as a strong ally, an extension of the unit itself to implement the programme with its clients.

However, it is important to highlight that this programme is not dedicated to all its clients, but only to those selected by the cooperative and approved by the chemical company. In Bebedouro, were selected the strategic cooperators who could start-up the programme and ensure its success while becoming influencers and an example for other producers. According to the manager of the cooperative's technical farming department and the Crop Protection Unit's special accounts consultant

> This choice was made jointly with the chemical company team in the region, so that we could associate this producer leadership in terms of region, in terms of power, of being an example, and also being a cooperator of the cooperative and also a the chemical company client. So, we tried to join all these links when choosing a producer. Because the idea is to make this learning about environmental recomposition be an advertisement for all our cooperators. It is a dream, but, well...

> We talked to the cooperative's technical body and defined some names of cooperators who we think, in the first instance, could be strategic for the Cooperative business, they are influential people, they are promoters of sustainable actions.

4.4 Structuring an implementation and management model for developing sustainable business in a network of social actors

To support the Crop Protection Unit in the implementation of the business strategy, the chemical company's Foundation structured an implementation and management model based on five core elements.

First, it is a *systems thinking-oriented model*, in two aspects:

(1) environmental compliance, aimed at offering technical support to agricultural professionals and guidance to rural producers regarding the recovery and mapping of permanent preservations and legal reservation areas and

(2) environmental education, which encourages behavioural change and the incorporation of socio-environmental values by people who live in the same region as the rural producers.

Both aspects, after the implementation cycle is closed, are self-sustainable; each benefited person (rural producers, teachers) may continue on their own to perform the activities and also to multiply, influence and facilitate the entry of new social actors, strengthening assertive actions. System orientation and system thinking are elements proposed by the transdisciplinary approach of Keen et al. (2005), where systemic learning considers interrelations and interdependencies between ecological and social systems to promote sustainability.

Second, it is a model based on *human, technological, financial and informational resource sharing*, since the Foundation is not structured to cover all the implementation needs of the programme. Therefore, it needs to form strong strategic partnerships – multiprofessional and multisectoral – that, during the implementation of the Programme for Environmental Compliance and Education assume different roles and responsibilities, as follows:

- providers of methodologies and tools;
- dialogue facilitators that act as impartial mediators, aiming to obtain the expected results or even conflict resolution;
- influential leadership, attracting more people to the programme through their example;
- disseminators to propagate and diffuse successful activities;
- multipliers to form and train other social actors;
- standardisers that suggest guidelines to direct actions and
- providers of financial resources and generators of knowledge.

Third, this model is based on *raising the awareness of social actors whilst qualifying them*, such as technicians at the cooperatives and farms, rural producers and teachers. These actors have the mission of applying methodologies and tools (didactic books, ecological trails), jointly developed by the Foundation and its partners, in rural properties and classrooms. Raising awareness is necessary to draw the attention of these actors and affect them with the target activities, to disseminate and multiply sustainable knowledge and environmental practices. Raising awareness is important to provoke interest and convince them that sustainable results are achievable, as long as there is

correct application and use of the methods and tools and that these are user-friendly instruments. The study on predicting and dealing with water eutrophication by Orderud and Vogt (2013, p. 412) shows that 'knowledge is one of the cornerstones underlying farmers' motives for taking actions, and farmers have a strong production mentality; that is, farmers are motivated by producing food and achieving a large output as well as good quality'.

Fourth, this is an *experience-oriented model to complete the qualification cycle*. For example, the social actors of the environmental compliance aspect – cooperative team, rural producers and technicians – learn by perceiving and feeling the results *in loco*, that is, the recovery of degraded areas with new vegetation. Gradually, these social actors perceive that, with the use of appropriate techniques, long-lasting goals can be reached, and therefore a local reality can be transformed into something better, as the interviewees report. This experience lasts approximately five years, when the implementation cycle is completed.

In the educational aspect, students and teachers learn through the various activities performed in classrooms using the Environmental Atlas book and material from the Ecological Trail; while crossing the forest during the Ecological Trail and on stage with the programme Theatre. The implementation of this aspect lasts approximately three years. As a result, there are changes in the behaviour and conduct of the communities involved with respect to environmental preservation, as evidenced by the interviewees' narratives.

In this way, the positive results of the chemical company's implementation and management model can be explained by the fact that it is not based on methodologies and tools of the 'apply yourself to your local reality' type. Instead, the support and guidance given to the various social actors occurred over the course of a cycle, which stretches from initial dialogues with the reality to be transformed (with rural landowners, students and teachers from the town of Bebedouro) through the monitoring phase, for results to be felt by the social actors involved in the process. This qualification – raising awareness – experience cycle occurs in various interlocution spaces, such as the following: launch events, organisational spaces at the Foundation and the Cooperative; itinerant stages; forests; schools and classrooms and farms.

For this reason, this implementation and management model, based on the use of various spaces that favour social learning for sustainable agriculture, can be classified as aligned with the relational practices proposed by Bouwen and Taillieu (2004, p. 144) as: 'any interactive project or exchange between at least two social actors' that 'has consequences for the relationship and some perceptible outcomes'. Also according to these authors, good relational practices signify the shared property of the task or project; personal, concrete communication and mutually energising and gratifying activity, all conditions for learning that were fostered by the project.

4.5 Coordinating complex implementation of a strategy to support sustainable business in a network of social actors

The operationalisation of this management and implementation model in the town of Bebedouro was relatively complex, involving various elements of the Programme for Environmental Compliance and Education. For this reason, a great *coordination campaign* was needed, especially on behalf of the Foundation, which is the actor responsible for managing the programme.

First, as can be seen in Figure 3 above, methodological strategy item, there are 23 social actors embedded in the programme. Second, these actors externalise several interests, as follows:

- the organisation's (the chemical company) interests: to meet the business strategy goals of winning client loyalty, supporting them in the development of sustainable business;
- the interests of the clients, such as the Cooperative, which are to support the rural producer, its cooperator, in the development of sustainable business, or of the rural landowners, which are to have sustainable agricultural production and comply with environmental legislation at low cost or preferably no cost;
- partner interests, which are to provide methodologies and tools of sustainable environmental and educational processes;
- community interests, such as those of teachers, which are to have interdisciplinary instruments and be duly qualified to raise awareness, and stimulate reflection and behaviour change in students regarding environmental preservation and
- government interests, which are to ensure compliance with environmental legislation.

Third, diverse contexts and interrelations exist, as follows:

- **A company** (Crop Protection Unit), where the business is planned and performed;
- **A non-governmental organisation** (Foundation), where the programme is managed;
- **A cooperative** with a portfolio of more than 20,000 associated rural producers, covering more than 500 towns in the states of São Paulo and Minas Gerais;
- **Public bodies** (IBAMA, DEMEC, Guaratinguetá Municipal Town Hall) responsible for the regulatory aspect;
- **A municipal school** public establishment for collective teaching;
- **A rural property,** where the recovery of the protection and legal reservation area occur;
- **The forests** (of the Bebedouro Citriculture Experimental Station and of Jurela), where the Ecological Trail training is conducted;
- **A stage** (Programme itinerant theatre and bus), for dissemination of socioeducational knowledge for the Bebedouro community;
- **A university** (Escola Superior de Agricultura Luiz de Queiroz (ESALQ/USP), responsible for providing the qualification in environmental recovery methodologies and creation of the Environmental Compliance Map for the rural properties).

Fourth, various power relations permeate the participation and engagement of this programme's 23 social actors. They range from a coercive relationship between the rural landowners and the government, due to the imposition of environmental legislation, to the co-active relationship between the Foundation, GIZ (the German government's international technical cooperation agency) and the DEG (German investment bank), as a result of joint action partnerships.

Having said that, the programme's strength lies in its capacity to establish and articulate relationships with all these social actors and other elements listed above, to meet its goals. This means coordinating to ensure engagement, participation, collaboration and negotiation (Keen et al. 2005), as well as coordinating to recognise the social identities of each actor and accommodate differences incompetencies, interests and power relations in meeting the programme's goals (Bouwen & Taillieu 2004).

Therefore, it was necessary to create a programme with systemic orientation and thinking, and one that was integrated (Keen et al. 2005), to enable it to join the social (environmental education in a region whose income comes from agricultural production); environmental (environmental education for rural producers) and economic (human, financial, technological and informational resources shared among the different partners, but with no additional costs for the rural producer and no cost for students and teachers) dimensions. Building a safe level of trust among the different social actors was also necessary to develop a common view of the programme's goals, problems and controversial subjects. Coordination was needed to resolve conflicts and arrive at solutions that were technically implemented in the environmental compliance and education actions (HarmoniCOP 2005).

For Hansmann et al. (2012, p. 458), the integration of the three pillars of sustainability often coincided with the occurrence of conflicts between them. But according to the discussion above, in the Programme for Environmental Compliance and Education, more synergies than conflicts existed between these three dimensions. These synergies meet the Principal Sustainability Components proposed by these authors (2012, p. 451), which are

- PSC 1: Product and Process Development: positive synergies between reduced and greater responsible use of natural resources and promotion of innovation, thus generating social and economic benefits;
- PSC 2: Education and Social Economics: reflects how educational activities and sociocultural

sustainability initiatives can simultaneously promote income and employment, social and human capital and free personal development;

- PSC 3: Protection of Nature and Humans: covers the synergetic benefits that protection of natural spaces and biodiversity and the reduction of environmental risks have for the protection of the population's health and safety.

5. Conclusions

In terms of theoretical implications, the results reveal how a profit-based organisation not only supports the resolution of complex environmental and social problems but also transforms them into an opportunity to generate sustainable products and services as part of its value chain. Thus, we can conclude that social learning for sustainability, from the viewpoint of a for-profit organisation, is as much a process (a means) as an end. As a process, engaging in dialogue with a reality and transforming it requires (1) a support strategy for the development of sustainable business in a network of social actors, (2) a systemic implementation and management model and (3) coordination capacity. As an end, the results are the development of competencies. In the case of the Chemical Company Crop Protection Unit, these competencies involved recovering ciliary forests. In sum, social learning for sustainable agriculture, as a process, revealed itself through the capacity for coordination and organisation on behalf of the Foundation, which allowed a joint decision-making process among the involved social actors regarding the problems they faced.

In the light of what has been discussed, we can conclude that social learning for sustainability (in this case, for sustainable agriculture) in a network of social actors, from the viewpoint of a for-profit organisation, means implementing collective actions to support the development of sustainable business over all or part of its value chain, based on a strategy founded on competencies developed by the organisation and anchored on a systemic implementation and management model; strong strategic partnerships as well as superior coordination capacity to manage multiple social actors, interests, contexts, learning spaces, partners, conflicts and power relations.

It must also be mentioned that the risk exists that this social learning process for sustainable agriculture at the chemical company will be interrupted in the town of Bebedouro. If the cooperative, for any reason, begins to buy products from the Chemical Company Crop Protection competitors and stops being a large client in this portfolio, then yes, the programme may be interrupted, even if only in part. This possible outcome reflects the fact that this business strategy was formulated on the basis of reciprocity between clients and the Chemical Company Crop Protection, and accordingly, the greater the mutual correspondence, the greater the availability of resources, especially financial ones. However, the results shown by

Wossen et al. (2013, p. 482) suggest that 'social learning is a very critical factor of farming technology adoption. In the absence of formal information sources, promoting social networks, informal community structures and social ties will therefore be important for the adoption of new technologies'. That is, the lesson learned from the experience and technology shared by the university in this programme can be multiplied among the rural landowners.

Furthermore, it is important to highlight the need to implement an approach for environmental and sustainability assessment in this programme, which embraces the programme's complexity and its several elements, as discussed above. For instance, Povedaa and Lipsetta (2014) suggests an integrated approach based on three areas of knowledge that are part of the Chemical Company's programme: (1) sustainable development theory and fundamentals to balance social, economic and environmental needs; (2) continual performance improvement by organisations or projects and (3) multi-criteria decision analysis through stakeholder engagement and participation as well as the design and implementation of a criteria weighting system. Such approaches can meet the programme's issues. In addition, the Foundation was responsible for the formation of strategic partnerships. Not to mention that the cooperative is a key part of the programme's implementation in the region, given its strength with the rural producers and the community in general. The cooperative may continue its work in the region, but for this to occur the cooperative would have to increase the Social and Cultural Investment Fund (FISC). If a rupture occurs for political reasons or due to a change in municipal management, there could also be a break in the programme's implementation.

As for the practical implications of the findings, some lessons learned from this case may be useful to other companies seeking social learning. The construction of multi-party, inter-organisational projects in search of answers to socio-environmental problems has proven to be a trend (Bouwen & Taillieu 2004); learning about the interdependencies in different interest groups presupposes giving a voice to participants and, in turn, developing the ability to listen to them. In the analysed experience, the sharing of knowledge and competencies, along with informational, methodological, financial, human and technological resources were the factors that propelled learning. The communicative process created the conditions for environmental change as a result of this forged understanding by the parties of social problems, dilemmas and conflicts and their implications, which allowed improvement strategies to emerge. It is worth remembering the warning given by Bouwen and Taillieu (2004, p. 143), for whom social learning is more than just 'community participation' or group learning, involving an understanding of the limitations of institutions and governance mechanisms. In other words, evaluating the consequences of each actor's behaviour and understanding is necessary, as well as understanding the influence of social structures and institutions in the way we think and act. This means creating situations where people can learn collectively how to act to improve the condition they live in.

But as Wals et al. (2007) explain that if the success of social learning depends largely on the collective goals and shared vision of those engaged in the learning process, this does not mean valuing a single way of thinking. It is fundamental to open up space for alternative visions that can lead to various levels of dissonance, as such divergences are needed to spark learning on individual and collective levels (Wals et al. 2007). Promoting meetings and events with different combinations of stakeholders and forming learning communities, virtual and face to face, are some possible suggestions to stimulate this type of action. The study experience demonstrated that the feeling of belonging to the Programme for Environmental Compliance and Education, revealed in the actors' narratives, allowed them to see themselves as part of the story as implied in the programme.

It is also worth considering that the organisational programme analysed here involved an educational orientation policy for teachers and the formation of new generations with a different mentality in relation to environmental matters, attributes that contributed to the programme's strength.

Finally, as a suggestion for future research, we recommend the study of social learning for sustainability in other profit-based organisations, however, covering other areas of the value chain, such as suppliers. We also recommend studies that reveal the development processes of organisational actors so that they can contribute to stronger social learning in their organisations.

Acknowledgements

This paper is part of the Pro-Administration Program (Pro-Adm) funded by the Special Project Coordination from CAPES (Coordination for the Improvement of Higher Education Personnel) under grant number 09/2008.

Note

1. In this paper, the company name was changed.

References

Antonacopoulou E, Chiva R. 2007. The social complexity of organizational learning: the dynamics of learning and organizing. Manage Learn. 38:277–295. doi:10.1177/1350507607079029

Bandura A. 1977. Social learning theory. Englewood Cliffs: Prentice Hall.

Boje DM. 2001. Narrative methods for organizational & communication research. London: Sage.

Boje DM. 2008. Storytelling organizations. London: Sage.

Bouwen R, Taillieu T. 2004. Multi-party collaboration as social learning for interdependence: developing relational knowing for sustainable natural resource management. J Community Appl Soc Psychol. 14:137–153. doi:10.1002/casp.777

Boyd R, Richerson PJ. 1985. Culture and the evolutionary process. Chicago: University of Chicago Press.

The Chemical Company. 2013 Mar 22. Programa de Adequaçãoe Educação Ambiental divulga balanço de 2012 [Internet]. [cited 2013 Oct 19]. Available from: http://www.basf.com.br/sac/web/brazil/pt_BR/imprensa/releases/20130322-R02

DeFillippi R, Ornstein S. 2003. Psychological perspectives underlying theories of organizational learning. In: Easterby-Smith M, Lyles MA, editors. Handbook of organizational learning and knowledge management. Oxford: Blackwell; p. 19–37.

Dessie Y, Wurzinger M, Hauser M. 2012. The role of social learning for soil conservation: the case of Amba Zuria land management, Ethiopia. Int J Sustain Dev World Ecol. 19:258–267. doi:10.1080/13504509.2011.636082

Elkjaer B. 2001. In search of a social learning theory. In: Easterby-Smith M, Burgoyne J, Araujo L, editors. Organizational learning and the learning organization: developments in theory and practice. London: Sage; p. 100–118.

Elkjaer B. 2003. Social learning theory: learning as participation in social process. In: Easterby-Smith M, Lyles MA, editors. Handbook of organizational learning and knowledge management. Oxford: Blackwell; p. 38–53.

Fiorino D. 2001. Environmental policy as learning: a new view of an old landscape. Public Adm Rev. 61:322–334. doi:10.1111/0033-3352.00033

Foundation. 2011. Resumo das atividades [Internet]. [cited 2012 Aug 30]. Available from: http://www.fundacaoespacoeco.com.br/sobre-a-fundacao/relatorio-de-atividades/relatorio2011/index.html

Friedmann J, Abonyi G. 1976. Social learning: a model for policy research. Environ Plann A. 8:927–940. doi:10.1068/a080927

Gardner GT, Stern PC. 1996. Environmental problems and human behaviour. Boston: Allyn and Bacon.

Glasser H. 2007. Minding the gap: the role of social learning in linking our stated desire for a more sustainable world to our everyday actions and policies. In: Wals AEJ, editor. Social learning: towards a sustainable world. Wageningen: Wageningen Academic.

Godoi CK, Freitas SF. 2008. Aprendizagem organizacional sob a perspectiva sociocognitiva: contribuições de Lewin, Bandura e Giddens [Organization learning under a socio-cognitive view: contributions from Lewin, Bandura and Giddens]. Rev Neg Blumenau. 13:40–55. (in Portuguese).

Goldstein H. 1981. Social learning and change: a cognitive approach to human services. Columbia: University of South Carolina Press.

Hansmann R, Mieg HA, Frischknecht P. 2012. Principal sustainability components: empirical analysis of synergies between the three pillars of sustainability. Int J Sustain Dev World Ecol. 19:451–459. doi:10.1080/13504509.2012.696220

Harmonising Collaborative Planning [HarmoniCOP]. 2005. Learning together to manage together: improving participation in water management. Osnabrück: University of Osnabrück, Institute of Environmental Systems Research.

Heclo H. 1974. Modern social politics in Britain and Sweden: from relief to income maintenance. New Haven: Yale University Press.

Keen M, Brown V, Dyball R. 2005. Social learning in environmental management: towards a sustainable future. London: Earthscan.

Kilvington MJ. 2007. Social learning as framework for building capacity to work on complex environmental management problems [Internet]. [cited 2008 Dec 3]. Available from: http://www.landcareresearch.co.nz/publications/research-pubs/Social_learning_review.pdf

Kilvington MJ. 2010. Building capacity for social learning in environmental management [PhD thesis]. Canterbury: Lincoln University.

Leal MS. 1998. Gestão ambiental de recursos hídricos: princípios e aplicações. Rio de Janeiro: Companhia de Pesquisa de Recursos Minerais.

Lee KN. 1995. Deliberately seeking sustainability in the Columbia river basin. In: Gunderson LH, Holling CS, Light SS, editors. Barriers and bridges to the renewal of ecosytems and institutions. New York: Columbia University Press; p. 215–238.

Leeuwis C, Pybyrn R. 2002. Wheelbarrows full of frogs: social learning in rural resource management. Assen: Koninklijke van Gorcum.

McKenzie-Mohr D, Smith W. 1999. Fostering sustainable behaviour: an introduction to community-based social marketing. Gabriola Island: New Society.

Orderud GI, Vogt RD. 2013. Trans-disciplinarity required in understanding, predicting and dealing with water eutrophication. Int J Sustain Dev World Ecol. 20:404–415. doi:10.1080/13504509.2013.814605

Pahl-Wostl C. 2002. Towards sustainability in the water sector – the importance of human actors and processes of social learning. Aquat Sci. 64:394–411. doi:10.1007/PL00012594

Pahl-Wostl C, Craps M, Dewulf A, Mostert E, Tabara D, Taillieu T. 2007. Managing change toward adaptive water management through social learning. Ecol Soc. 12:30. [Online].

Parson EA, Clark WC. 1995. Sustainable development as social learning: theoretical perspectives and practical challenges for the design of a research program. In: Gunderson LH, Holling CS, Light SS, editors. Barriers and bridges to the renewal of ecosystems and institutions. New York: Columbia University Press; p. 428–460.

Peteraf M, Shanley M. 1997. Getting to know you: a theory of strategic group identity. Strategic Manage J. 18:165–186. doi:10.1002/(SICI)1097-0266(199707)18:1+<165::AID-SMJ914>3.3.CO;2-R

Povedaa CA, Lipsetta MG. 2014. An integrated approach for sustainability assessment: the Wa-Pa-Su project sustainability rating system. Int J Sustain Dev World Ecol. 21:85–98. doi:10.1080/13504509.2013.876677

Robinson J. 2003. Future subjunctive: backcasting as social learning. Futures. 35:839–856. doi:10.1016/S0016-3287(03)00039-9

Rosenthal TL, Zimmerman BJ. 1978. Social learning and cognition. New York: Academic Press.

Silva JAA, Nobre AD, Manzatto CV, Joly CA, Rodrigues RR, Skorupa LA, Nobre CA, Ahrens S, May PH, Sá TDA, et al. 2011. O código florestal e a ciência: contribuições para o diálogo. Sociedade Brasileira para o Progresso da Ciência, Academia Brasileira de Ciências [Internet]. [cited 2012 Dec 5]. Available from: http://www.abc.org.br/IMG/pdf/doc-547.pdf

Swartling GÅ, Lundholm C, Plummer R, Armitage D. 2011. Social learning and sustainability: exploring critical issues in relation to environmental change and governance. Stockholm: Stockholm Environment Institute, Stockholm Resilience Centre.

Wals AFJ, Krasny M, Hart P. 2007. Social learning, sustainability and environmental education research. Paper presented at: Annual Meeting of the North American Association for Environmental Education [Internet]; Virginia, US. [cited 2009 Oct 18]. Available from: http://citation.allacademic.com/meta/p_mla_apa_research_citation/1/8/6/9/0/pages186905/p186905-1.php

Webler T, Kastenholz H, Renn O. 1995. Public participation in impact assessment: a social learning perspective. Environ Impact Assess Rev. 15:443–463. doi:10.1016/0195-9255(95)00043-E

Wegner E. 1999. Communities of practice: learning, meaning and identity. Cambridge (UK): Cambridge University Press.

Wossen T, Berger T, Mequaninte T, Alamirew B. 2013. Social network effects on the adoption of sustainable natural resource management practices in Ethiopia. Int J Sustain Dev World Ecol. 20:477–483. doi:10.1080/13504509.2013.856048

Evaluating losses in ecosystem services in nature reserves in Sichuan, China

Yan Wang[a,b], Jixi Gao[a,b], Jinsheng Wang[a], Yuanzhi Wu[c], Changxin Zou[b], Meirong Tian[b] and Hao Zheng[a,b]

[a]College of Water Science, Beijing Normal University, Beijing, PR China; [b]Nanjing Institute of Environmental Science, Ministry of Environmental Protection, Nanjing, Jiangsu Province, PR China; [c]Shandong Provincial Key Laboratory of Soil Conservation and Environmental Protection, Linyi University, Linyi, Shandong Province, PR China

Nature reserves have developed rapidly over the decades in China and play a significant role in the function of ecosystem services. The function of ecosystem services in nature reserves, however, has tended to decline in recent years due to natural hazards and human activities. Based on land use, the variation of ecosystem services value (ESV) during 2000–2010 in national nature reserves in Sichuan was evaluated. We analyzed the comprehensive effects of natural disasters and human activities on the decline of ESVs. Total ESV in the national nature reserves in Sichuan was approximately 2741.35 million US$ in 2000, 2616.81 million US$ in 2005, and 2499.06 million US$ in 2010, representing a decrease of 242.29 million US$, or 8.84%, in the decade. Forestland, grassland, wetland, and water bodies played vital roles in the function of ecosystem services, with an aggregated ESV of 99% of the total. The largest proportion of the total ESV was the protection of biodiversity at 48.6%. ESV of all land use types and single ecosystem services continued to decline during 2000–2010. A mechanism of adaptable risk prevention should be established, and unreasonable human activities should be avoided to protect ecosystems and to improve the functions of ecosystem services.

1. Introduction

Ecosystems provide a range of services, many of which provide important benefits for humans, including the maintenance of conditions conductive to human health, livelihoods, welfare, and inputs to the economy (Costanza & Daly 1992; MEA 2005; TEEB 2010). Nature reserves have rich biological resources and diverse ecosystems and play a significant role in the functions of ecosystem services (ESs). Frequent natural disasters and the scales of human population and economic activity, however, now cause negative feedbacks to the biosphere, which reduces its complexity and diversity and its ability to perform the ecosystem functions that deliver human benefits (Ekins 2011). Ecological life-support systems are declining worldwide (MEA 2005; Ewing et al. 2010; Nielsen 2012). The degradation of ecosystems undermines their functioning and resilience and thus threatens their ability to continuously supply the flow of ESs for present and future generations. Degradation will increase with climate change and our ever-increasing consumption of resources (de Groot et al. 2012).

Climate change and land use/cover change (LUCC) were recognized as the main causes of global environmental problems (Pielke 2005; Boyd et al. 2008). Climate change is a direct cause of many natural hazards such as landslides, debris flows, droughts, floods, and freeze injuries. LUCCs are the result of changes in natural conditions (many caused by natural hazards) and human activity and are an important aspect of the International Geosphere-Biosphere Program and the most direct link between humans and nature. They will inevitably affect the structure and function of ecosystems and have an effect on ESs (Liu et al. 2009). The identification and measurement of variations in ESs as a consequence of changes in land use cover and climate appear to be viable means of evaluating the environmental costs and benefits of land-planning decisions and the ecological consequences of climate change (Barral & Oscar 2012).

The appetite for further economic growth has not diminished even in the richest countries, despite the deterioration of ecosystems caused by the large increase in human economic activity since the start of industrialization. Economic development to eliminate poverty and hunger and to satisfy our basic material needs inevitably comes at the cost of ecosystem degradation, especially in developing countries. Anthropogenic pressures have reached a scale where the risk of abrupt disruptions of global ecological environments can no longer be excluded (Rockström et al. 2009). Achieving this growth in the long term, though, clearly requires a radical reduction in the damage to ecosystems caused by current economic activity; that is, such activity must be made 'sustainable' (Ekins 2011). The strategic endorsement of ES valuation has acquired an increasingly dominant position as the environmental movement attempts to look for novel strategies of conservation, where traditional strategies have failed, to halt the loss of biodiversity and habitats (Armsworth et al. 2007; Daily et al. 2009). Environmental science and policy have increased their efforts in the last two decades to valuate ESs in monetary terms, articulating such values through markets to create economic incentives for conservation (Balmford et al. 2002; Barbier et al. 2009; Pascual et al. 2010). The concept of ES can be used as a revelatory metaphor to overcome the ecological blindness of conventional economic accounts and to demonstrate the impossibility of perpetual economic growth. ESs can also indicate the prerequisite necessity of conserving ecosystems for long-term economic sustainability.

As a typical region in southwestern China, Sichuan province has suffered a high frequency of natural disasters, such as earthquakes, landslides, mudflows, droughts, and floods. Natural disasters cause huge losses, which becomes restricting factors for the ecological environment and economic development. For example, the ecosystem services value (ESV) in the central zone of the Wenchuan earthquake of May 2008 decreased by approximately 520.04×10^6 US\$ (Chen et al. 2012). In the Wenchuan earthquake, the proportions of severe damage in important regions of water conservation and biodiversity were 4.15% and 2.85%, respectively, and the proportions of decreased ESs were 9.2% and 7.63%, respectively (Wang et al. 2008). Various natural hazards can damage ecosystems and affect the functioning of ESs. Moreover, rapid economic development can influence ecosystems. Frequent construction and large-scale economic activity have nevertheless degraded ecosystems through soil erosion, degradation of vegetation, and reduction of biodiversity, which also affect the functioning of ESs. Conservation efforts, early risk warning, prevention, and emergency recovery systems must therefore be established to provide an effective ecological barrier from human society. More attention should also be given to assessing the risk of ecosystem degradation caused by climate change and human activity. Some ecosystems such as wetlands and water bodies are sensitive to climate change and human activity, and an adaptable mechanism of risk prevention must be quickly established to protect these ecosystems.

Nature reserves are created to safeguard and maintain wildlife resources, preserve biodiversity, integrate protective and developmental activities, cultivate ecological education and boost the development of ecological tourism (Moswete et al. 2012). The establishment of nature reserves has become the preferred means of reducing the loss of global biodiversity (Xie et al. 2012). Nature reserves have rich biological resources and diverse ecosystems and play a significant role in the functions of ESs. Previous studies on ESV have mainly focused on simple evaluations of economic value or changes caused by human activity, but few have accounted for the comprehensive effects of nature and humans on ESV. These two factors cannot be ignored, and more relevant research, such as this study, is needed to understand ecosystems, warn populations, prevent disasters, and reduce risks to protect ecosystems and serve humanity better.

The economic approach of this study seeks to calculate the monetary value of the damage to ecosystem functions caused by economic activity and natural hazards. Ecological degradation and destruction cannot be understood independent of the fluctuations in ESV due to both natural hazards and economic activities. This study estimated the ESV of national nature reserves during 2000–2010 in Sichuan, south-central China, using remotely sensed data, value coefficients, and ArcGIS10.0 (ESRI) (http://www.esrichina.com.cn/softwareproduct/EI//), a platform for analyzing geographic information. Our objectives were to: (1) analyze the changes in land use in national nature reserves during the decade, (2) assess the variation of ESV, and (3) discuss the variation in ESV in response to natural hazards and human activities.

2. Materials and methods

2.1. Study area

The study area (26°36'–34°12' N, 97°22'–108°27' E) is located in Sichuan, south-central China, on the upper reaches of the Yangtze River, and includes 24 national nature reserves (Figure 1). The climate of this subtropical region is variable due to the variety of terrain and monsoon circulation. The total area is 27,844.05 km^2, accounting for approximately 5.1% of the area of Sichuan. The annual average temperature is 5–20°C, and annual rainfall

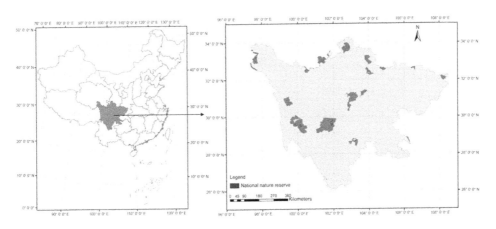

Figure 1. Location of the study area.

is 400–1800 mm. According to the classification system of China (Xue et al. 1994), the multitype nature reserves in the study area include forest ecosystem, inland wetland, and wildlife reserves that harbor more than 5000 species of plants and animals. A large variety of natural resources provide many ESs that play an important part in the ecological health of the Yangtze River basin.

2.2. Data collection and land use classification

A data set for the changes in land use was extracted from geographic information system (GIS) and remote sensing (RS) data from Landsat Thematic Mapper imagery for 2000 and 2005 and from environmental satellite data (http://www.secmep.cn/secPortal/portal/index.faces) for 2010. After converting the data to the unified coordinate system and projection, the Krasovsky ellipsoid and the Transverse Mercator projection of ENVI 4.8 (http://www.esrichina.com.cn/softwareproduct/EI/) were used to perform RS image radiation correction and geometry correction, respectively. When completing the pretreatments, ArcGIS 10.0 was used to consolidate and analyze the land use data with a background of raster images. We used the maximum likelihood classifier of supervised classification method for classification with ENVI 4.8. For the confusion matrix for classification accuracy, we controlled qualitative errors of precision for deciphering the RS data for different years at the 90% level. The interpreted results were compared with those for typical points of the field survey result. All classification accuracies were above 90%, and all total kappa coefficients were greater than the accepted minimum (0.7). The accuracy could thus meet the monitoring accuracy of the demands for land use change. The data set contained seven classified land use types that were listed in the resource and environmental database established by the Chinese Academy of Sciences (Table 1). We used ArcGIS 10.0 and SPSS 19.0

Table 1. Definition of land use type in the national nature reserves in Sichuan.

Type	Definition
Forestland	Arbor, bush forestland, broad-leaved forestland, coniferous forestland, and mixed forestland
Grassland	Meadow and steppe
Farmland	Dry land, irrigable land, and crop fields
Wetland	Herbaceous swamp and thicket swamp
Water body	Rivers, ponds, reservoirs, and lakes
Construction land	Land used for industry, residences, and transportation
Unused land	Bare soil, bare rock, and saline-alkali soil

(http://www.microsoft.com/zh-cn/default.aspx) for the statistical analyses.

The data sets for the normalized difference vegetation index (NDVI) were obtained from the Goddard Space Flight Center (NASA), (http://ladsweb.nascom.nasa.gov/data/search.html). The climatic data sets, including the monthly records from 122 radiation stations and 756 ground-based meteorological and automatic stations, were obtained from the China Meteorological Data Sharing Service System (Figure 2) (http://cdc.cma.gov.cn/index.jsp). Data for vegetation types were got from GLC2000 land cover database (http://solargis.info/doc/32).

2.3. Land use dynamics

We used images of the national nature reserves in Sichuan in 2000, 2005, and 2010 to estimate the land use changes in the past decade. The figures of land use type for 2000, 2005, and 2010 and the dynamics of land use were calculated by the Map Algebra function of ArcGIS 10.0. The rate (R) of land use change was calculated as:

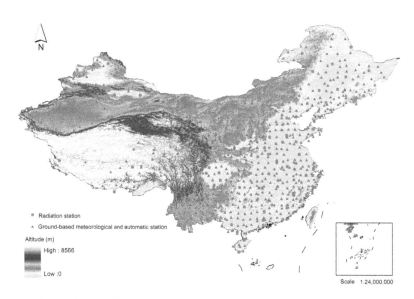

Figure 2.   Distribution of weather stations in China.

Table 2. Equivalent value per unit area of ecosystem services in China (Xie et al. 2008).

	Forestland	Grassland	Farmland	Wetland	Water body	Unused land
Gas regulation	4.32	1.50	0.72	2.41	0.51	0.06
Climate regulation	4.07	1.56	0.97	13.55	2.06	0.13
Water supply	4.09	1.52	0.77	13.44	18.77	0.07
Soil formation and protection	4.02	2.24	1.47	1.99	0.41	0.17
Waste treatment	1.72	1.32	1.39	14.40	14.85	0.26
Biodiversity protection	4.51	1.87	1.02	3.69	3.43	0.40
Food production	0.33	0.43	1.00	0.36	0.53	0.02
Raw material	2.98	0.36	0.39	0.24	0.35	0.04
Recreation and culture	2.08	0.87	0.17	4.69	4.44	0.24
Total	28.12	11.67	7.90	54.77	45.35	1.39

$$R = \frac{A_1 - A_0}{A_0} \times 100\% \qquad (1)$$

where A_0 and A_1 stand for the initial and final areas of a given land use, respectively.

2.4. ESV assessment

The equivalent value per unit area (Table 2) that was practicable in China was determined by Costanza and Folke's (1997) theory and a survey of 500 Chinese ecologists, which has the widespread use of ES assessment (Li et al. 2010; Liu et al. 2012; Wu et al. 2013). The ESV of one equivalent weight factor was estimated by the following (Xie et al. 2003):

$$VC_0 = \frac{1}{7} \times q_i \times \frac{1}{10} \sum_{i=1}^{10} p_i \qquad (2)$$

where VC_0 stands for the economic value of one equivalent weight factor (Yuan ha^{-1} year^{-1}; 1 Yuan = 0.16 US\$), q_i stands for the average grain price nationwide (Yuan kg^{-1}), p_i stands for the yield per unit area of crops in year i (kg ha^{-1} year^{-1}), and i stands for the year.

Since species resources particularly for rare species are much richer inside than outside nature reserves, it is essential to adjust the equivalent value per unit area of biodiversity protection. A database of 3337 rare and endangered species in China was determined from the International Union for Conservation of Nature (IUCN) endangered species level 3.1, the Convention on International Trade in Endangered Species appendix, the IUCN Red List of Threatened Species, a list of China's endemic species, and lists of national key protected wildlife species. According to information of species protection in 861 nature reserves in China, the distributions of 2157 rare and endangered species were established for the nature reserves. Given the information about protection in national nature reserves accounted for 96.2% of the objects and 99.7% of the area, the calculated value per unit area represented the important species well. Thus, the density of important species as a parameter for correction was determined as:

$$V_b = \frac{d}{D} \times V_{b0} \qquad (3)$$

where V_b stands for the equivalent value per unit area of biodiversity protection in nature reserves, d stands for the density of important species in nature reserves (species ha^{-1}), D stands for the average distribution density of important species on the national scale (species ha^{-1}), and V_{b0} stands for the equivalent value per unit area of biodiversity protection in China.

Since the equivalent value per unit area of ES is based on the national average, it is necessary to calibrate regional differences for ESV estimation of a local area. A correction factor is based on net primary production (NPP) to adjust the estimation of ESV, for ESV is closely related to ecosystem productivity (Wang et al. 2014). It revealed the difference in NPP caused by the climate variations between local areas and the whole country. ESV of per unit area for one year was estimated as:

$$VC_i = \frac{b_i}{B_i} \times VC_0 \qquad (4)$$

where b_i and B_i stand for the average NPP values of ecosystems in the study areas and the country in year i, respectively, and i is 2000, 2005, or 2010.

The Carnegie-Ames-Stanford Approach (CASA) affirms that plant productivity is related to the amount of photosynthetically active radiation absorbed or intercepted by green foliage (Monteith & Moss 1977; Potter et al. 1993). Based on the model, it is easy to get transformation to the regional scales for evaluating the annual dynamic change in NPP values. Some parameters of the vegetation were obtained from the RS data. The parameter FPAR meeting NPP calculation was obtained from NDVI time-series data from the MODIS spectroradiometer aboard the EOS satellites. The climatic data, e.g., average temperature, total solar radiation, and duration of sunshine, were got from 122 radiation stations and 756 ground-based meteorological and automatic stations in China (Wang et al. 2014). The equations for NPP estimation were shown as:

$$NPP(x, t) = APAR(x, t) \times \varepsilon(x, t) \qquad (5)$$

$$APAR\,(x,t) = FPAR\,(x,t) \times PAR\,(x,t) \qquad (6)$$

$$\varepsilon\,(x,t) = \varepsilon_{max} \times T_{\varepsilon 1}\,(x,t) \times T_{\varepsilon 2}\,(x,t) \times W_{\varepsilon}\,(x,t) \qquad (7)$$

where APAR stands for photosynthetically active radiation (mJ m^{-2}); ε *stands for the actual light use efficiency of vegetation* (g mJ^{-1}); x and t are location and time, respectively; PAR stands for the total incident photosynthetically active radiation (mJ m^{-2}); FPAR stands for the fraction of PAR absorbed by the vegetation canopy; ε_{max} stands for the maximum light use efficiency under ideal conditions (g mJ^{-1}); $T_{\varepsilon 1}$ and $T_{\varepsilon 2}$ are stress effects of low and high temperatures on the use efficiency of light energy, respectively; and W_{ε} stands for the water stress influence coefficient, representing the influence of moisture conditions.

Then, the ESV of each land use type and each service function and the total ESV were determined as:

$$ESV_k = \sum_{f} A_k \times VC_{ikf} \qquad (8)$$

$$ESV_f = \sum_{k} A_k \times VC_{ikf} \qquad (9)$$

$$ESV = \sum_{k} \sum_{f} A_k \times VC_{ikf} \qquad (10)$$

where ESV_k, ESV_f, and ESV stand for the ESV of land use type k, service function f, and all the ecosystems (Yuan ha^{-1} year^{-1}), respectively; A_k stands for the area of land use type k (ha) and VC_{ikf} stands for the value coefficient for land use type k with ES function type f (Yuan ha^{-1}) in year i.

We used the contribution rate to assess the effect of ESV variation on land use change. It was calculated as (Costanza & Folke 1997):

$$S_{kt} = \frac{|\Delta ESV_{kt}|}{\sum_{k=1}^{n} |\Delta ESV_{kt}|} \times 100\% \qquad (11)$$

where S_{kt} stands for the percentage of the absolute value of ESV variation of land use type k in the period t to the total amount of ESV variation of land use type k in the period t.

2.5. Sensitivity analysis of ESV

It is valid for the coefficient of sensitivity (CS) to validate the land use types representative of ecosystem types and certainties in the value coefficients (Kreuter et al. 2001; Wang et al. 2004; Li et al. 2007). The response of ESV to the ecological value of changes in unit price can be taken by CS as a measure of the degree of sensitivity of ESV to a coefficient. It was determined as:

$$CS = \left| \frac{(ESV_j - ESV_i)/ESV_i}{(VC_{jk} - VC_{ik})/VC_{ik}} \right| \qquad (12)$$

where ESV_i and ESV_j refer to the initial and adjusted total ESVs, respectively, and VC_{ik} and VC_{jk} refer to the initial and adjusted value coefficients, respectively. ESV is considered rigid, and the results will be reliable when CS < 1; ESV is considered elastic related to the coefficient when CS > 1, and higher values of CS will confirm more accurate VCs.

3. Results

3.1. Changes of land use

The changes of land use in the national nature reserves in Sichuan during 2000–2010 are shown in Table 3 and Figures 3 and 4. The area of grassland and forestland – the main land use types in the reserves – occupied approximately 85% of the total area. The areas of construction land, forestland, and grassland increased in 2000–2005 by 17.13, 0.14, and 0.04%, respectively, while the areas of farmland, wetland, unused land, and water bodies decreased by 2.89, 0.92, 0.25, and 0.02%, respectively. The areas of forestland and wetland decreased in 2005–2010 by 0.93 and 0.07%, respectively, and the areas of the other land use types all increased. The areas of grassland and construction land continued to grow throughout 2000–2010, by 0.36 and 38.35%, respectively, while the area of wetland decreased by 1.00%. The areas of forestland, wetland, and farmland ultimately shrank during the past decade by 0.79, 1.00, and 2.80%,

Table 3. Areas of land use types in the national nature reserves in Sichuan in 2000, 2005, and 2010.

Land use type	2000		2005		2010	
	Area (ha)	Percentage (%)	Area (ha)	Percentage (%)	Area (ha)	Percentage (%)
Forest land	1,032,049.86	41.89	1,033,488.89	41.95	1,023,899.37	41.56
Grassland	1,045,988.34	42.46	1,046,375.48	42.48	1,049,721.90	42.61
Farmland	25,378.82	1.03	24,646.52	1.00	24,666.95	1.00
Wetland	74,200.81	3.01	73,516.38	2.98	73,461.72	2.98
Water body	74,085.68	3.01	74,068.58	3.01	74,127.77	3.01
Unused land	211,034.61	8.57	210,516.69	8.55	216,579.21	8.79
Construction land	733.19	0.03	858.77	0.03	1014.38	0.04
Total	2,463,471.30	100.00	2,463,471.30	100.00	2,463,471.30	100.00

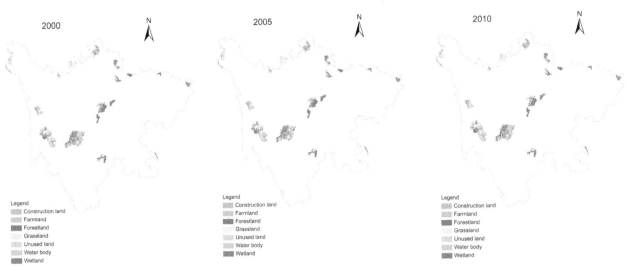

Figure 3. Distribution of the land use types in the national nature reserves in Sichuan during 2000–2010.

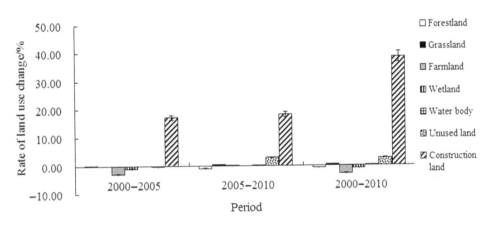

Figure 4.   Dynamic rates of each land use type during 2000–2010.

respectively, and the areas of grassland, water bodies, unused land, and construction land expanded by 0.36, 0.06, 2.63, and 38.35%, respectively. The growth rate of construction land was highest during 2000–2010. The absolute increase was not large (281.2 ha) because of the small cardinality, slightly more than the increase in the area of water bodies (42.1 ha) and far less than the increases in the areas of unused land (5544.6 ha) and grassland (3733.6 ha).

The study area is prone to earthquakes, and more than 10 earthquakes of magnitude 4.8 or higher occurred in Sichuan in 2000–2010, eight of which measured over 5.0 and three measured over 6.0. Droughts, floods, and geological hazards (e.g., landslides, collapses, and debris flows) also frequently occurred during this period. These natural hazards disrupted the structures of ecosystems, resulting in reduced areas and ecosystem degradation. Furthermore, the Three Gorges Dam (TGD) Project, the world's largest hydroelectric project to date, affects 20 county-level administrative regions with a total area of 58,000 km^2, and the surface area of the reservoir is over 1080 km^2 with a water level of 175 m (Fu et al. 2010).

This huge project led to changes of land use in the relevant regions, including Sichuan. The area of forestland subsequently decreased, and the areas of grassland and unused land increased substantially during 2000–2010.

3.2. Changes of ESV

The variation of ESVs in the various ecosystems of the nature reserves in Sichuan is shown in Table 4. The structure of the total ESV composition remained stable during the decade and was mainly contributed by the ESVs of forestland, grassland, wetland, and water bodies. The aggregated ESV of forestland, grassland, wetland, and water bodies was approximately 99% of the total ESV, indicating that these ecosystems played vital roles in ES function. Even though the area of forestland was similar to that of grassland, the ESV of forestland was much higher than that of grassland because forestland had a higher value coefficient and was the highest ESV of all land use types. The areas of wetland and water bodies were approximately 6% of the total area, but their ESVs were

Table 4. Ecosystem service values (ESVs) and their variation for each land use type in the national nature reserves in Sichuan in 2000, 2005, and 2010.

Land use type	2000 ESV (10^7 US$\cdot$year^{-1})	2000 Percentage (%)	2005 ESV (10^7 US$\cdot$year^{-1})	2005 Percentage (%)	2010 ESV (10^7 US$\cdot$year^{-1})	2010 Percentage (%)
Forestland	1674.93	61.10	1600.75	61.17	1521.56	60.89
Grassland	704.23	25.69	672.35	25.69	647.14	25.90
Farmland	10.63	0.39	9.85	0.38	9.46	0.38
Wetland	177.83	6.49	168.15	6.43	161.21	6.45
Water body	151.18	5.51	144.25	5.51	138.51	5.54
Unused land	22.54	0.82	21.46	0.82	21.18	0.85
Construction land	0	0	0	0	0	0
Total	2741.35	100.00	2616.81	100.00	2499.06	100.00

approximately 12% of the total ESV due to their high value coefficients.

The total ESVs of the nature reserves were approximately 2741.35 million US$ in 2000, 2616.81 million US$ in 2005, and 2499.06 million US$ in 2010 (Table 4). Declines in forestland and grassland were the main cause of the total decline in ESV (Figure 5). The decline in the ESVs of forestland and grassland from 2000 to 2005 totaled 106.07 million US$, which reduced the total ESV by 85.17%. As a result, the total ESV decreased by 124.53 million US$, or 4.54%. The combined ESV of forestland and grassland decreased by 104.4 million US$ from 2005 to 2010, which reduced the total ESV by 117.75 million US$, or 4.50%. The total ESV decreased by 242.29 million US$ (8.84%) from 2000 to 2010. This decrease was mostly due to the impacts on both forestland and grassland (Figure 5). Natural hazards directly destroyed the structures of ecosystems and reduced ES functions. In addition, the TGD Project negatively affected the ecological environment, further reducing ES functions. For example, the project slowed the flow of water and reduced the ability of water bodies to purify the water.

The values of single ESs in the nature reserves are shown in Figure 6. The ESV of biodiversity protection represented the largest proportion of the total ESV,

approximately 48.6%, followed by the ESVs of water supply (10.1%) and climatic regulation (8.6%). The ESVs of food production and raw materials had the least influence, with proportions of approximately 1.1 and 4.3%, respectively, indicating that the effects of food production and raw materials were less significant than the effects of the other ESs under the principles of protection and control in nature reserves.

The ESV of each ES continued to decrease throughout 2000–2010. The ESV of each ES decreased from 2000 to 2005 by an average of 4.56%, in which the ESVs of biodiversity protection, water supply, and climatic regulation decreased the most, with reductions of 60.1, 12.76, and 10.93 million US$ or 4.51, 4.60, and 4.61%, respectively. The ESV of each ES decreased less during 2005–2010 (average of 4.48%) than during the 2000–2005 prophase (average of 4.56%). The ESV of biodiversity protection decreased the most by 57.39 million US$. Over the entire decade, the ESVs of biodiversity protection, water supply, and climatic regulation decreased the most by 117.49, 24.5, and 21.13 million US$, respectively. The Wilcoxon signed-rank test of SPSS 19.0 analysis showed that the ESVs of various land use types decreased significantly in different periods ($P = 0.028 < 0.05$), and the ESVs of each individual ES decreased quite drastically in different periods

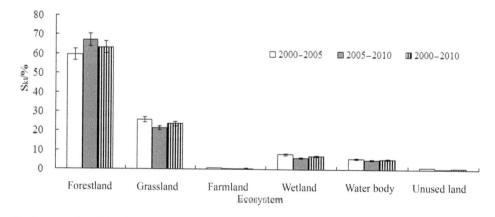

Figure 5. Contribution rate of each land use type during 2000–2010.

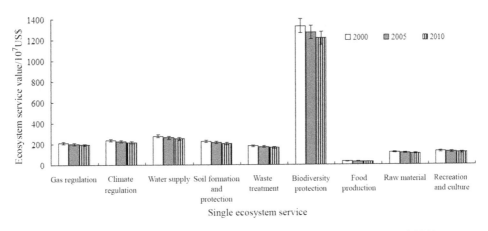

Figure 6. Values of ecosystem services in the national nature reserves in Sichuan in 2000, 2005, and 2010.

($P = 0.008 < 0.01$). These changes indicated that the ESVs of the study area decreased significantly during 2000–2010. Natural hazards directly threatened species resources and their habitats, resulting in a decrease of biodiversity. The TGD Project affected biodiversity and ecological processes in the area through both an immediate loss of habitat area and an increased isolation of the remaining patches of habitat (Wu et al. 2003). The loss of biodiversity occurred not only on land but also in the water; 25 species of endemic fish became endangered in this area, accounting for 27% of all endangered species of freshwater fish in China (Xie 2003).

3.3. Analysis of ecosystem sensitivity

The percent changes in calculated total ESV and the CS were estimated for a 50% adjustment in the value coefficients and are presented in Table 5. To ensure the reliability of our results, the sensitivity of ESV to changes in the value coefficients must be quite small (Equation (12)), i.e., lower than 1.

As is shown in Table 5, the CS in each case was less than 1, indicating that the estimated ESVs were rigid relative to changes in the value coefficients. The CS for forestland (0.61), with a large area and high value coefficient, was higher than the CSs of the other types of land use. The CS for grassland was the next highest. The area

of unused land was relatively large, about three times larger than for wetland and water bodies, but the CSs for wetland and water bodies were approximately six times higher than that for unused land with a high value coefficient. From the estimated CS, we can conclude that the calculated ESV was responsible for all the uncertainties in the value coefficients.

4. Discussion

Techniques for assessing ESVs can be broadly classified into biophysical methods and preference-based methods (TEEB 2010). The biophysical methods are based on ecosystem processes and mechanisms, estimating ESVs through a series of models (Leh et al. 2013). The biophysical methods, however, require much basic data, especially long-term observational and experimental data, so evaluating ESVs quickly and effectively is difficult. Moreover, due to the restriction of management and conditions in some areas (e.g., nature reserves), some data are quite difficult to obtain. In comparison, the preference-based methods are more flexible and convenient for evaluating ESV. Based on the widely used contingent valuation method (Park et al. 2013), our method requires relatively few data, and ESV can be estimated through the equivalent factor method by some parameter correction that can be conveniently achieved. The method of

Table 5. Variation of the estimated total ecosystem services value (ESV) and the coefficient of sensitivity (CS) resulting from a 50% adjustment in the value coefficients in the national nature reserves in Sichuan in 2000, 2005, and 2010.

Land use type	Variation of ESV			CS		
	2000	2005	2010	2000	2005	2010
Forestland	±30.55%	±30.59%	±30.44%	0.61	0.61	0.61
Grassland	±12.84%	±12.85%	±12.95%	0.26	0.26	0.26
Farmland	±0.19%	±0.19%	±0.19%	0.00	0.00	0.00
Wetland	±3.24%	±3.21%	±3.23%	0.06	0.06	0.06
Water body	±2.76%	±2.76%	±2.77%	0.06	0.06	0.06
Unused land	±0.41%	±0.41%	±0.42%	0.01	0.01	0.01
Construction land	±0.00%	±0.00%	±0.00%	0.00	0.00	0.00

evaluation was first proposed by Costanza and Folke (1997), was modified by Xie et al. (2008) to apply to China, and has been widely and flexibly applied to quickly and efficiently reflect trends of variation of ESV (Huang et al. 2010; Li et al. 2010; Song et al. 2011). RS data can economically and efficiently estimate ESV at large scales and over long time periods. They are especially suitable for the dynamic assessment of ESV to find ecological problems quickly and efficiently.

Different methods of evaluation can provide different results. For example, both Peng et al. (2005) and Li et al. (2010) evaluated the ESV of Shenzhen for the same year, giving estimates of 126.5 billion and 2.9 billion Yuan, respectively. Absolute numbers of ESVs have less meaning, and the dynamics of ESVs are commonly indicating ecological problems (Wang et al. 2014).

The existing evaluations based on the equivalent factor method were adopted with the same value coefficient, ignoring the difference caused by spatial heterogeneity, which would inevitably lead to the results (Li et al. 2010; Liu et al. 2012). Compared with the existing evaluations, our method paid more attention to regional-difference correction to improve the accuracy of the value coefficient, making it better suited to the practice of the study area. Nature reserves are much richer than other areas in biodiversity, ecosystem productivity, and important species; hence correcting for factors of species and NPP, as we have, is essential. Some spatial heterogeneity remains for the same ecosystems in the region, despite the complexity and heterogeneity of the ecosystems (Limburg et al. 2002; Turner et al. 2003). The appropriate parameters should thus be used for reasonably adjusting the factors.

The biomes that have been used as proxies for the land use types, however, have clearly not been perfect matches in each case (Kreuter et al. 2001). For example, evergreen broadleaved forestland and sparse shrubbery are both regarded as forestland but generally differ substantially in biomass. Some calculations of ESV have thus produced similar value coefficients as one type of land use, and value coefficients of construction land can be zero, ignoring some service functions of culture and esthetics, which can lead to rough ESV estimations with imprecise values for recreation and culture. The determination of the value coefficient is the key to this method.

The ESV of the national nature reserves in the study area, comprehensively influenced by natural disasters and human activity, decreased by 242.29 million US$, or 8.84%, from 2000 to 2010. Ecosystems provided a variety of ecological functions but were also threatened by natural hazards and human activity. The frequent occurrence of natural hazards in recent years and the effects of climate change have caused major losses of life and property in many regions.

More than 4000 natural hazards such as floods, droughts, earthquakes, and hurricanes have occurred worldwide in the past decade, affecting more than one million people and costing at least 1.2 billion US$ in damage (WEF 2012). These events quickly and directly damaged ecosystems to different degrees, but human activity has affected ecosystems more profoundly and extensively and has substantially increased potential risks. For example, the disappearance of coral reefs and coastal mangrove ecosystems caused by human activity has weakened their capacity to protect against floods and storm surges (WEF 2012). Sichuan, with complex climatic conditions, a fragile ecological environment, a large population, and frequent natural disasters, is especially vulnerable to climate change.

ESV is determined by the area of an ecosystem and its value coefficient. The area of ecosystems affected by natural disasters (earthquakes, landslides, mud-rock flows, etc.) with strong ES function, such as forested land, wetland, and farmland, all decreased, especially for forested land, directly leading to the decline of the total ESV and a reduction in area of 8150.5 ha. In the Wenchuan earthquake in 2008, for example, 69 nature reserves in the country were damaged and much infrastructure and ecosystems were destroyed. In Sichuan, the earthquake and its secondary geological disaster caused the loss of 65,584 ha of giant panda habitat, with a loss ratio of 5.92%, in which the loss in nature reserves was 34,737 ha that accounted for 6.02% of the total habitat area. The Baishui River, Longxihongkou, and Wolong national nature reserves were the most seriously damaged, with decreases in area of habitat of 7859, 7354, and 5606 ha and loss ratios of 47.8, 32.2, and 6.6%, respectively (Ouyang et al. 2008). Forest ecosystems were destroyed the most, which not only threatened the survival of the giant panda but also caused the decline of ESV.

The area increase of construction land in the nature reserves was mainly due to the construction of infrastructure, such as corridors (for the giant panda), roads, protection stations, posts, observatories, and laboratories. In addition, the planning of village construction and post-disaster reconstruction in nature reserves play another important role in the increase. The older houses in the nature reserves were built of wood and so were more vulnerable to the local humid climate and frequent natural disasters (earthquakes, landslides, mud-rock flows, etc.). With social economic development and the growth of personal income, many rural houses were planned or rebuilt in nature reserves, resulting in an increase in the area of construction land to some extent.

About 30 million poor people live inside or adjacent to nature reserves in China, leading to the dilemma of how to protect biodiversity yet achieve sustainability and a balanced development (Li et al. 2001; Chowdhury et al. 2013). Economic activities in nature reserves are dominated by construction projects, including projects for tourism, water conservation, transportation, and resource exploitation. These projects are responsible for the adjustment number for the national nature reserves approaching 15% of the total (Jiang et al. 2009). In the Wolong national nature reserve, for example, man-made landscapes accounted for 30% of the total area, and road construction, hydroelectric power generation, and the production and impact from the local population caused direct damage and had an impact on the forest and giant panda habitat, in which the construction and operation of the hydroelectric power station had the strongest influence on the local ecosystems (Liu et al. 2001; Zeng et al. 2001).

A change in value coefficient mainly depends on the productivity of an ecosystem. The TGD had an impact on both climate and ecosystem productivity in the region. An analysis by NASA indicated that the change in land use associated with the construction of the TGD increased precipitation in the region between the Daba and Qinling mountains and reduced precipitation in the vicinity of the Yangtze River after the water level behind the dam rose abruptly by 135 m in June 2003. The effects of man-made reservoirs, such as that produced by the TGD, on climate are on regional (100 km) rather than local (10 km) scales, as projected in previous studies (Wu et al. 2006). The temperature, fluctuations of precipitation, and stability of relative humidity of the region also tended to increase after the TGD was built (Chao et al. 2011). The large size of the TGD has also been claimed to have changed the water table in the Yangtze basin (Foster 2011). The changes in the stability of climate and groundwater level have directly affected ecosystem productivity, causing the inevitable decrease in ESV.

The TGD is the major trigger of environmental change in the Yangtze River valley, which consists of Sichuan province. Some other practices of land use and management also contribute to environmental change. Water and sediment flux, biodiversity, water quality, dam operation, and regional development are mutually and closely related in time and space. The ecological and environmental effects of the TGD are thus certainly complex and uncertain (Fu et al. 2010).

5. Conclusions

Nature reserves provide us with abundant and various ESs. Economic development, climate change, human activity, and natural disasters are threatening our nature reserves and can reduce ES functions. An improved method of assessment and an analysis of changes in land use have enabled us to assess the changes in ESV in the national nature reserves in Sichuan from 2000 to 2010. The total ESVs of the reserves were approximately 2741.35 million US$ in 2000, 2616.81 million US$ in 2005, and 2499.06 million US$ in 2010, representing a decrease of 242.29 million US$ (8.84%) from 2000 to 2010. The total ESV decreased throughout 2000–2010, mostly by the impact from forestland and grassland. The aggregated ESV of forestland, grassland, wetland, and water bodies was approximately 99% of the total ESV, indicating that these ecosystems played vital roles in ES functions. The ESV of biodiversity protection represented the largest proportion of the total ESV, approximately 48.6%, followed by water supply (10.1%) and climatic regulation (8.6%). The ESVs of biodiversity protection, water supply, and

climatic regulation decreased the most during 2000–2010, by 117.49, 24.5, and 21.13 million US$, respectively. The ESV of each land use type and single ESs decreased throughout the decade. An analysis of ecosystem sensitivity indicated that the estimated ESV was responsible for all the uncertainties in the value coefficients and that the results were reliable.

The complex climatic conditions and frequent natural disasters render nature reserves especially vulnerable to climate change. Large-scale human activities such as the TGD Project and China's Western Development also negatively affect the ecosystems in nature reserves. ES functions have tended to decline due to the comprehensive influence of natural disasters and human activity, warning that an adaptable mechanism of risk prevention should be established and that unreasonable human activities should be avoided to protect our ecosystems and to improve ES function. Further research should be conducted on how to prevent and minimize the effect of natural hazards on ecosystems

Acknowledgements

We are grateful to the staff of the report of the key techniques for monitoring and conserving important biological species and for demonstrating its application in China [No. 2008BAC439B00].

Funding

This research was financially supported by the National Special Scientific Research of Environmental Protection Public Welfare Project (grant no. 201209027, grant no. 201409055), the National Science and Technology Support Project (grant no. 2012BAC01B00) and Remote Sensing Investigation and Assessment on the National Ecological Environment Change over Decade (2000–2010).

References

Armsworth PR, Chan KM, Daily GC, Ehrlich PR, Kremen C, Ricketts TH, Sanjayan MA. 2007. Ecosystem-service science and the way forward for conservation. Conserv Biol. 21:1383–1384. doi:10.1111/j.1523–1739.2007.00821.x.

Balmford A, Bruner A, Cooper P, Costanza R, Farber S, Green RE, Jenkins M, Jefferiss P, Jessamy V, Madden J, et al. 2002. Economic reasons for conserving wild nature. Science. 297:950–953. doi:10.1126/science.1073947.

Barbier EB, Baumgärtner S, Chopra K, Costello C, Duraiappah A, Hassan R, Kinzig AP, Lehman M, Pascual U, Polasky S, et al. 2009. The valuation of ecosystem services. In: Naeem S, Bunker D, Hector A, Loreau M, Perrings C, editors. Biodiversity, ecosystem functioning, and human wellbeing: an ecological and economic perspective. Oxford: Oxford University Press; p. 248–262.

Barral MP, Oscar MN. 2012. Land-use planning based on ecosystem service assessment: a case study in the Southeast Pampas of Argentina. Agric Ecosyst Environ. 154:34–43. doi:10.1016/j.agee.2011.07.010.

Boyd E, Corbera E, Estrada M. 2008. UNFCCC negotiations (pre-kyoto to COP-9): what the process says about the politics of CDM-sinks. Int Environ Agreements. 8:95–112. doi:10.1007/s10784–008–9070-x.

Chao T, Xue JL, Wang Y 2011. The relationship between the Three Gorges and local climate change: an empirical analysis based on Sichuan and Chongqing meteorological data [Internet]. [cited 2013 Nov 13]. Available from: http://www.docin.com/p-725143813.html.

Chen L, Wu F, Yang W, Zhang J. 2012. A comparison on ecosystem services before/after "5.12" Wenchuan earthquake. Acta Ecol Sin. 32:271–273. doi:10.1016/j.chnaes.2012.07.002.

Chowdhury MSH, Koike M, Rana MP, Muhammed N. 2013. Community development through collaborative management of protected areas: evidence from Bangladesh with a case of Rema-Kalenga Wildlife Sanctuary. Int J Sustain Dev World Ecol. 20:63–74. doi:10.1080/13504509.2012.755480.

Costanza R, Daly H. 1992. Natural capital and sustainable development. Conserv Biol. 6:37–46. doi:10.1046/j.1523-1739.1992.610037.x.

Costanza R, Folke C. 1997. Valuing ecosystem services with efficiency, fairness, and sustainability as goals. In: Daily GC, editor. Nature's services: societal dependence on natural ecosystems. Washington (DC): Island Press; p. 49–68.

Daily GC, Polasky S, Goldstein J, Kareiva PM, Mooney HA, Pejchar L, Ricketts TH, Salzman J, Shallenberger R. 2009. Ecosystem services in decision making: time to deliver. Frontiers Ecol Environ. 7:21–28. doi:10.1890/080025.

de Groot R, Brander L, van der Ploeg S, Costanza R, Bernard F, Braat L, Christie M, Crossman N, Ghermandi A, Hein L, et al. 2012. Global estimates of the value of ecosystems and their services in monetary units. Ecosyst Serv. 1:50–61. doi:10.1016/j.ecoser.2012.07.005.

Ekins P. 2011. Environmental sustainability: from environmental valuation to the sustainability gap. Progress Phys Geogr. 35:629–651. doi:10.1177/0309133311423186.

Ewing B, Moore D, Goldfinger S, Oursler A, Reed A, Wackernagel M. 2010. The ecological footprint Atlas 2010. Oakland: Global Footprint Network.

Foster P. 2011. China's Yangtze River closed to ships by severe drought. The Telegraph [Internet]. [cited 12 May 2011]; World, China: [1 screen]. Available from: http://www.telegraph.co.uk/news/worldnews/asia/china/8509516/Chinas-Yangtze-river-closed-to-ships-by-severe-drought.html

Fu BJ, Wu BF, Lu YH, Xu ZH, Cao JH, Niu D, Yang GS, Zhou YM. 2010. Three Gorges Project: efforts and challenges for the environment. Progress Phys Geogr. 34:741–754. doi:10.1177/0309133310370286.

Huang X, Chen YN, Ma JX, Chen YP. 2010. Study on change in value of ecosystem service function of Tarim River. Acta Ecol Sin. 30:67–75. doi:10.1016/j.chnaes.2010.03.004.

Jiang MK, He ZH, Wang Z, Qin WH. 2009. Environmental management of construction projects involving nature reserve. J Ecol Rural Environ. 25:101–105. Chinese.

Kreuter UP, Harris HG, Matlock MD, Lacey RE. 2001. Change in ecosystem service values in the San Antonio area, Texas. Ecol Econ. 39:333–346. doi:10.1016/S0921-8009(01)00250-6.

Leh MDK, Matlock MD, Cummings EC, Nalley LL. 2013. Quantifying and mapping multiple ecosystem services change in West Africa. Agric Ecosyst Environ. 165:6–18. doi:10.1016/j.agee.2012.12.001.

Li JC, Wang WL, Hu GY, Wei ZH. 2010. Changes in ecosystem service values in Zoige Plateau, China. Agric Ecosyst Environ. 139:766–770. doi:10.1016/j.agee.2010.10.019.

Li JW, Cui GF, Li JQ. 2001. Income and managing problems of the protected areas in China. J Forestry Res. 12:195–200. doi:10.1007/BF02856706.

Li RQ, Dong M, Cui JY, Zhang LL, Cui QG, He WM. 2007. Quantification of the impact of land-use changes on ecosystem services: a case study in Pingbian County, China. Environ Monit Assess. 128:503–510. doi:10.1007/s10661-006-9344-0.

Limburg KE, O' Neill RV, Costanza R, Farber S. 2002. Complex systems and valuation. Ecol Econ. 41:409–420. doi:10.1016/S0921-8009(02)00090-3.

Liu JG, Linderman M, Ouyang ZY, An L, Yang J, Zhang HM. 2001. Ecological degradation in protected areas: the case of Wolong Nature Reserve for giant pandas. Science. 292:98–101. doi:10.1126/science.1058104.

Liu JH, Gao JX, Nie YH. 2009. Measurement and dynamic changes of ecosystem services value for the Tibetan plateau based on remote sensing techniques. Geog Geo-Inform Sci. 25:81–84. Chinese.

Liu Y, Li J, Zhang H. 2012. An ecosystem service valuation of land use change in Taiyuan City, China. Ecol Modell. 225:127–132. doi:10.1016/j.ecolmodel.2011.11.017.

[TEEB] The Economics of Ecosystems and Biodiversity TEEB: mainstreaming the economics of nature: a synthesis of the approach, conclusions and recommendations of TEEB [Internet]. Geneva: The Economics of Ecosystems and Biodiversity; [cited 2010]. Available from: http://www.teebweb.org/Portals/25/TEEB%20Synthesis/TEEB_SynthReport_09_2010_online.pdf.

[MEA] Millennium Ecosystem Assessment. 2005. Ecosystems and human well-being: synthesis. Washington (DC): Island Press.

Monteith JL, Moss CJ. 1977. Climate and the efficiency of crop production in Britain [and discussion]. Philos Trans Royal Soc B: Biol Sci. 281:277–294. doi:10.1098/rstb.1977.0140.

Moswete NN, Thapa B, Child B. 2012. Attitudes and opinions of local and national public sector stakeholders towards Kgalagadi Transfrontier Park, Botswana. Int J Sustain Dev World Ecol. 19:67–80. doi:10.1080/13504509.2011.592551.

Nielsen G. 2012. Capacity development in protected area management. Int J Sustain Dev World Ecol. 19:297–310. doi:10.1080/13504509.2011.640715.

Ouyang ZY, Xu WH, Wang XZ, Wang WJ, Dong RC, Zheng H, Li DH, Li ZQ, Zhang HF, Zhuang CW. 2008. Impact assessment of Wenchuan Earthquake on ecosystems. Acta Ecol Sin. 28:5801–5809.

Park SY, Yoo SH, Kwak SJ. 2013. The conservation value of the Shinan Tidal Flat in Korea: a contingent valuation study. Int J Sustain Dev World Ecol. 20:54–62. doi:10.1080/13504509.2012.742472.

Pascual U, Muradian R, Brander LM, Gomez-Baggethun E, Martin-Lopez B, Verma M, Armsworth P, Christie M, Cornelissen H, Eppink F, et al. 2010. The economics of valuing ecosystem services and biodiversity. In: Kumar P, editor. The economics of valuing ecosystem services and biodiversity: ecological and economic foundation. London: Earthscan; p. 183–256.

Peng J, Wang YL, Chen YF, Li WF, Jiang YY. 2005. Economic value of urban ecosystem services: a case study in Shenzhen. Acta Sci Nat Univ Pekin. 41:594–604.

Pielke RA. 2005. Atmospheric science: land use and climate change. Science. 310:1625–1626. doi:10.1126/science.1120529.

Potter CS, Randerson JT, Field CB, Matson PA, Vitousek PM, Mooney HA, Klooster SA. 1993. Terrestrial ecosystem production: a process model based on global satellite and surface data. Global Biogeochem Cycles. 7:811–841. doi:10.1029/93GB02725.

Rockström J, Steffen W, Noone K, Persson Å, Chapin III FS, Lambin EF, Lenton TM, Scheffer M, Folke C, Schellnhuber HJ, et al. 2009. A safe operating space for humanity. Nature. 461:472–475. doi:10.1038/461472a.

Song G, Fu C, E Y. 2011. The analysis of ecosystem service value's change in Yueqing Bay Wetland based on RS and GIS. Proc Environ Sci. 11:1365–1370. doi:10.1016/j.proenv.2011.12.205.

Tianhong LI, Wenkai LI, Zhenghan Q. 2010. Variations in ecosystem service value in response to land use changes in

Shenzhen. Ecol Econ. 69:1427–1435. doi:10.1016/j.ecolecon.2008.05.018.

Turner RK, Paavola J, Coopera P, Farber S, Jessamya V, Georgiou S. 2003. Valuing nature: lessons learned and future research directions. Ecol Econ. 46:493–510. doi:10.1016/S0921-8009(03)00189-7.

Wang WJ, Pan YZ, Xu WH, Wang JJ, Bai X. 2008. Analysis on ecosystem destroy and its ecological impact caused by earthquake in Wenchuan, Sichuan Province. Res Environ Sci. 21:110–116 (Chinese).

Wang Y, Gao J, Wang J, Qiu J, Bond-Lamberty B. 2014. Value assessment of ecosystem services in nature reserves in Ningxia, China: a response to ecological restoration [Internet]. PLoS ONE. 9:e89174. doi:10.1371/journal.pone.0089174. Available from: http://www.plosone.org/article/info%3Adoi%2F10.1371%2Fjournal.pone.0089174

Wang ZM, Zhang SQ, Zhang B. 2004. Effects of land use change on value of ecosystem services of Sanjiang Plain. China Environ Sci. 24:125–128.

[WEF] World Economic Forum. 2012. World risk report 2012. Berlin: Bündnis Entwicklung Hilft.

Wu JG, Huang JH, Han XG, Xie ZQ, Gao XM. 2003. Ecology: Three-Gorges Dam—experiment in habitat fragmentation? Science. 300:1239–1240. doi:10.1126/science.1083312.

Wu KY, Ye XY, Qi ZF, Zhang H. 2013. Impacts of land use/land cover change and socioeconomic development on regional ecosystem services: the case of fast-growing Hangzhou metropolitan area, China. Cities. 31:276–284. doi:10.1016/j.cities.2012.08.003.

Wu LG, Zhang Q, Jiang ZH. 2006. Three Gorges Dam affects regional precipitation [Internet]. Geophys Res Lett. 33:Jul 7. doi:10.1029/2006GL026780. Available from: http://onlinelibrary.wiley.com/doi/10.1029/2006GL026780/full

Xie GD, Lu CX, Leng YF, Zheng D, Li SC. 2003. Ecological assets valuation of the Tibetan Plateau. J Nat Resour. 18:189–196. Chinese.

Xie GD, Zhen L, Lu CX, Xiao Y, Chen C. 2008. Expert knowledge based valuation method of ecosystem services in China. J Nat Resour. 23:911–919. Chinese.

Xie P. 2003. Three-Gorges Dam: risk to ancient fish. Science. 14:1149–1150.

Xie Z, Liu J, Ma Z, Duan X, Cui Y. 2012. Effect of surrounding land-use change on the Wetland landscape pattern of a natural protected area in Tianjin, China. Int J Sustain Dev World Ecol. 19:16–24. doi:10.1080/13504509.2011.583697.

Xue DY, Jiang MK, Wang XB: Principle for categories and grades of nature reserves. [Internet]. Beijing: Ministry of Environmental Protection, The People's Republic of China; [cited 1994 Jan 1]. Available from: http://www.mep.gov.cn/image20010518/4593.pdf (Chinese).

Zeng H, Kong NN, Li SJ. 2001. Human impacts on landscape structure in Wolong Natural Reserve. Acta Ecol Sin. 21:1994–2001.

Index